D1547497

THE AMERICAN ROAD TO NUREMBERG

THE AMERICAN ROAD TO NUREMBERG

The Documentary Record 1944–1945

Bradley F. Smith

Hoover Institution Press
Stanford University, Stanford, California

The Hoover Institution on War, Revolution and Peace, founded at Stanford University in 1919 by the late President Herbert Hoover, is an interdisciplinary research center for advanced study on domestic and international affairs in the twentieth century. The views expressed in its publications are entirely those of the authors and do not necessarily reflect the views of the staff, officers, or Board of Overseers of the Hoover Institution.

HOOVER PRESS PUBLICATION 248

International Standard Book Number: 0-8179-7481-4
Library of Congress Catalog Card Number: 80-83830
Printed in the United States of America
Design by P. Kelley Baker

In Memory of Raymond J. Sontag,
Teacher, Scholar, Friend

Contents

Abbreviations and Short References

Asst. Sect.: RG 107, Assistant Secretary of War, 000.5, War Crimes, Modern Military Branch, National Archives of the United States.

Report of Robert H. Jackson: *Report of Robert H. Jackson, United States Representative to the International Conference on Military Trials, London, 1945* (Washington: 1949).

Rosenman Papers War Crimes: Papers of Samuel I. Rosenman, Box 7, War Crimes File, Harry S. Truman Library, Independence, Missouri.

Preface

Even while the International Military Tribunal (IMT) was still hearing the Allied case against the major Nazi war criminals (Hermann Goering et al.) at Nuremberg in 1945–46, books began to appear describing and explaining the proceedings. Over the next 35 years the number of new secondary accounts and memoirs of participants flowed and ebbed, with cresting points in the late 1940s and during the Vietnam War. However, the course followed in the publication of documentary materials related to the main Nuremberg trial has been rather different. Although the American government published one edition of prosecution materials during the trial (*Nazi Conspiracy and Aggression*), the most important documents by far all appeared in print during 1949. In that year Justice Robert H. Jackson released 400 pages of background papers in his report on the London war crimes conference that had been held in the summer of 1945. Of even greater significance was the publication (also in 1949) of a 42-volume record of the proceedings before the IMT.[1] From their first appearance until the mid-1970s, these volumes were the necessary foundation for every serious consideration of the Nuremberg Trial.

Beginning in 1971, under the "25" and "30" rules that apply to the declassification of most government documents in the United States and Great Britain a vast new storehouse of information began to become available for research. Within a few years, the first secondary account based on a portion of these materials was published, and it seems likely that we are now at the start of an era of re-examination and re-evaluation of Nuremberg.[2] The appearance at this point of a volume of documents setting out the development of the trial plan (to parallel a narrative account on the same subject)[3] should therefore require no additional justification. What could be more appropriate than that the materials related to the beginning of the story appear at the point of this new beginning?

It should be noted in passing that the significance of these documents differs in one important respect from that of most published collections of historical materials. Since the IMT was a judicial body, the intent of those who set forth the legal system upon which it rested is of major importance in evaluating later reverberations. Heretofore those called upon to deal with Nuremberg's impact on international law have been forced to gauge the intent of its founders on little besides the published London conference records and the charter of August 1945. The present volume takes a large step into the origins of the basic plan that came to be embedded in the London Charter.

The main feature of this story is that what the world now knows as the Nuremberg trial system was primarily developed in late 1944 and early 1945, almost exclusively by a group of American government officials. Working to counter the harsh occupation policy for Germany recommended by Henry Morgenthau, this handful of planners developed a system that they believed would punish the guilty, eliminate the threat of a Nazi revival in Germany, and avoid the dangers inherent in the economic destruction of central Europe. Passing through a series of conferences and political maneuvers, the system gradually took shape and was revised in draft after draft.

The most important formulations of the system made between September 1944 and May 1945 are reproduced below, together with some additional documents that throw light on the atmosphere and circumstances shaping the revisions. To make more comprehensible both the course of events and the course of the redrafting, the materials have been grouped into three time periods, with a short explanatory essay introducing each of the three groups of documents.

Before setting off down the Nuremberg road, however, a short comment on the editorial approach employed in this volume is in order. The editor holds that in explanatory notes, less is often actually more. Since intent is in many ways the crucial issue raised by these materials, the editorial comments have tried, as far as possible, not to usurp the function of evaluating what the "Nuremberg fathers" were trying to do and have left it to the reader. Hypothesizing about possible motive has been kept to a minimum in the essays, and the explanatory notes have been used chiefly to provide information essential to understanding what is being said in the documents. The notes and editorial comments have sought only to provide, in Carlyle's phrase, a "garment for thought." If when putting the book down, readers feel that they have received enough information to help them wrestle effectively with the questions of how and why the Nuremberg system developed the way it did, then the editorial work will have performed its intended purpose.

Acknowledgments

Archivists and librarians from a number of institutions helped to make this volume possible, especially Agnes F. Peterson, Hoover Institution, Stanford University; Marilla Guptil, John Mendelsohn, Edward Reese, William Cunliffe, and Robert Wolfe (Chief) Modern Military Branch and Patricia Dowling Diplomatic Branch, National Archives of the United States; James Miller and James Hastings, Federal Records Center, Suitland Maryland; Harry Clark and Philip D. Lagerquist, Harry S. Truman Library; Jon Kepler, Dwight D. Eisenhower Library; David Crosson and Gene Gressley, University of Wyoming; Mary K. Hembree, Thomas Marvin, and John Martin, United States Justice Department; Alice Prochaska, Public Records Office, London.

Permission to publish specific documents has been graciously granted by Yale University (Stimson Papers), Mrs. Roberta Wohlstetter (Edmund M. Morgan papers), and the Controller of Her Majesty's Stationery Office (official papers in the Public Records Office).

Some of the research for this volume was tucked into the corners of grants intended for two other works by the Mabel McLeod Lewis Memorial Fund of Stanford University and the Hoover Institution of Stanford University.

A final special thanks is due to the very helpful people at the Hoover Press.

PHASE I

I

Documents

August to November 1944

Editor's Note

The printed version of these documents conforms as closely as possible to the original versions, including wording, punctuation, and spelling. Exceptions are in the document headings, lists, outlines, and ornaments which have been arranged in consistent format for the reader's convenience.

I

Introduction

August to November 1944

During the years of mortal struggle with the Third Reich, the Allied nations made a number of general statements denouncing Nazi war crimes and atrocities. The scale of the horror perpetrated by Hitler and his minions was so vast that it fairly cried out for such condemnation. In addition, Allied peoples were genuinely shocked by the nightmare of bloodshed and suffering that Hitler's forces had brought to Europe, and they wanted these acts publicly censured.

However, the leaders of the United Nations were reluctant to be too specific in their condemnations as long as the Germans retained the power to retaliate against the Allied prisoners in their hands. The governments of the United States and Britain were especially cautious and, while excoriating Nazi deeds, were extremely circumspect about what would actually be done to the Nazi leaders. Not until November 1943, in the Moscow Declaration (document 1), did the Allies publicly announce that most of those who were responsible for atrocities committed in the occupied territories would be taken back to face justice at the scenes of their crimes. But even in this declaration, nothing specific was said about what was to be done to the major Nazi leaders, except that their fate would be subsequently determined by joint decision of the Allies.

This reticence regarding the specific punishment that awaited Hitler and his top aides was not a subtle propaganda ploy intended to lull suspicion and facilitate capitulation. As we now know, until the summer of 1944 neither the British nor the American government had reached a definite decision on what was to be done with Nazi war criminals. In fact, only after the D-Day invasion was serious high-level consideration of the general occupation policies to be employed in Germany begun in London and Washington. Even these efforts lacked a note of urgency until the breakout from Normandy in July-August

1944. Then, with Anglo-American forces racing eastward, decisions had to be made about the policies to be followed when the German frontier was crossed. Since the armies of Britain and the United States would bear the primary responsibility for the procedures to be applied in western Germany, it was only natural that the military authorities took the lead in this policy development. In August, the American War Department planners hurriedly completed a draft interim directive on occupation policy for Germany (document 2) and a "handbook" (document 3) to guide officers charged with the task of implementing the directive. Although both the handbook and the interim directive were thick, dense documents—the handbook contained hundreds of pages of detailed information—they did not throw much light on the course that the United States would follow in regard to Nazi war criminals. The handbook and interim directive merely ordered the American army occupation authorities to intern the officers and noncommissioned officers of Nazi organizations such as the Gestapo and the S.S., and also to take into custody Hitler, his top aides, and all those suspected of "war crimes." What was ultimately to happen to these detainees, the handbook and interim directive did not say. Since the American generals would be swamped with the administrative duties of occupation while battling their way across western Germany, they were more than happy to leave to the future every question that did not cry out for an immediate decision.

However, other organizations and individuals were not so cautious about war crimes policy planning once it appeared that the Allies might be close to victory over Germany. In late 1943, the Anglo-American governments had bowed to the demands of public opinion, and the entreaties of the Allied governments in exile, to create a United Nations War Crimes Commission (UNWCC). London and Washington were not overly enthusiastic about the commission's activities, wishing to retain the decision-making power in their own hands and to keep general policy matters quiet until action was absolutely necessary. The Soviet Union was even more critical of the UNWCC and refused to join, alleging that the inclusion of the dominions gave the British over-representation. Nonetheless, the commission met in London throughout 1944, preparing lists of war criminals and debating possible ways to deal with Nazi malefactors, while the Anglo-American governments nervously watched and tried to ease the proceedings into harmless byways. By the late summer of 1944, things had developed so far, however, that a formal proposal was before the commission recommending that the Allies create a special treaty court to try the major Nazi war criminals. The London and Washington governments were then requested to take a stand in support of the proposal. The British adamantly opposed the idea, contending that it was impractical, unnecessary, and too innovative. On August 19, 1944, the United Kingdom requested that the United States join the London government in rejecting the treaty court proposal (document 4).

Pressure on Washington to state clearly what would be done to Nazi war criminals was also building within the United States during the early fall of 1944. Not only were large elements of the press calling for punitive action, but the American Jewish Conference, now in possession of numerous reports of the Holocaust, demanded in late August that the United States government establish procedures to guarantee that those responsible for atrocities would be severely punished (document 5). More significantly, the powerful secretary of the treasury, Henry Morgenthau, Jr., returning from a tour of inspection to Europe in late August, was nearly obsessed by the conviction that American policymakers were inclined to be too soft on the Germans. Morgenthau believed not only that Germany should be economically crippled—the infamous pasturalization plan to deindustrialize the country—but that all those who had produced the evils of the Third Reich should be ruthlessly punished. Along with general purges of German, especially Nazi, institutions, Morgenthau wanted to forego trials for the Nazi leaders, leaving it to advancing army units to dispose of Hitler and his paladins through "summary execution."

Morgenthau was a tough, intelligent—and often charming—political combatant, willing and able to fight aggressively for what he wanted. In late August and early September 1944, he feverishly threw himself into the task of convincing his associates, especially Secretary of State Cordell Hull and Secretary of War Henry Stimson, as well as the president, that it was time to take a hard line on postwar Germany and German war criminals. Of all the officials in Washington, the man put most directly on the spot by Morgenthau's agitation was Stimson, because the army was at the gates of Germany and wanted carte blanche to apply the occupation procedures set forth in the interim directive and the handbook. On August 24, Stimson began turning over in his mind the broad question of what should be done about Nazi war criminals and organizations like the Gestapo. He did not totally spurn summary execution, but did reject anarchic killings. If American army units were to execute without trial, Stimson was convinced that, at the very least, officers would have to have "definite instructions" (document 6).

The secretary of war was jolted out of these leisurely ruminations on August 26 by a sharply worded letter from President Roosevelt strongly criticizing the army's occupation handbook (document 7). Henry Morgenthau had made use of his close personal association with the president to inflame Mr. Roosevelt's anti-German feelings and to convince him that the army was inclined to be overly easy on Germany. In a long discussion at the White House on August 25, Morgenthau had vigorously pushed his case, and had armed the president with a memorandum detailing the allegedly "soft" provisions of the handbook.

Roosevelt's letter to Stimson of August 26, parroting Morgenthau's objections to the handbook and calling for the use of stern measures in Germany, greatly increased the pressure on the War Department to justify, or modify, its occupation plans. Specifically, Stimson and his associates were being forced to take a stand on Morgenthau's economic proposals and on the general issue of war criminal policy. On August 28, an additional push was applied in the same direction by John Pehle, a Morgenthau associate and director of the war refugee board. In a letter to the secretary of state, which was sent on to Stimson, Pehle insisted that the U.S. government immediately develop procedures that would provide for the punishment, not only of German officials guilty of traditional war crimes, but also of those who had carried out prewar and wartime persecutions of German nationals (document 8).

In response to this pressure, Stimson sought to block Morgenthau by demonstrating the economic folly of deindustrialization and by asserting that a comprehensive war crimes program would be the most effective means of making Germany safe and democratic. On August 28, Stimson and Assistant Secretary of War John J. McCloy discussed the matter by telephone, and agreed that a war crimes program should rest on the twin principles of trial (rather than summary execution) and internment for members of Nazi organizations such as the Gestapo (document 9). A week later, Stimson buttressed his case by securing a telephone declaration from the army's chief legal officer, Major General Myron C. Cramer (the judge adjutant general), that some form of trial was essential; Cramer also indicated that it should be possible to use simplified court procedures (document 10).

However, when Stimson tried his arguments out on his colleagues in the policy committee for Germany (Morgenthau, Hull, and Mr. Roosevelt's confidential adviser, Harry Hopkins), they met with universal opposition. In a September 5 meeting, not only did Hopkins support Morgenthau, but even Hull turned away from his earlier advocacy of lowering international economic barriers and endorsed the idea of obliterating German economic power. Hull and his State Department colleagues were also prepared to accept any war criminal program that made certain that the Nazi leaders were "tried and executed" (document 11).

In the aftermath of this encounter, the participants sent position papers to Mr. Roosevelt setting out their respective positions. The State Department, with a qualified endorsement from Hopkins, reiterated its call for harsh economic measures and its support for a perfunctory trial and execution plan. Morgenthau dispatched to the White House a long memorandum detailing the "Morgenthau Plan" of summary execution and deindustrialization (document 12). In contrast, Stimson's letter to the president contended that no

Carthaginian economic plan would work and that Morgenthau's deindustrialization/summary execution scheme would merely act as a depressant on the world economy while producing dangerous resentment within Germany. Rather than conducting random executions and smashing the economic structure of central Europe, the secretary of war saw a comprehensive war criminal trial system, systematically punishing Nazi leaders and organizations, as the best means of settling the Allies' score with the Third Reich and securing the future peace of the world (document 13).

By fighting hard and making full use of his eloquence, Stimson succeeded in deterring the President from formally endorsing the State Department or Morgenthau occupation plans in two meetings that the Committee for Germany held with Mr. Roosevelt on September 5 and 9. But even though the president did not give his official approval to the Morgenthau plan in these sessions, he was definitely more inclined to the "radicals" than to Stimson. And the secretary of war, though he sharply condemned the proposals of his rivals, was forced to admit that he did not have in hand a war crimes trial plan that would produce a full-scale purge of Nazi Germany. Not only had the drafting work for such a system not been done, but Mr. Stimson granted that—under prevailing international law—he did not see how it would be possible to prosecute the Nazis for prewar persecutions or any other atrocities committed against German nationals (document 14).

Therefore, at the time Mr. Roosevelt met with Prime Minister Churchill at Quebec in mid-September 1944, he was leaning toward a Morgenthauesque German occupation policy, and the circumstances and mood of the conference tipped the scales more heavily in that direction. Neither Stimson nor Secretary of State Hull was in Quebec, but the president brought Morgenthau into the discussions, ostensibly to deal with the problem of postwar economic aid to Britain.

In the course of the conference, the secretary of the treasury and the president broadened the economic issues under consideration to include the treatment of postwar Germany. A wedge was thereby inserted for Morgenthau to advance his deindustrialization and summary execution scheme. Although British officials were sharply divided on the wisdom of Morgenthau's economic plans for Germany, they were more sympathetic toward his proposal that political execution be used to do away with Hitler and his aides. The British Cabinet had been intermittently wrestling with the question of war crimes policy in recent months and, although reaching no formal conclusion, had tended to hold that the liabilities of holding a state trial were so great that summary execution would be the wiser course. Reflecting that tendency, the lord chancellor, Sir John Simon, had prepared a paper setting out the case for political execution, and this memorandum was shown to the Americans at Quebec, although it had not been approved by the War Cabinet or even been seen by the Foreign Office (document 15). The upshot of the whole free-wheeling affair in Quebec was that the president and the prime minister finally initiated a summary of Morgenthau's economic plan and also agreed to send a copy of Simon's war crimes memorandum to Marshal Stalin, with a request that the three powers jointly prepare a list of top Nazis to be dispatched by summary execution.

Morgenthau's political victory at Quebec, though dazzling, quickly revealed itself as pyrrhic. In private, Stimson bitterly castigated the decisions of the conference, and Secretary Hull, outraged by the slapdash procedures that had been used and miffed that he had been excluded from the deliberations, rallied to Stimson's side. Then, in late September, the proverbial porosity of the Washington security system resulted in wholesale leaks to the press. Throughout the country the media spread stories of a deep Administration conflict over German-occupation policy, and the public was regaled with juicy details of the deindustrialization plan. Attempts to defend Morgenthau were lost in a chorus of American press criticism of what were seen as inhumane and unrealistic measures. On the other side of the world, Nazi Propaganda Minister Josef Goebbels seized on the controversy to threaten the German people, saying that if they did not struggle on to victory, the Western Allies, inspired by vindictive men like Morgenthau, would exterminate them. With the American presidential election but six weeks away and the Allied offensive temporarily, and most inopportunely, stalled just inside the German border, Franklin Roosevelt was caught in a very awkward political position. Marshaling all his subtlety and charm, he took the obvious step and began backing away from the Morgenthau plan. Although not formally repudiating the deeds of Quebec, the president henceforth did his best to pretend that nothing of importance had happened there.

The questions of German-occupation and war crimes policy were again thrown wide open, and Stimson and his War Department colleagues immediately moved in to take advantage of the new opportunity. In mid-September, Lieutenant Colonel Murray C. Bernays, chief of the Special Projects Office of the Personnel Branch (G-1), had completed a memorandum setting forth a new plan to prosecute the Nazi war criminals. Under the "Bernays plan," the leaders of the Third Reich, as well as certain "criminal" organizations such as the Gestapo, would be charged before an Allied tribunal with conspiracy "to commit murder, terrorism, and destruction of peaceful populations in violation of the laws of war." Not only would this approach allow the Allies to punish the Nazi chiefs and the broad mass of organization members for wartime violations of the traditional laws of war, it would also make admissible "everything done in furtherance of the conspiracy . . . including domestic atrocities induced or procured by the German Government to be committed by other Axis nations against their respective nationals." By introducing the concepts of conspiracy (heretofore virtually unknown in international law) and organizational criminality (which posed serious civil-liberties dangers in regard to guilt by association) Bernays had developed a plan that would enable the Allies to condemn the Nazi culprits for all their misdeeds in one gigantic trial, while leaving to secondary proceedings the task of meting out punishment to members of "criminal" organizations. The Bernays plan thus appeared to be the answer to the War Department's prayer—a method of purging Nazi Germany, not through Morgenthau's deindustrialization scheme, but by judicial action.

On September 15 the chief of the Personnel Branch approved a sketch of the Bernays plan and sent the first formulation of what came to be known as the Nuremberg trial system up the War Department's chain of command. Barely two weeks later, after a discussion of the plan in the office of the assistant secretary of war, John J. McCloy, on September 27, McCloy's assistant executive officer, Colonel Ammi Cutter, was given the task of evaluating the Bernays proposal. The Cutter critique, completed on October 1, indicated concern over the "fairly radical departures" from existing legal practice advocated by Bernays, but concluded that the approach was "ingenious" and worthy of additional study (document 17).

After three weeks, during which the plan was circulated and examined in various offices of the Pentagon, on October 24 Bernays gave an oral report on his proposal to Secretary Stimson and other high War Department officers and officials. Although this meeting did not produce immediate formal War Department approval of Bernays conspiracy/criminal-organization scheme, Henry Stimson was very enthusiastic about it. A few days later (October 27), when the secretary sent Secretary of State Hull a formal letter discussing various war crimes issues being considered by the two departments, he used the occasion to set forth a summary of the conspiracy/criminal-organization plan. While noting that the plan had not yet been endorsed by the War Department, Stimson also sent Hull a copy of Bernays' original memorandum of September 15 and urged that the State and War departments, and perhaps the Navy Department as well, begin immediate joint consideration of the proposal (document 18).

On November 9, 1944, a general meeting of the representatives from the three departments, presided over by Assistant Secretary of War McCloy, gave "in principle" agreement to the idea and authorized the War Department to prepare a draft memorandum to serve as the basis of future discussion. Colonel Bernays, possibly assisted by Colonel Cutter, quickly set to work preparing the first detailed formulation of the conspiracy/organization plan. The memorandum, which was finished on November 11, initially set out the various war crimes difficulties facing the planners, such as the enormous scale of Nazi offenses and the legal obstacles standing in the way of traditional prosecution of prewar persecutions and other atrocities. It then summarized the main elements of the conspiracy/criminal-organization plan and recommended that, after approval by the secretaries of the three departments, the proposal be forwarded to the president. Although the tone and content of the memorandum was favorable to the conspiracy/criminal-organization approach, the paper did contain two sections that would immediately produce questions and controversies. First, in summarizing the Nazi acts that should be taken as constituting elements of a criminal conspiracy, it included not only traditional war crimes and crimes against humanity, but also the assertion that the ultimate aim of the conspiracy was the "achieving of world domination"—a phrase that opened up the question of the criminality of aggressive war. Second, in order to protect the Allies from charges of too-radical innovation and "legal insufficiency," the memorandum also recommended that the tribunal created to hear the case be established by international treaty. In the opinion of those preparing the memorandum, although the drafting, negotiation, and ratification of such a treaty might be difficult, it would be the only really safe way to secure the legal underpinnings of an international trial (document 19).

The completion of the November 11 War Department memorandum marked the end of the first phase in the evolution of American war crimes policy. The basic proposal was now down on paper. Together with other memoranda setting out various formulations of the conspiracy/criminal-organization plan, it would be the battleground on which departmental controversies would be fought out and through which the official American policy would gradually take shape.

DOCUMENT 1

THE MOSCOW DECLARATION

November 1, 1943[1]

The United Kingdom, the United States and the Soviet Union have received from many quarters evidence of atrocities, massacres and cold-blooded mass executions which are being perpetrated by the Hitlerite forces in the many countries they have overrun and from which they are now being steadily expelled. The brutalities of Hitlerite domination are no new thing and all the peoples or territories in their grip have suffered from the worst form of government by terror. What is new is that many of these territories are now being redeemed by the advancing armies of the liberating Powers and that in their desperation, the recoiling Hitlerite Huns are redoubling their ruthless cruelties. This is now evidenced with particular clearness by monstrous crimes of the Hiterlites on the territory of the Soviet Union which is being liberated from the Hitlerites, and on French and Italian territory.

Accordingly, the aforesaid three allied Powers, speaking in the interests of the thirty-two United Nations, hereby solemnly declare and give full warning of their declaration as follows:—

At the time of the granting of any armistice to any government which may be set up in Germany, those German officers and men and members of the Nazi party who have been responsible for, or have taken a consenting part in the above atrocities, massacres and executions, will be sent back to the countries in which their abominable deeds were done in order that they may be judged and punished according to the laws of these liberated countries and of the free governments which will be created therein. Lists will be compiled in all possible detail from all these countries having regard especially to the invaded parts of the Soviet Union, to Poland and Czechoslovakia, to Yugoslavia and Greece, including Crete and other islands, to Norway, Denmark, the Netherlands, Belgium, Luxemburg, France and Italy.

Thus, the Germans who take part in wholesale shooting of Italian officers or in the execution of French, Dutch, Belgian or Norwegian hostages or of Cretan peasants, or who have shared in the slaughters inflicted on the people of Poland or in territories of the Soviet Union which are now being swept clear of the enemy, will know that they will be brought back to the scene of their crimes and judged on the spot by the peoples whom they have outraged. Let those who have hitherto not imbrued their hands with innocent blood beware lest they join the ranks of the guilty, for most assuredly the three allied Powers will pursue them to the uttermost ends of the earth and will deliver them to their accusers in order that justice may be done.

The above declaration is without prejudice to the case of the major criminals, whose offences have no particular geographical localisation and who will be punished by the joint decision of the Governments of the Allies.

ROOSEVELT STALIN CHURCHILL

DOCUMENT 2

From INTERIM DIRECTIVE FOR MILITARY GOVERNMENT OF GERMANY

August 21, 1944

POLICY DIRECTIVES, I 5, NAZI OFFICIALS, WAR CRIMINALS AND OTHER CRIMINALS[1]

POLICY — Nazi officials and war criminals will be apprehended and detained.

RESPONSIBILITIES — a. Adolf Hitler, his chief Nazi and Fascist associates and collaborators and all persons suspected of having committed war crimes, including those who appear on lists drawn up by the United Nations, which will be communicated to you by Supreme Headquarters, shall be arrested and held for investigation and subsequent disposition.

b. The heads of all ministries and other high political functionaries of the German Reich and those Germans who have held high position in German occupied countries will be interned and held pending further instructions.

c. You will also detain any national of any of the United Nations who is alleged to have committed an offence against his national law relating to the conduct of the war[2] such persons will be turned over to the appropriate National authority. You will also detain any other person whose name or designation appears on lists to be drawn up by the United Nations and communicated to you by Supreme Headquarters.

DOCUMENT 3

WAR DEPARTMENT HANDBOOK OF MILITARY GOVERNMENT FOR GERMANY, (SEPTEMBER 1, 1944)[1] TABLE "D"—NAZI POLICE, PARTY, PARA-MILITARY AND GOVERNMENTAL OFFICERS TO BE INTERNED

[FOR INFORMATION ONLY]

The following categories of Nazi officers will be arrested and detained upon the entry into Germany of the Allied Occupational Forces.[2] The figures shown are an estimate of the number of persons who will be detained in Germany as a whole. The estimate of the number in the Western Zone, is roughly, one half of each group.

1. *The Secret State Police* (GESTAPO), All personnel 15,000
2. *Security Service of the SS (SD)*, All personnel 15,000
3. *Police Officials*:
   a. Police Presidents and Directors 100
   b. Befehlshaber der ORPO and der SIPO[3] 60
   c. Technische Nothilfe[4] 50
   d. Police Officers in Key Posts 320
      (1) Höherer SS and Polizeiführer[5]
      (2) Inspekteur der ORPO[6]
      (3) Inspekteur der SIPO und SD[7]
4. *Nazi Party Officials*:
   a. Administrative officials of the Party on the Reich, Gau and Kreis[8] levels down to the post of Kreishauptstellenleiter.
   b. All other members of the Party holding rank of Bereichsleiter[9] or higher. 30,000
   c. Ortsgruppenleiter[10] 27,000
5. *Para-Military Officers*:
   a. Waffen SS (all officers)[11] 60,000
   b. Allgemeine SS (all officers and non-commissioned officers from Scharführer upwards)[12] 8,000
   c. SA (officers holding the rank of Sturmbannführer or higher)[13] 30,000
   d. Hitler Jugend (officers holding the rank of Sturmführer or higher)[14] 20,000

e. NSKK (officers holding the rank of Staffelführer or higher)[15]	10,000
f. NSFK (officers holding the rank of Sturmbannführer or higher)[16]	5,000
g. RAD (headquarters officials)[17]	250

DOCUMENT 4

BRITISH AIDE-MÉMOIRE

THE BRITISH AMBASSADOR (HALIFAX) TO THE SECRETARY OF STATE (HULL).[1]

August 19, 1944

His Majesty's Ambassador presents his compliments to the Secretary of State and has the honour to refer to previous correspondence regarding the scope of the activities of the United Nations War Crimes Commission.[2]

2. Lord Halifax has now been informed that on May 30, 1944, Sir Cecil Hurst, the United Kingdom representative on the Commission, and concurrently its Chairman, addressed a formal letter to His Majesty's Principal Secretary of State for Foreign Affairs[3] drawing attention to public demand that some machinery should be established for dealing with atrocities committed on racial, political, or religious grounds in enemy territory. The letter stated that if machinery for this purpose already exists the Commission feels that a public announcement to this effect would be helpful. If, on the other hand, the Governments of the United Nations have no plan in view for bringing the authors of such crimes to justice, the Commission is prepared to undertake the task if desired. Sir Cecil Hurst suggests that Mr. Eden should take the initiative in promoting any further discussion that may be required on the subject between the Governments of the United Nations.

3. His Majesty's Government have considered this question and have decided that in their view the War Crimes Commission should confine itself to collecting evidence of atrocities of this nature, e.g. those against Jews, only when perpetrated in occupied countries. It is felt that a clear distinction exists between offences in regard to which the United Nations have jurisdiction under International Law, i.e. war crimes, and those in regard to which they had not. Atrocities committed on racial, political or religious grounds in enemy territory fell within the latter category. The United Nations should, therefore, in the opinion of His Majesty's Government in the United Kingdom, not themselves assume any formal obligation in regard to the punishment of those responsible for such atrocities. Any attempt on their part to do

so or to attempt to enforce specific provisions for the prosecution of offenders by enemy authorities would give rise to serious difficulties of practice and principle.

4. On the other hand successor Governments in enemy countries after the war will have jurisdiction in such cases and the United Nations will be in a strong position to exert pressure upon them to exercise it. There would appear to be a strong case for leaving the door open for the exercise of such pressure.

5. His Majesty's Government accordingly propose that their attitude in this question should be as follows:

(A) Sir Cecil Hurst should be informed that His Majesty's Government cannot agree to any extension of the terms of reference of the United Nations War Crimes Commission to enable it to deal with atrocities committed on racial, political or religious grounds in enemy territory.

(B) The United Nations should not assume any formal commitment to ensure the trial of those responsible for such atrocities; nor should they impose upon the enemy any formal obligation to try them or surrender them for trial. The United Nations should, however, be prepared to bring pressure to bear upon successor Governments in enemy countries to ensure that criminals are brought to justice. The War Crimes Commission should be informed of the general intentions of the United Nations in this respect.

6. Lord Halifax has been instructed to enquire whether the United States Government concur in the foregoing conclusions and, if so, whether they approve the lines of the proposed reply to Sir Cecil Hurst's letter.[4]

7. It is not the intention of His Majesty's Government to consult the other Allied Governments in this matter.

WASHINGTON

DOCUMENT 5

STATEMENT ON WAR CRIMINALS SUBMITTED BY THE AMERICAN JEWISH CONFERENCE TO THE SECRETARY OF STATE[1]

August 25, 1944

Since their rise to power, the leaders of the Nazi regime in Germany have repeatedly and consistently proclaimed the extermination of the Jewish people as a major aim. Both before and since the beginning of the war, they have pursued this aim with unrelenting vigor and brutality, utilizing every measure of degradation and despoilation, including forced labor, starvation, deportation and mass murder. This campaign of terror and annihilation has been carried out with unexampled bestiality in consort with Axis allies and associates, and with the connivance of Nazi followers and subordinates in their home countries and their collaborators in occupied territories. These crimes cannot go unpunished without destroying the legal and moral foundations upon which our civilization rests.

The United Nations, being aware of the manifold crimes committed by the Axis powers against the Jewish people, have solemnly and officially affirmed as their policy toward all those guilty of these crimes the exaction of full and just retribution.

Thus, the Inter-Allied Declaration signed at St. James' Palace on January 13, 1942, though not making express reference to the Jews, proclaimed that the signatory powers "place among their principal war aims the punishment, through the channel of organized justice, of those guilty and responsible for these crimes (against civilians), whether they have ordered them, perpetrated them, or in any way participated in them."

Subsequently, in a Joint Declaration issued simultaneously at London and Washington on December 17, 1942, the United Nations took formal cognizance of the fact that "the German authorities . . . are now carrying into effect Hitler's oft-repeated intention to exterminate the Jewish people in Europe," and therefore "reaffirm their solemn resolution to ensure that those responsible for these crimes shall not escape retribution, and to press on with the necessary practical measures to this end."

In conjunction with the historic Moscow Conference, the heads of the governments of the United States, the U.S.S.R., and Great Britain, "speaking in the interests of 32 United Nations," issued on November 1, 1943, "a solemn public declaration." As Secretary of State Cordell Hull stated on November 18, 1943, before a Joint Meeting of the Senate and the House of Representatives, the Declaration promised that "due punishment will be administered . . . to the perpetrators of the bestial and abominable crimes committed by the Nazi leaders against the harassed and persecuted inhabitants of occupied territories—against people of all races and religions, among whom Hitler has reserved for the Jews his most brutal wrath."

On March 24, 1944, this policy was clearly and emphatically reiterated when President Roosevelt, with the approval of Prime Minister Churchill and Premier Stalin, made a public pronouncement calling attention to the fact that the extermination of the Jewish people was "begun by the Nazis in the day of peace and multiplied by them a hundred times in time of war," and stating in part: "We . . . again proclaim our determination that none who participate in these acts of savagery (against Jews and other civilians) shall go unpunished. The United Nations have made it clear that they will pursue the guilty and deliver them up in order that justice be done. That warning applies not only to the leaders but also to their functionaries and subordinates in Germany and in the satellite countries. . . . All who share the guilt will share the punishment."

In view of the solemn and unequivocal declaration of policy embodied in these and similar official statements, which leave no doubt as to the intention of the United Nations to visit just punishment upon those guilty of crimes against civilian populations, and notably against the Jewish people, the American Jewish Conference, representing the Jewish community of the United States of America, urges that in carrying out this policy the United Nations take cognizance of and proper action upon the following considerations:

1. Among the crimes to be made punishable under this policy, there be expressly included the publicly announced intent of the Axis nations and their allies and associates to annihilate the Jewish people, and all acts whereby they sought to accomplish this aim, before and during the war, within their own and occupied territories.

2. In all trials of those guilty of crimes against civilian populations, criminal acts performed against the Jewish people shall be duly specified as part of the indictment.

3. Those charged with specific crimes against individual Jews, or with acts designed to bring about the ultimate annihilation of Jewish communities, such as deprivation, starvation, deportation, unendurable forced labor, and mass murder by whatever means, in territories occupied by the enemy, shall be prosecuted with the utmost energy and vigor in the national courts of the states where such crimes were committed, irrespective of the nationality of the accused or of the victims.

4. The prosecution of those guilty of these acts against Jews in Germany and in the territories of her allies and associates, as well as of crimes not confined to single territories, shall be within the jurisdiction of the contemplated international court for the trial of war criminals.

5. The United Nations shall agree among themselves to declare as common criminals, and shall so declare, all those guilty of these acts against the Jews, and shall require the Axis nations, their allies and associates, the neutral nations and any other country where the criminals may seek asylum, to surrender or extradite all persons thus designated. Provisions for the surrender of these criminals by the Axis Powers, their allies and associates, shall be included in the terms of the armistice.

7.[2] Representatives of the respective Jewish communities shall be consulted in the preparation of evidence against these criminals, and shall be recognized in the national courts as *amici curias*[3] before the contemplated international prosecuting body and the international court for the trial of war criminals. The constituting acts of these bodies shall contain the necessary provisions to this effect.

8. The Commission for the Investigation of War Crimes,[4] or such other body as may be constituted for this purpose by the United Nations, shall receive and give due consideration to all suggestions which may be submitted to it by a representation of the Jewish people, and it shall grant such a representation a *locus standi*.[5]

DOCUMENT 6

FROM NOTES OF HENRY L. STIMSON FOR A CONFERENCE WITH THE PRESIDENT[1]

August 25, 1944

3. Policy vs. liquidation of Hitler and his gang.
   Present instructions seem inadequate beyond imprisonment.
   Our officers must have the protection of definite instructions if shooting is required.
   If shooting is required it must be immediate; not postwar.
4. Treatment of Gestapo? To include what levels?

DOCUMENT 7

PRESIDENTIAL MEMORANDUM FOR THE SECRETARY OF WAR[1]

August 26, 1944

This so-called "Handbook"[2] is pretty bad. I should like to know how it came to be written and who approved it down the line. If it has not been sent out as approved, all copies should be withdrawn and held until you get a chance to go over it.

It gives me the impression that Germany is to be restored just as much as The Netherlands or Belgium, and the people of Germany brought back as quickly as possible to their pre-war estate.

It is of the utmost importance that every person in Germany should realize that this time Germany is a defeated nation. I do not want them to starve to death but, as an example, if they need food to keep body and soul together beyond what they have, they should be fed three times a day with soup from Army soup kitchens. That will keep them perfectly healthy and they will remember that experience all their lives. The fact that they are a defeated nation, collectively and individually, must be so impressed upon them that they will hesitate to start any new war. . . .

The following are a few extracts of things which have caught my eye in a very hurried reading of this "Handbook". There are doubtless many others.

"Your main and immediate task, to accomplish your mission, is to get things running, to pick up the pieces, to restore as quickly as possible the official functioning of the German civil government in the area for which you are responsible. . . ."

There exists a school of thought both in London and here which would, in effect, do for Germany what this government did to its own citizens in 1933 when they were flat on their backs. I see no reason for starting a WPA, PWA, or a CCC for Germany when we go in with our Army of Occupation.[3]

Too many people here and in England hold to the view that the German people as a whole are not responsible for what has taken place—that only a few Nazi leaders are responsible. That unfortunately is not based on fact. The German people as a whole must have it driven home to them that the whole nation has been engaged in a lawless conspiracy against the decencies of modern civilization.

Please let me see the revision of this and also let me have this original copy back.

FDR

DOCUMENT 8

MEMORANDUM FOR MR. STETTINIUS FROM JOHN W. PEHLE, EXECUTIVE DIRECTOR, THE WAR REFUGEE BOARD[1]

August 28, 1944

As you know, a major activity of the War Refugee Board has been psychological warfare designed to induce and persuade the enemy to cease the persecution of the Jews and other minorities. The basis of this program, which has been carried out in cooperation with the State Department, Office of War Information[2] and other agencies, has been the threat to punish every Axis war criminal who has participated, directly or indirectly, in such persecution. Threats of this nature had been made by the United Nations, including various Branches of this Government, even before the War Refugee Board was established, and they have since been repeated with increasing tempo. For your information we have collected and are attaching hereto those declarations which specifically set forth the determination of the United States and of the other United Nations to punish the perpetrators of atrocities and other crimes against Jews and other minorities even where the victims are or were nationals of Germany or of a satellite power.[3]

We had assumed that one of the primary functions of the United Nations Commission for the Investigation of War Crimes, which was created in 1943, would be to devise procedures for the gathering of evidence and the ascertainment, trial and punishment of those enemy nationals who had participated in such war crimes. Much to our surprise we were informed by our General Counsel, Mr. Josiah E. DuBois,[4] upon his return from London recently that he understood from a conversation with Mr. Pell,[5] the United States representative on the Commission, that the Commission takes the view that war crimes under international law do not include crimes committed by an Axis nation or its nationals against its own subjects or the subjects of another Axis nation.[6] Accordingly, it appears that the Commission is not making any provision for the just punishment of such war criminals.

Needless to say, it would be a fearful miscarriage of justice if such war criminals were permitted to escape punishment for their inhuman crimes. Moreover, the failure to implement the numerous threats of punishment would not only subject to ridicule the authors thereof, but would render it far more difficult to deter similar criminal conduct in the future. The failure to punish the criminals of World War I may well have removed a deterrent to the commission of brutalities against civilian populations in this war, including the mass murder of the Jews.

According to Mr. DuBois' report, Mr. Pell is not satisfied with this position of the United Nations Commission for the Investigation of War Crimes, but seems not to have received instructions from this Government in the matter. Mr. Pell believes that the most effective way of inducing the Commission to broaden the scope of its work to include the punishment of all Axis war criminals, including those guilty of crimes against persons in the above categories, would be to have the United States Government instruct him to urge the Commission to include such crimes in its program and, if possible, to have the other governments represented on the Commission instruct their representatives along similar lines. Another suggested step would be to publicize such an instruction by releasing it to the press.

Accordingly, we suggest that the Department advise Mr. Pell along the lines of the proposed cable attached hereto[7] indicating clearly that the declared policy of the United States Government is to ensure the just punishment of all Axis war criminals, including those guilty of crimes against the Jews and other minorities whether or not the victims of such crimes are of the same nationality as the evildoers; and that Mr. Pell should insist upon the formulation of a program by the Commission effectuating this policy.

J. W. Pehle
Executive Director

DOCUMENT 9

REPORT BY THE ASSISTANT SECRETARY OF WAR (McCLOY) OF A TELEPHONE CONVERSATION WITH SECRETARY OF WAR STIMSON, 12:30 PM[1]

August 28, 1944

Four Propositions.

1. Swift punishment should be visited on the Nazi leaders in respect to war crimes.

2. We should then go down by steps into the subordinates responsible for such crimes, beginning with the leaders of the Gestapo[2] and investigating their individual responsibility and punishing it accordingly.

3. As a preliminary step to the above we should immediately upon the occupation of Germany arrest and intern the entire Gestapo and institute careful investigation into individual responsibility for these crimes. Encourage the making of such charges by the German people.

4. Institute at once an investigation as to the responsibility of the Storm Troopers[3] and their leaders for similar war crimes. Consider also the method of proceeding against the Storm Troopers in a way similar to that taken against the Gestapo. We should always have in mind the necessity of punishing effectively enough to bring home to the German people the wrongdoing done in their name, and thus prevent similar conduct in the future, without depriving them of the hope of a future respected German community. (Those are the two alternatives.) Remember this punishment is for the purpose of prevention and not for vengeance. An element in prevention is to secure in the person punished the conviction of guilt. The trial and punishment should be as prompt as possible and in all cases care should be taken against making martyrs of the individuals punished.

How far can we go under the Geneva Convention[4] in educating war prisoners against Nazism?

How far can we go in protecting the remainder of the Germans from the contagion of the Nazis?

DOCUMENT 10

TELEPHONE CONVERSATIONS BETWEEN THE SECRETARY OF WAR (HENRY STIMSON) AND THE JUDGE ADVOCATE GENERAL (MAJOR GENERAL MYRON C. CRAMER)[1]

September 5, 1944

FIRST CONVERSATION

Cramer: Good morning, Mr. Secretary, General Cramer.

Stimson: Good morning, General. I wanted to ask you a question or two. Is it possible for the Allies to set up criminal courts in Germany consisting of civilians—I mean American civilians—allied civilians—and have them dispense justice—in order to form a military tribunal. The question comes up with dealing with the war criminals right off. What's your advice in regard to that?

Cramer: Well, off hand I would see no legal objection to putting some civilians on but it should be fundamentally military. It's possible to have civilians on these military commissions—for instance, Mr. Biddle was not a member of the commission, he was one of the prosecutors in that saboteur trial.[2]

Stimson: Yes I know but he was not a member of the court.

Cramer: He was not a member of the court, no sir. I would have to check back on that before I could give you a positive answer. I can possibly give you an answer in a few minutes.

Stimson: Are you at your office?

Cramer: Yes sir.

Stimson: Well if you would look that up—I mean that the court is put on regional military tribunals throughout Germany—in the different regions consisting perhaps of one American, one Briton and one Russian. Would they have to be military or not? And the Russians in their investigations are putting in a pretty high type of men. It might be advisable that we put in a well-known man, politically well-known, or professionally well-known.[3]

Cramer: Are they putting in civilians or military?

Stimson: What they are doing is not in their courts—I mean the investigation they made of these atrocities has been done by pretty good men I'm told and it would be well for us to follow that example if we could.

Cramer: Well these investigations of war criminals that we've been carrying on over in England or from there are composed mostly of civilians.[4]

Stimson: Yes, I know we've got that sort of tribunal but that is not—that's a grand jury so to speak. I just want quickly your advice—the tribunal must be absolutely free of the restrictions of courts-martial. I understand that's so from experience with the saboteur case. It can make its own rules. Of course, as a matter of fact—this will be my advice—this will give them simply the skeleton of what we call the requisitional fair trial. They must have some sort of charge against them—they must have some sort of an opportunity to reply to that charge. I'm not even sure of counsel but of course counsel can be given to them by the court but it must be slender enough but substantial—it must give them—well we must not put ourselves in the position where it can be said we convicted these people without a trial. But it must be free from all the delays that would go with the technicalities of courts-martial or the United States jurisprudence procedure should go in, absolutely. There are lots of cases, for instance—oh well in all kinds of quasi tribunals, police courts or police magistrates and things like that where they give them elements of what is fair play and such things, and in general as I remember it, a man brought up must know what he's charged of, must have a chance to say what he wants to say in regard to it and perhaps to a certain extent—well as to calling witnesses I won't say yes, that might tie it up.

Cramer: As to calling witnesses?

Stimson: Whether he would have the power to call witnesses.

Cramer: I think offhand you'd have to give them that.

Stimson: Well probably so but tell me what you think. It's got to be cut down to its bare bones.

Cramer: All right. Now you want that right away I take it.

Stimson: I'm at my house Adams 8030.

Cramer: Yes sir.

Stimson: I'm going over to Mr. Hull's.[5]

Cramer: You want it before you go there?

Stimson: Yes I want it if I could before I go there.

Cramer: What time are you leaving for there?

Stimson: Shortly after nine o'clock.

Cramer: All right, sir. I'll have some kind of an answer for you before nine.

SECOND CONVERSATION

Stimson: Yes?

Cramer: This is General Cramer again, Mr. Secretary. In regard to the matter about which you just talked to me we are satisfied that legally such commissions as you speak of can be appointed.

Stimson: That is, commissions of part or whole civilians?

Cramer: Well, mostly part although there would be no legal objection to make it all civilians. But it seems to me that there should be some military men on there, at least one.

Stimson: Yes. Well I'll bear that in mind.

Cramer: Of course those things are more or less military and the more military men you have the more military it is. Now as to rules of evidence and so on that of course can be loosened to a certain extent but I do think that the evidence should be taken down verbatim for future records and so on, because we have had I understand one—I mean we've seen one record that's come from Italy and it's only really a summary of testimony.

Stimson: Let me put this down. The Judge Advocate General thinks that we can make military tribunals for the judgment of war criminals in Germany composed of civilians instead of military although he strongly advises that at least one military man [be included]; second, he strongly urges the keeping of record verbatim testimony of what takes place at the trial for future use. Now anything further?

Cramer: The other question of course that you raised about witnesses—I think they should be permitted to bring on any witnesses they please because otherwise you'll have—

Stimson: Should be permitted to produce witnesses.

Cramer: What I want to provide against is any charges of railroading these people.

Stimson: To prevent any chance of railroading the people?

Cramer: Would there be any charges to that effect you see.

Stimson: A great many people think that the question of the guilt of some of these people is already decided. I'm taking the position that they must have the substance of a trial. I just wanted to know whether you agreed with me.

Cramer: I agree with you absolutely.

Stimson: All right. Well then we can go into the details afterwards. I'm in such a hurry now I can't unfortunately go into those details now. This should include the production of witnesses and the keeping of records?

Cramer: Yes, sir.

Stimson: I see. Thank you very much.

Cramer: Well now there's one thing, Mr. Secretary, if you're interested in having a copy of the *American Bar Association Journal* for June 1944 there's about a four page article by Major Cowles on the trial of war criminals by military tribunals.[6]

Stimson: I'd like to see that very much—will you send it around to my office at the Pentagon Building?

Cramer: All right, sir.

Stimson: Marked for me immediate. Thank you very much.

Cramer: All right, I'll do that, sir.

Stimson: I'm very much obliged to you.

DOCUMENT 11

FROM STATE DEPARTMENT MEMORANDUM FOR THE CABINET COMMITTEE ON GERMANY[1]

September 5, 1944

2(b) *Dissolution of the Nazi Party and all affiliated organizations.*[2] Large groups of particularly objectionable elements, especially the SS and the Gestapo, should be arrested and interned and war criminals should be tried and executed.

DOCUMENT 12

FROM HENRY MORGENTHAU JR. TO PRESIDENT ROOSEVELT (THE MORGENTHAU PLAN)[1]

September 5, 1944

APPENDIX B

PUNISHMENT OF CERTAIN WAR CRIMES AND TREATMENT OF SPECIAL GROUPS.

A. *Punishment of Certain War Criminals*[2]

(1) *Arch-criminals.*

A list of the arch-criminals of this war whose obvious guilt has generally been recognized by the United Nations shall be drawn up as soon as possible and transmitted to the appropriate military authorities. The military authorities shall be instructed with respect to all persons who are on such list as follows:

(a) They shall be apprehended as soon as possible and identified as soon as possible after apprehension, the identification to be approved by an officer of the General rank.

(b) When such identification has been made the person identified shall be put to death forthwith by firing squads made up of soldiers of the United Nations.

(2) *Certain Other War Criminals*

(a) Military commissions shall be established by the Allied Military Government for the trial of certain crimes which have been committed against civilization during this war. As soon as practicable, representatives of the liberated countries of Europe shall be included on such commissions. These crimes shall include those crimes covered by the following section and such other crimes as such military commissions may be ordered to try from time to time.

(b) Any person who is suspected of being responsible for (through the issuance of orders or otherwise), or having participated in causing the death of any human being in the following situations shall be arrested and tried promptly by such military commissions, unless prior to trial one of the United Nations has requested that such person be placed in its custody for trial on similar charges for acts committed within its territory:

(i) The death was caused by action in violation of the rules of war.

(ii) The victim was killed as a hostage in reprisal for the deeds of other persons.

(iii) The victim met death because of his nationality, race, color, creed, or political conviction.

(c) Any person who is convicted by the military commissions of the crimes specified in paragraph (b) shall be sentenced to death, unless the military commissions, in exceptional cases, determine that there are extenuating circumstances, in which case other punishment may be meted out, including deportation to a penal colony outside of Germany. Upon conviction, the sentence shall be carried out immediately.

B. *Detention of Certain Groups*

All members of the following groups should be detained until the extent of the guilt of each individual is determined:

(a) The S.S.

(b) The Gestapo.

(c) All high officials of the police, S.A. and other security organizations.

(d) All high Government and Nazi Party officials.

(e) All leading public figures closely identified with Nazism.

C. *Registration of Males*

An appropriate program will be formulated for the re-registration as soon as possible of all males of the age of 14 or over. The registration shall be on a form and in a manner to be prescribed by the military authorities and shall show, among other things, whether or not the person registering is a member of the Nazi Party or affiliated organizations, the Gestapo, S.S., S.A. or Kraft Korps.[3]

D. *Labor Battalions*

Apart from the question of established guilt for special crimes, mere membership in the S.S., the Gestapo and similar groups will constitute the basis for inclusion into compulsory labor battalion to serve outside Germany for reconstruction purposes.

E. *Dissolution of Nazi Organizations*

The Nazi Party and all affiliated organizations such as the Labor Front, The Hitler Youth, The Strength-through-Joy, etc.[4] should be dissolved and their properties and records confiscated. Every possible effort should be made to prevent any attempts to reconstitute them in underground or disguised form.

F. *Prohibition on Exercise of Certain Privileges*

All members of the following groups should be dismissed from police office, disenfranchised and disqualified to hold any public office or to engage in journalist, teaching, and legal professions, or, in any managerial capacity in banking, manufacturing or trade:

(1) The Nazi Party.

(2) Nazi sympathizers who by their words or deeds materially aided or abetted the Nazi program.

(3) The Junkers.[5]

(4) Military and Naval officers.

G. *Junker Estates*

All Junker estates should be broken up and divided among the peasants and the system of primogeniture and entail should be abolished.[6]

H. *Prohibition on Emigration*

(1) A Proclamation shall be issued prohibiting any person resident in Germany from leaving or attempting to leave Germany, except with permission from the Allied Military Government.

(2) Violation of this Proclamation shall be an offense triable by military commissions of the Allied Military Government and heavy penalties shall be prescribed, including death.

(3) All possible steps shall be taken by the military authorities to prevent any such person from leaving (without permission).

HENRY MORGENTHAU JR.

DOCUMENT 13

FROM HENRY L. STIMSON TO HENRY MORGENTHAU JR.[1]

September 5, 1944

It is primarily by the thorough apprehension, investigation, and trial of all the Nazi leaders and instruments of the Nazi system of terrorism such as the Gestapo with punishment delivered as promptly, swiftly and severely as possible that we can demonstrate the abhorrence which the world has for such a system and bring home to the German people our determination to expiate it and all its fruits forever. . . .

My basic objection to the proposed methods of treating Germany which were discussed this morning was that in addition to a system of preventive and educative punishment they would add the dangerous weapon of complete economic oppression. Such methods, in my opinion, do not prevent war, they tend to breed war.

DOCUMENT 14

SECRETARY OF WAR (STIMSON) TO THE PRESIDENT[1]

September 9, 1944

[After discussing his disagreement with Henry Morgenthau Jr. regarding deindustrialization of Germany, Mr. Stimson continued:]

The other fundamental point upon which I feel we differ is the matter of the trial and punishment of those Germans who are responsible for crimes and depredations. Under the plan proposed by Mr. Morgenthau,[2] the so-called arch-criminals shall be put to death by the military without provision for any trial and upon mere identification after apprehension. The method of dealing with these and other criminals requires careful thought and a well-defined procedure. Such procedure must embody, in my judgment, at least the rudimentary aspects of the Bill of Rights, namely, notification to the accused of the charge, the right to be heard and, within reasonable limits, to call witnesses in his defense. I do not mean to favor the institution of state trials or to introduce any cumbersome machinery but the very punishment of these men in a dignified manner consistent with the advance of civilization, will have all the greater effect upon posterity. Furthermore, it will afford the most effective way of making a record of the Nazi system of terrorism and of the effort of the Allies to terminate the system and prevent its recurrence.

I am disposed to believe that at least as to the chief Nazi officials, we should participate in an international tribunal constituted to try them. They should be charged with offenses against the laws of the Rules of War in that they have committed wanton and unnecessary cruelties in connection with the prosecution of the war. This law of the Rules of War has been upheld by our own Supreme Court and will be the basis of judicial action against the Nazis.

Even though these offenses have not been committed against our troops, I feel that our moral position is better if we take our share in their conviction. Other war criminals who have committed crimes in subjugated territory should be returned in accordance with the Moscow Declaration to those territories for trial by national military commissions having jurisdiction of the offense under the same Rules of War. I have great difficulty in finding any means whereby military commissions may try and convict those responsible for excesses committed within Germany both before and during the war which have no relation to the conduct of the war. I would be prepared to construe broadly what constituted a violation of the Rules of War but there is a certain field in which I fear that external courts cannot move. Such courts would be without jurisdiction in precisely the same way that any foreign court would be without jurisdiction to try those who were guilty of, or condoned, lynching in our own country . . .

DOCUMENT 15

MEMORANDUM, "MAJOR WAR CRIMINALS," BY THE BRITISH LORD CHANCELLOR SIR JOHN SIMON[1]

September 4, 1944

I was asked by the War Cabinet[2] to consider further, and to report upon, proposals for dealing with the *major*[3] war criminals. The following appear to be some of the principal considerations to be borne in mind:

1. The Moscow Tri-partite Declaration (Nov. 1st, 1943) concluded with the statement that it was made "without prejudice to the case of the major criminals, whose offenses have no particular geographical localisation, and who will be punished by the joint decision of the Governments of the Allies". This statement has as yet never been amplified either by public announcement, or (as far as I know) by consultation between the Allies.

2. In view of the progress made towards final victory over Germany, has not the time arrived to raise—with President Roosevelt, at any rate—certain questions connected with the carrying out of this announcement of intended punishment? It is much to be hoped that the principal criminals may, before the end, be disposed of by the people whom they have led to destruction, or may take their own lives—but if they fall alive into the hands of the Allies, what is to be done with them?

3. I am strongly of opinion that the method by trial, conviction, and judicial sentence is quite inappropriate for notorious ringleaders such as Hitler, Himmler, Goering, Goebbels and Ribbentrop. Apart from the formidable difficulties of constituting the Court, formulating the charge, and assembling the evidence, the question of their fate *is a political, not a judicial, question*. It could not rest with judges, however eminent or learned, to decide finally a matter like this, which is of the widest and most vital public policy. The decision must be "the joint decision of the Governments of the Allies". The Moscow Declaration, indeed, has already said so.

4. I am equally clear that these leading and notorious criminals cannot be left untouched, while lesser people who have committed atrocities and war-crimes under their orders and with their approval are tried and heavily punished. Such a course would be universally, and rightly, condemned. It may not be essential to make a precise public announcement of Allied intentions as regards the major criminals at present—the Moscow Declaration is itself a general indication, and a new statement might evoke reprisals against Allied individuals in German hands—but it seems to me most desirable to open confidential consultations on the subject with some of our Allies, and to get a decision now as to what is to be done. Otherwise, when the time comes, there may be a disastrous difference of view.

5. The list of war criminals who might be dealt with without trial, which was prepared by the Foreign Secretary,[4] was criticised in some quarters for its omissions,[5] but I am disposed to think that this method will only be considered appropriate and justified in the case of the small group of leaders who are known to have been responsible for the conduct of the war, and who have at headquarters authorized, approved or acquiesced in the horrible atrocities that have been committed.

6. A formula which might meet the Prime Minister's suggested views[6] would be as follows:—

> "The Moscow Tri-partite Declaration of November 1st, 1943 announced that the Allies intended to arrange for the trial and punishment of enemy war criminals who had already been captured or who fell into their hands, but the Moscow Declaration was stated to be made "without prejudice to the case of the major criminals, whose offenses have no particular geographical localisation, and

who will be punished by the joint decision of the Governments of the Allies." The time has come to announce that among these major criminals are Hitler, Himmler, Goering, Goebbels and Ribbentrop, but the Allies reserve the right to add to their number. Upon any of these major criminals falling into Allied hands, the Allies will decide how they are to be disposed of, and the execution of this decision will be carried out immediately.

[LONDON] S[IMON]

DOCUMENT 16

SUBJECT: TRIAL OF EUROPEAN WAR CRIMINALS (BY COLONEL MURRAY C. BERNAYS, G-1)[1]

September 15, 1944

THE GENERAL PROBLEM[2]

1. a. There will be many thousands of war criminals who should be tried for crimes committed all over Europe. Their offenses range from the establishment of policy at the center of the Nazi organization, down to scattered individual acts of criminality. Some offenders are guilty as principals, some as accessories. In many cases it will be difficult to establish the individual's identity or to connect him with the particular act charged. Witnesses will be dead and scattered, and the gathering of proof will be laborious and costly. The offenders will become subject to trial under many and divergent codes and procedures. The applicable basic law, law as to justification (e.g., orders of duly constituted superiors), procedures, and rules of evidence will vary from jurisdiction to jurisdiction. The paper work will be enormous, the liaison and coördination singularly difficult.

b. Undoubtedly, the Nazis have been counting on the magnitude and ingenuity of their offenses, the numbers of the offenders, the law's complexities, and delay and war weariness as major defenses against effective prosecution.[3] Trial on an individual basis, and by old modes and procedures, will go far to realize the Nazi hopes in this respect.

THE MINORITIES PROBLEM

2. a. Many of the Axis atrocities were committed before there was a state of war. These cannot be categorized as war crimes under existing law.

b. Some of the worst outrages were committed by Axis powers against their own nationals on racial, religious, and political grounds. As to these, the offenders can plead justification under domestic law. Also, to call these atrocities war crimes would set the precedent of an international right to sit in judgment on the conduct of the several states toward their own nationals. This would open the door to incalculable consequences and present grave questions of policy.

c. However, widely publicized statements of the highest leaders have been interpreted as assuring that the above atrocities would be prosecuted by the United Nations as war crimes.[4]

3. a. It may be expected that even though the above acts cannot be reached as war crimes, the Axis authorities who committed them will be punishable in many cases with equal or greater severity for offenses which are war crimes. This, however, will not necessarily cover all the cases, and in any event it will not satisfy the insistence of the minority groups that recognition should be given to the criminal character of the specific acts and policies of which they complain.

b. The alternative has been suggested of bringing pressure to bear on successor Governments in the Axis countries to punish the offenders through their own legal processes.[5] Even if all the successor Governments should be so inclined, and should be able to do so under their several legal systems, it is hardly likely that all of them can be counted on to be as vigorous and effective as they should be. Furthermore, such a course would not meet the demand that the United Nations make good their apparent assurance that these acts would be stamped as criminal by international judgment, and punished accordingly.

4. To let these brutalities go unpunished will leave millions of persons frustrated and disillusioned. The fact that these acts are believed to be outside the jurisdiction of the United Nations War Crimes Commission as presently constituted has already aroused vigorous protest.[6] Strong pressure is being brought upon the United States and British Governments by organized Jewish groups, representing their co-religionists and undoubtedly also expressing the views of many others who are not of their faith, to have these acts categorized and treated as war crimes.[7] It must be anticipated that the pressure will grow stronger with time.

DEFICIENCIES OF CERTAIN SUGGESTED SOLUTIONS

5. Perhaps because of the apparently prohibitive complexities involved, the suggestion has been made that when the arch-Nazis (Hitler, Himmler, *et al.*) are apprehended and authoritatively identified, they be executed out of

hand. The justification is, presumably, that proof of their guilt would be the merest formality. However, this suggestion would not solve the problem of punishing the thousands of less outstanding culprits. Furthermore, it would do violence to the very principles for which the United Nations have taken up arms, and furnish apparent justification for what the Nazis themselves have taught and done. It would also help the Nazis elevate Hitler to martyrdom. The suggested procedure would taint an essential act of justice with false color of vindictiveness.

6. The alternative suggestion has been made that the offenders be given "streamlined" trials. The intention, presumably, would be to limit the proof, perhaps to the extent of keeping it down to the bare essentials of a *prima facie* case with regard to the particular atrocities charged. This could be done without injuring the substance of justice. However, it would not solve the problems discussed in the preceding sections.

7. The basic difficulty with the suggestions heretofore considered is in the approach. It will never be possible to catch and convict every Axis war criminal, or even any great number of them, under the old concepts and procedures. Even if this could be done it would not, of itself, be enough. The ultimate offense, for example, in the case of Lidice, is not alone the obliteration of the village, but even more, the assertion of the right to do it. The ordinary thug does not defend on the ground that thuggery is noble; he only contends that the police have arrested the wrong man. Behind each Axis war criminal, however, lies the basic criminal instigation of the Nazi doctrine and policy. It is the guilty nature of this instigation that must be established, for only thus will the conviction and punishment of the individuals concerned achieve their true moral and juristic significance. In turn, this approach throws light on the nature of the individual's guilt, which is not dependent on the commission of specific criminal acts, but follows inevitably from the mere fact of voluntary membership in organizations devised solely to commit such acts.

BASIC OBJECTIVES

8. a. The punishment of Axis war criminals should aim at three prime objectives: *first*, the establishment of a solemnly considered international judgment that alleged high interests of state are not acceptable as justification for national crimes of violence, terrorism, and the destruction of peaceful populations; *second*, bringing home to the world the realities and menace of racism and totalitarianism; and *third*, arousing the German people to a sense of their guilt, and to a realization of their responsibility for the crimes committed by their government.

b. If these objectives are not achieved, Germany will simply have lost another war. The German people will not know the barbarians they have supported, nor will they have any understanding of the criminal character of their conduct and the world's judgment upon it. The Fascist potential will thus remain undiminished both in Germany and elsewhere, and its scope unimpaired. If, on the other hand, the approach suggested herein is adopted, the victory can be turned to more valuable use than merely putting off the Fascist menace to another day.

PROPOSED SOLUTION

9. The following is therefore recommended for consideration:

a. The Nazi Government and its Party and State agencies, including the SA, SS, and Gestapo, should be charged before an appropriately constituted international court[8] with conspiracy to commit murder, terrorism, and the destruction of peaceful populations in violation of the laws of war.

b. For the purposes of trial before the above court, the prosecuting Nations should bring to the bar only such individual defendants, considered to be representative of the defendant organizations, as they elect.

c. The proceedings should be public and widely publicized, and the evidence should be full enough to prove the guilty intent (Nazi doctrine and policy) as well as the criminal conduct (atrocious acts in violation of the laws of war).

d. The judgment should adjudicate:

(1) That the Nazi Government and its mentioned agencies are guilty as charged.

(2) That every member of the Government and organizations on trial is guilty of the same offense. Such adjudication of guilt would require no proof that the individuals affected participated[9] in any overt act other than membership in the conspiracy.

e. Sentence would be passed by the court on the individual defendants before it.

f. Thereafter, every member of the mentioned Government and organizations would be subject to arrest, trial and punishment in the national courts of the several United Nations. Proof of membership, without more, would establish guilt of participation in the mentioned conspiracy, and the individual would be punished in the discretion of the court. Proof of the commission of other criminal acts would subject the individual to additional punishments conformably to local law.

10. It is particularly noted, in connection with the foregoing:

a. That in view of the nature of the charge, everything done in furtherance of the conspiracy from the time of its inception would be admissible, including domestic atrocities against minority groups within Germany, and domestic atrocities induced or procured by the German Government to be committed by other Axis Nations against their respective nationals.

b. That once the conspiracy is established, each act of every member thereof during its continuance and in furtherance of its purposes would be imputable to all other members thereof.

DOCUMENT 17

MEMORANDUM FOR MR. McCLOY FROM COLONEL AMMI CUTTER, ASSISTANT EXECUTIVE OFFICER, OFFICE OF THE ASSISTANT SECRETARY OF WAR[1]

SUBJECT: WAR CRIMES

October 1, 1944

1. *Two files*[2] are presented with letters submitted for the signature of the Secretary:

(a) File dated 15 Sept. 1944, "Trial of War Criminals",[3]

(b) File dated 12 Sept. 1944, "Persecution of Racial Minorities as a War Crime".[4]

2. *File (a)* originated in G-1 and states concurrence by CAD,[5] suggests sending a memorandum (apparently prepared in G-1) to the Secretary of State with copy to Navy for consideration. The memo:

(a) points out the magnitude of the war criminal problem and the difficulty of individual trials.

(b) indicates the difficulty of trying prosecutions of enemy nationals as war crimes.

(c) calls attention to the public resentment at the view that persecutions of enemy minorities are outside the jurisdiction of United Nations War Crimes Commission.

(d) suggests (par. 7, p. 4)[6] that the real war crime is the "basic criminal instigation of Nazi doctrine and policy".

(e) suggests a sort of "class representative" prosecution of a number of representatives (in effect as representing and in behalf of others similarly situated) of each Nazi group, (e.g. Nazi government, S.A., S.S., Gestapo), proof in each class case of the criminality of the organization, adjudication (by a sort of declaratory judgment *in rem*[7] as to the organization and all its members) of that fact, sentence of the individual representative defendants in the class

case, and thereafter sentence of all other members of the class on proof of the fact of membership—on the theory that membership is proof of criminality or at least of criminal conspiracy.
3. The discussion in file (a) is ingenious. The proposal however, involves fairly radical departures from existing theories, (i) of individual criminality and criminal responsibility and (ii) of prosecution procedures. It also contemplates one (or a series) of grandiose state trials, which have obvious disadvantages in providing opportunities for the manufacture of national martyrs, giving the defense an effective public platform for use in propaganda, etc.[8]

Recommendation: If the file is to be sent to State and Navy, a clearer indication should be given that the memorandum does not yet represent War Department policy and is merely transmitted as an interesting individual study and suggestion. A more informal type of transmittal might be desirable. . . .

DOCUMENT 18

THE SECRETARY OF WAR (STIMSON) TO THE SECRETARY OF STATE (HULL)[1]

October 27, 1944

My dear Mr. Secretary:

Two communications from your office on the subject of war crimes and related matters have been under consideration for some time, as follows:

a. Your letter of 4 September 1944, LE 740.00116 EW, enclosing a memorandum from Mr. Pehle of the War Refugee Board dated 28 August 1944, regarding the punishment as war crimes of atrocities committed by Axis powers against the Jews and other minorities and suggesting that such atrocities be investigated by the United Nations War Crimes Commission.[2]
b. Your letter of 8 September, LE 740.00116 ES/8-25-44, enclosing a "Statement on Punishment of War Criminals" submitted to the Department of State by the American Jewish Conference.[3]

The War Department understands that the United Nations War Crimes Commission was formed to deal only with war crimes in the technical sense. An atrocity committed by an Axis government against its own nationals would not ordinarily come within the usual legal definition of the term "war crime."

Accordingly, the War Department would suppose that if such atrocities are to be investigated by the War Crimes Commission an extension of the jurisdiction of the Commission would be necessary. Whether this should be done would seem to be primarily a political question.

The War Department does not feel that certain of the proposals in the memorandum from the American Jewish Conference are presented in sufficient detail or with adequate definiteness to enable the War Department to comment at this time. Among such proposals are the suggestions as to procedures to be followed in the prosecution of war criminals before international tribunals and national courts. The further proposal in this memorandum that the terms of the armistice should provide for surrender of offenders by the Axis powers would appear to be a matter for first consideration by the European Advisory Commission.[4]

The suggestion that the Jewish people shall have special representation on the United Nations War Crimes Commission, on the international prosecuting body, and upon the proposed international court, is a matter which does not appear to involve any military interest. The War Department, therefore, expresses no view upon it at this time.

The broad problem of war crimes and their prosecution is, however, a matter of very great interest to the War Department and has been receiving careful attention. The Judge Advocate General of the Army has been instructed to establish an agency in his office to act for the Army in collecting evidence of war crimes committed against members of our armed forces or other Americans, including the people of any dependencies of the United States and the Philippines. The War Department also has been trying to foresee the problems which will arise in connection with the prosecution of war crimes upon the occupation of enemy territory and to determine what military participation in these prosecutions will be desirable.

The conduct of the war by the Nazis has involved the commission of offenses against citizens of the United Nations on a wholesale basis without precedent in the history of modern war. The large volume of these crimes, many of them committed by members of enemy organizations like the Gestapo and SS, presents wholly novel problems of prosecution. Not only are there difficulties in arresting and trying such a large number of offenders but the fact that the offenses seem to have been planned on a national scale and as part of a national program makes necessary the adoption of new methods.

The nature of the broad Nazi program, of which these war crimes seem to form an essential part, has led some to the suggestion that prosecution of these crimes be on a basis analogous to the prosecution of a criminal conspiracy in this country. A memorandum, a copy of which I enclose for your consideration, has been prepared, setting forth certain proposals and theories of prosecution which seem to me to deserve careful study.[5] This memorandum has not yet been considered fully in the War Department or officially approved. I feel, however, that it will be advantageous to have the State Department consider the proposals at this time.

You will observe that the memorandum deals in part with the possible prosecution of enemy nationals for atrocities committed against other enemy nationals, particularly minority groups. The proposal is that these atrocities, whether committed before or after the formal declaration of war, be regarded as steps in the execution of a general conspiracy to which all members of certain enemy organizations were parties. Obviously any such theory demands very close scrutiny of the evidence relied on as proof of the conspiracy.

The enclosed memorandum proposes the prosecution of totalitarianism by trying the organizations which have made total war possible through their coercion of a whole people. It recognizes the unity of criminal purpose in all the acts of Naziism which have carried out the scheme outlined in "Mein Kampf." It treats on a parity, and as part of the same conspiracy, both the acts of criminal aggression against neighboring countries and the persecutions of minority groups within enemy territory. I think the proposals set out in the memorandum are worthy of complete investigation and may serve as the basis of an interdepartmental conference on the general war crimes problem, which should be held as soon as possible. I suggest that the appropriate representative of the State Department arrange such a conference with the Assistant Chief of Staff G-1, at your convenience.[6]

One other possible method of dealing with the prosecution of enemy nationals, for offenses against other enemy nationals, has been brought to my attention. The Judge Advocate General has informally advised that such offenses committed by officials of an enemy power against its own citizens may, during the period of military occupation of enemy territory, be prosecuted before military tribunals. During military occupation of enemy territory the courts of the occupied country are closed or sit to hear such cases only as the occupying power permits. Military tribunals of the occupying power thus have full jurisdiction to try offenses against local laws and will then be in a position to deal with enemy nationals who killed or injured other enemy nationals at any time in violation of the local enemy law.[7] There are, of course, substantial questions as to the extent to which such military tribunals would find it necessary to consider pleas in defense or justification based upon decrees or orders of enemy officials which themselves were of a nature outraging the sense of international decency. This possibility of prosecuting Axis nationals during the occupation period for earlier persecutions of minority groups also deserves study.

The prompt punishment of war crimes and similar offenses, by fair judicial methods, is clearly a necessary step in the destruction of totalitarianism. Punishment is essential, not as retribution, but as an expression of civilization's condemnation of the Nazi philosophy and aggression which have relentlessly plunged the world into war. That condemnation must be achieved in a fair manner which will meet the judgment of history. I do not believe that we can start the work of preparation too soon.

In view of the interest of the Secretary of the Navy[8] in these matters, I am sending him a copy of this letter and its enclosures.

Sincerely yours,

Henry L. Stimson
Secretary of War

DOCUMENT 19

DRAFT MEMORANDUM FOR THE PRESIDENT FROM THE SECRETARIES OF STATE, WAR AND NAVY
SUBJECT: TRIAL AND PUNISHMENT OF EUROPEAN WAR CRIMINALS[1]

November 11, 1944

We have been giving consideration to ways and means for carrying out the United States policy regarding the trial and punishment of war criminals, as established in your statement on the subject dated October 7, 1942, the United Nations Declaration on Persecution of Jews of December 17, 1942, and the Moscow Statement on Atrocities of November 1943.[2]

DIFFICULTIES INHERENT IN SEPARATE TRIALS FOR INDIVIDUAL OFFENSES[3]

The attempt to try these crimes on the basis of the separate prosecutions of large numbers of individuals will only make good the Nazi assumption that their crimes would go unpunished if they committed them on a sufficiently grandiose scale. The practical difficulties of proceeding on this basis are almost prohibitive. The crimes to be punished have been committed the world over, and have been participated in by many hundreds of thousands of offenders. Millions of victims and witnesses to these offenses have perished.

Moreover, the United States policy as established in the pronouncements mentioned above contemplates trying and punishing not only technical violations of the laws and customs of war, but also (1) atrocities committed by the

Nazis before there was a state of war, and (2) atrocities committed by them against their own nationals on racial, religious, and political grounds. These are not cognizable as war crimes in the technical sense. Also the prosecution of Axis leaders for offenses against their own nationals might be opposed as setting the unacceptable precedent of outside interference in the domestic relationships between a sovereignty and its nationals.

NAZI ATROCITIES, BOTH PRE-WAR AND SINCE, COMMITTED PURSUANT TO CRIMINAL CONSPIRACY AND PUNISHABLE AS SUCH

The criminality with which the Nazi leaders and groups are charged does not consist of scattered individual outrages such as may occur in any war, but represents the results of a purposeful and systematic pattern created by them to the end of achieving world domination. The objective in the prosecution of Nazi war crimes should be not only to punish the individual criminals, but also to expose and condemn the criminal purpose behind each individual outrage.

The writings and statements of the Nazi leaders themselves indicate that beginning even prior to the assumption of power by the Nazis in Germany, there has been a continuing conspiracy necessarily involving the commission of the atrocities which the United Nations have pledged themselves to punish. We believe that further research will develop the full scope of this conspiracy and enable its demonstration according to accepted judicial standards before a fair tribunal.

To such a state of facts the well recognized principles of the law of criminal conspiracy are plainly applicable, and may be employed. An indictment upon a charge of conspiracy will properly include the leaders of State, the governmental and party agencies such as the SS and Gestapo, and other individuals and groups who during the time in question have been in control of formulating and executing Nazi policy. Under such a charge, there would be properly admissible in evidence the acts of any of the conspirators done in preparation for, in furtherance of, and in consummation of the conspiracy, regardless of the fact that, separately considered, certain of these acts could not be prosecuted as war crimes in the accepted and most limited definition of that term. The pertinent proof would include, among other things, the atrocities committed before there was a state of war, and those committed by the Nazis against their own nationals on racial, religious, and political grounds.

CONSPIRACY CHARGE COULD BE DISPOSED OF IN SINGLE TRIAL

The conspiracy charge could be disposed of in a single trial. The United Nations would physically bring to the bar in this trial only those individual defendants, considered to be fairly representative of the defendant groups and organizations, such as they deem necessary. A judgment would be sought which adjudicates the existence, nature, and purposes of the conspiracy, its results, and the identity of the participants in it. The judgment would be binding upon all the individuals, groups and organizations against whom it is directed, and there would remain only the further requirements of identifying individual members of the groups and organizations whose criminality had been thus adjudicated, determining their respective degrees of guilt, and awarding appropriate punishments accordingly. This procedure could be remitted to the civil or military courts of the several United Nations, and could be carried out by them expeditiously, without prohibitive efforts or expense.

The proceeding will be judicial rather than political. It will rest securely upon traditionally established legal concepts. Not only will the guilty of this generation be brought to justice according to due process of law, but in addition, the conduct of the Axis will have been solemnly condemned by an international adjudication of guilt that cannot fail to impress the generations to come. The Germans will not again be able to claim, as they have been claiming with regard to the Versailles Treaty, that an admission of war guilt was exacted from them under duress.[4] It may be noted, in addition, that those of the criminals who have been or may hereafter be taken prisoners of war will lose their protected status under the Geneva Prisoners of War Convention, and can be dealt with freed from the restrictions of that Convention.[5]

RECOMMENDATION

We recommend that you approve this method of dealing with the basic war crimes problem.

CREATION OF TREATY COURT FOR TRIAL OF CONSPIRACY CHARGE

We favor a court constituted by international treaty for the trial of this charge. In such a treaty the crime will be defined, the jurisdiction of the court established, and provision made to insure that all dilatory and irrelevant technicalities are eliminated, without, however, impairing the essentials of due process. The treaty should be a simple document, and, by limiting the jurisdiction of the court to the trial of the charge described above, will avoid long-term and unforseeable commitments. The court itself may consist of military or civilian personnel, or both, and should be representative of the interested United Nations.

In making this recommendation, we have given due consideration to the possible difficulties which might arise in the consummation of the necessary treaty. The process of ratification might be time-consuming. When the proposed treaty comes before some ratifying bodies, such as the United States Senate, there might be suggestions of undesirable reservations. The publicity might lead to anticipatory retaliations by the Axis on United Nations personnel in their custody. We believe, however, that these objections can be obviated in part by restricting the treaty to the simple and limited scope which has been described, and, for the rest, by deferring its public announcement and presentation to the necessary ratifying bodies until so doing would no longer hazard the safety of United Nations personnel in German custody. In the meantime, the terms of the treaty could well be negotiated and agreed upon by the interested United Nations.

RECOMMENDATION

We recommend that you approve the preparation and negotiation of a treaty as described above.

OTHER ESTABLISHED PROCEDURES NOT FORECLOSED

The program which we have described does not foreclose other available procedures for dealing with particular offenses. Thus, for example, atrocities against our nationals by identifiable Axis individuals will remain subject to trial by United States military and naval commissions. The military and civilian tribunals of the other United Nations will probably be employed to try other individual crimes, under either international or local law. These procedures present no new problems of law or policy, and are mentioned only for the sake of completeness. They do not require further action on your part at this time.

SECRETARY OF STATE SECRETARY OF WAR SECRETARY OF THE NAVY

PHASE II

II

Documents

November 1944 to January 1945

II

Introduction

November 1944 to January 1945

John J. McCloy and his associates went ahead during the third week of November 1944, trying to weave the conspiracy/criminal-organization prosecution system into the fabric of the army's occupation program for Germany (document 20). But a reservation about one feature of the plan was soon registered within the War Department. After two months of deliberation, on November 22 the judge advocate general (General Cramer) finally gave the Bernays scheme a cautious and qualified mark of approval. But Cramer added, with heavy emphasis, that the system was so unorthodox that a treaty foundation would be indispensable if subsidiary cases against members of criminal organizations were to be heard in United States civil or military courts (document 21).

Outside the War Department, the draft memorandum of November 11 encountered sharper criticism. The initial reaction of navy officials was so cool that the supporters of the proposal found it prudent to shelve the idea of a three-department recommendation to the president and concentrated instead on reaching agreement between the State and War departments. Although he was generally sympathetic to the plan, the State Department's legal advisor, Judge Green H. Hackworth, also had doubts and reservations. Hackworth felt revision was necessary, first because the November 11 memorandum was unclear about the nature of the conspiracy that was to be prosecuted. At one point, the draft indicated that the conspiracy was aimed at world domination, while in another place the conspiracy was said to have been directed at the perpetration of atrocities. The State Department legal advisor furthermore believed that the War Department had made a mistake by recommending the use of a treaty court. Hackworth contended that such a plan was likely to run into trouble with the British and, in any event, it would be impossible to keep the proposal secret—an essential consideration for the protection of Allied prisoners in German hands—if negotiation and ratification of a treaty were attempted before the end of hostilities.

Consequently, in late November the basic War Department memorandum was redrafted. In addition to incorporating some stylistic improvements, the revision tried to meet Hackworth's complaint that the conspiracy charge was inconsistent. The new formulation blended together hints of prosecution for aggressive war and for atrocities, contending that the Nazis had conspired to "achieve domination of other nations and peoples by deliberative violation of the rules of war . . ." But this was the only concession made to Hackworth. On the basic issue of reliance on a treaty court, the new War Department memorandum followed the advice of General Cramer and, while discounting the threat of British opposition, reiterated the indispensability of a treaty foundation for the conspiracy/criminal-organization prosecution system (document 22).

Without making further attempts to mollify the State Department or to guarantee that the new draft would be acceptable to the Judge Advocate General's Office (JAG), on December 4 McCloy sent copies of the redrafted memorandum to the State and Justice departments, as well as to Harry Hopkins in the White House. Even before this was done, there were signs that the war crimes issue was becoming increasingly complicated and that great prudence and finesse would be required to secure approval for the War Department plan.

Once again, the initial complication was an outgrowth of action by the UNWCC. During the fall, that organization had begun to consider a motion proposing to prosecute aggressive war as a crime. A subcommittee of the UNWCC debated the issue, and concluded that the Nazi leaders should be tried for the "crime" of preparing and waging aggressive war. Before a final vote was taken by the whole commission, however, the representatives of the member states were given an opportunity to ask for instructions from their governments. When the request for instructions by the American representative (Herbert Pell) reached Washington in mid-November, State immediately asked the advice of the War Department. Following recommendations made by the personnel branch and seconded by McCloy, Henry Stimson strongly advised in reply that America use whatever influence it had on the UNWCC to delay a vote on the question. Noting that the matter was controversial and touched on elements of the conspiracy/criminal-organization plan, Stimson contended that further public debate or action by the commission would only make more difficult the clarification of American war crimes policy (document 23). The American representative on the UNWCC was thereupon directed to stall, and the Anglo-Americans succeeded in muzzling international discussion of the matter for the time being.

No sooner was the basis laid for quieting the aggressive-war question abroad, than the same issue blew up inside Stimson's own department. On November 28, Colonel William C. Chanler, the deputy chief of the Civil Affairs Division and a close personal and legal associate of Stimson, sent the secretary a long memorandum on war crimes policy. Chanler advanced an argument claiming that the Nazi leaders could be prosecuted for collateral violations of the 1928 Kellogg-Briand (Paris) Pact. The colonel contended that it would be possible to skirt the controversial question of whether or not the Kellogg-Briand Pact had made aggression a crime by asserting that by breaching the pact, the Nazis had forfeited their right to the protections of lawful belligerency in respect both to neutrals and to the victims of their attacks. In Chanler's scheme, one of the Nazi's victims, such as Poland, should demand that Hitler and his aides be turned over to it for trial on the grounds that the invading forces of the Third Reich had not been lawful belligerent armies, but merely illegal bands of looters and murderers. The colonel hoped that the United Nations would then hold something in the nature of an extradition hearing to deal with such a request, and in that hearing an international court would conclude that violators of the Kellogg-Briand Pact were liable to criminal punishment (document 24).

Stimson conceded that Chanler's views were probably in advance of prevailing legal opinion, but he nonetheless directed John J. McCloy to circulate the colonel's memorandum through the War Department. The appearance of the Chanler paper, wending its way through the Pentagon, provided critics of aggressive-war prosecution and legal innovation with a convenient point of attack. Sensing the danger, McCloy tried to neutralize possible opposition by invoking the aid of a prestigious and hopefully neutral War Department observer. But the scheme backfired. When, at McCloy's invitation, the army's deputy fiscal director (and postwar secretary of the army) Brigadier General Kenneth C. Royall completed his appraisal on December 14, he concluded that the Nazi war criminals should be tried on the basis of a slightly modified form of the traditional military trial system. Royall accepted the idea of a limited prosecution of criminal organizations, but rejected the notion of charging the German leaders with prewar persecutions, atrocities committed against German nationals, or the crime of aggressive war (document 25).

The appearance of the cautious and critical Royall memorandum was the overture to a series of attacks on innovative war crimes trial planning launched from both inside and outside the War Department. The most significant internal assault consisted of a draft critique sharply critical of the theory that the preparation and waging of an aggressive war was a punishable offense. Completed in the JAG on December 18, the long technical memorandum concluded that even though public opinion would probably be outraged, there was actually no basis in existing law to prosecute the Nazis, or anyone else, for aggression, because aggressive war was not a crime under international law (document 26). Despite a series of counter memoranda from Chanler and Bernays, this JAG paper condemning aggressive war prosecution definitely put the war crimes policy innovators on the defensive.

Then, in late December 1944, McCloy, Bernays, and their colleagues were met by another critical blast, this time from the Justice Department. On December 29, the War and State departments, as well as the White House, received a formal paper on war crimes policy prepared by Assistant Attorney General Herbert Wechsler. Taking as his basis the late November War Department memorandum that set forth the conspiracy/criminal-organization plan, Wechsler moved through the document section by section, pointing to a multitude of reasons why the Bernays plan should be sharply modified or abandoned. Contending that much of the proposal constituted an attempt to apply ex post facto law, Wechsler specifically objected to the use of the concept of conspiracy because it was virtually unknown outside of Anglo-American law, and he also doubted whether any court could do a respectable job of adjudicating what were in reality the major historical issues in the life of Europe and much of the world during the period from 1933 to 1945 (document 27). The documentary record indicates that Mr. Wechsler's criticisms were more than a matter of personal opinion. Apparently Attorney General Francis Biddle was at this point also far from enthusiastic about the conspiracy/criminal-organization plan. He too seems to have had doubts about the use of conspiracy and, like many other critics, believed that it would be unwise to try to prosecute prewar persecutions or acts committed against German nationals in an international trial (document 28).

Surrounded by criticism, the proponents of the conspiracy/criminal-organization plan and the advocates of aggressive-war prosecution were in a tight corner by the end of 1944. They were saved from defeat, however, by the impact of the Malmédy massacre, which occurred on December 17, and by the need of Washington planners in early 1945 to provide the president with a policy statement on war crimes for possible use at the forthcoming Crimean conference. When the First S.S. Panzer Regiment slaughtered some seventy American prisoners at Malmédy, Belgium, during the darkest days of the Battle of the Bulge, the incident persuaded many American officials, including Attorney General Francis Biddle, that the Nazis were actually involved in a lawless conspiracy to commit war crimes by use of criminal organizations such as the S.S. (That Biddle was apparently still criticizing the conspiracy/criminal-organization plan on January 5 [document 28] was probably due to a delay in full reports of the atrocity reaching Washington and to the fact that the Malmédy fever took time to reach its full heat.) This shift in attitude in favor of the basic principles of the Bernays plan came at a most opportune moment for its proponents, because only two months remained before Roosevelt was scheduled to meet with Prime Minister Churchill and Marshal Stalin at Yalta, and war crimes might well be a topic of discussion by the Big Three.

The new push toward the development of an American war crimes position paper that ensued in early 1945 was complicated and confused by the fact that Harry Hopkins had stepped down as the White House adviser on war crimes policy and had been replaced in this capacity by two other confidants of the president, Ambassador Joseph E. Davies and Judge Samuel I. Rosenman. Ambassador Davies soon revealed himself to have little sympathy for the Bernays plan or any other form of innovative war crimes program, but Judge Rosenman strongly favored the principles of the conspiracy/criminal-organization plan and fought hard to have it adopted as the basic American policy.

Judge Rosenman first seems to have made his supportive influence felt on January 3, 1945, when Roosevelt directed an inquiry to the State Department regarding war crimes policy. On every other occasion, the president was extremely tight-lipped about what he wanted done with the Nazi leaders, but on January 3, for the first and only time, he indicated that he would look sympathetically on a conspiracy trial that charged Hitler and his top subordinates with the crime of aggressive war (document 29). It seems likely that Judge Rosenman persuaded the president to give this sign that a form of the conspiracy/criminal-organization plan might gain his favor.

But Judge Rosenman's influence and the presidential sign of January 3 were not sufficient to sweep away all criticism. Opposition within the JAG had so deepened and hardened that in a meeting with McCloy, Cutter, and Bernays on January 4, the deputy chief of JAG, Major General John M. Weir, not only condemned the idea of prosecuting the Nazis for aggressive war, but also denounced the whole conspiracy/criminal-organization plan. McCloy and his aides, nonetheless, decided to gird themselves and push ahead on their effort to secure interdepartmental approval of the plan while making but one noteworthy concession to the critics in the JAG. After preparing a paper that set out all possible arguments favoring unrestricted prosecution of aggressive war as a crime, Bernays and one of his assistants tempered their conclusion in deference to the criticism of General Weir and recommended that such prosecution be carried out only in cases where the Nazis had attacked victims without issuing prior warning or making a declaration of war (document 30).

Yet when the first of the showdown meetings of representatives from the various departments and agencies concerned with war crimes policy finally took place, it was so packed with men who favored the conspiracy/criminal-organization plan that there seemed no reason to make extensive concessions to the opposition. McCloy, Bernays, Hackworth, and the converted Herbert Wechsler, gathered in Judge Rosenman's office on January 8, and they easily brushed aside criticism from the JAG. The result was a redraft of the basic plan developed between January 8 and January 13 by Colonel Bernays. This memorandum incorporated technical changes recommended by Mr. Hackworth and Mr. Wechsler, and also included a summary of the probable war crimes policies of the United Kingdom and the Soviet Union, as requested by Judge Rosenman. But the distinguishing feature of the January 13 draft was its enthusiastic endorsement of a treaty court proposal and of unlimited prosecution of aggression. Apparently emboldened by the signs of strong support for the general conspiracy/criminal-organization approach manifested in the interdepartmental meeting of January 8, Bernays had pulled out all the stops. He had swept aside the earlier compromise with JAG on limited aggressive-war prosecution and ignored the doubts and reservations expressed earlier by Wechsler and Hackworth regarding a treaty court. The draft of January 13 showed no sign of moderation and displayed the most radical features of the conspiracy/criminal-organization plan in bold relief (document 31).

Bernays' excessive zeal offered opponents of the plan a new point of attack. For weeks the JAG had been assiduously gathering ammunition for use against the conspiracy/criminal-organization plan, and among other items it had acquired a critical appraisal by the acting dean of the Harvard Law School and former JAG lieutenant colonel, Edmund M. Morgan (document 32). In the third week of January, JAG recruited Ambassador Davies as an ally to help in assaulting the new January 13 draft and passed on all of their documentary and legal projectiles to him, including a copy of the critique by Dean Morgan.

But the supporters of the conspiracy/criminal-organization plan had also not been idle in the aftermath of the first interdepartmental meeting of January 8. Although some of those involved, including Colonel Cutter, were highly critical of features of the new draft, Judge Rosenman showed a sure hand in moving the conspiracy/criminal-organization system on to victory. The judge deftly sidestepped a last-minute effort by Henry Morgenthau to participate in the deliberations, and then carefully arranged the makeup of the meeting of January 18 that would consider Bernays' new draft. Ambassador Davies and General Weir were invited to participate, but everyone else scheduled to be in the room supported the basic principles of conspiracy and criminal-organization prosecution. Rosenman had made certain that War Department influence was not too obvious (neither McCloy nor Stimson participated), and the only Cabinet member in attendance was another convert to the plan, Attorney General Francis Biddle.

With the casting and choreography complete, Judge Rosenman took the assembled group through his script on January 18, 1945. The new draft of the conspiracy/criminal-organization plan was laid on the table, and criticisms or counter proposals were invited. General Weir, speaking for the JAG, presented an alternate draft that recommended use of a slightly expanded form of traditional war crimes prosecution. Under the JAG plan, an international military tribunal would be used to hear charges that the Nazis had committed atrocities in the occupied territories and had launched aggressive wars without warning or declaration. Accusations of conspiracy to commit such atrocities and limited acts of aggression would also be heard, but there would be no prosecution of prewar acts or atrocities committed against German nationals. Nazi organizations, as such, would also not be tried (document 33).

Ambassador Davies brought forth another counter plan, or at least an alternate strategy. Instead of arming the president with a complete formulation of the conspiracy/criminal-organization proposal to guide him during his talks with Stalin and Churchill, Davies wanted the war crimes policy group to advise Mr. Roosevelt to support a general declaration by the Big Three that the Nazi leaders would be punished, but to leave to the three foreign ministers the task of developing a concrete trial plan. The ambassador emphasized, however, that whatever trial procedure was ultimately agreed upon, it should not invoke ex post facto law and should not contain legal innovations such as those included in the conspiracy/criminal-organization plan (document 34).

The assault mounted by the JAG and Ambassador Davies was enough to force the group in Judge Rosenman's office to pause and make concessions, but not sufficiently powerful to disrail completely the conspiracy/criminal-organization plan. Too many important people had rallied to the plan's support for it to be totally discarded at this late date, especially when the propositions advanced by Davies and the JAG did not go to the root of the problems that the Bernays plan had been created to solve—the need to purge German society by other means than the Morgenthau plan and the general public demand that the Nazi leaders be punished for the whole gamut of their atrocious acts, not just for traditional war crimes. Consequently the meeting ended with a consensus decision that the January 13 memorandum should be redrafted by an incongruous team composed of Colonel Bernays and General Weir. In its new form the conspiracy/criminal-organization plan would be sustained but as many of its legal innovations as possible would be stripped away.

The resulting memorandum, which after some slight rephrasings was signed by the secretaries of war and state as well as by the attorney general and was forwarded to the president on January 22, 1945, was a cautious endorsement of Bernays' basic ideas. While preserving the concept of a criminal-organization trial, it substituted—as Wechsler had suggested—the prosecution of "joint participation in a criminal enterprise" for the peculiarly Anglo-American conspiracy approach. The memorandum retained prewar atrocities, acts against German nationals, and the waging of an aggressive war among the constituent elements of the "criminal enterprise." But accusations of planning, preparing, and initiating aggression were eliminated, and the memorandum also dropped advocacy of a treaty court, recommending instead that an international military tribunal be established by an executive agreement concluded between the Allied Big Three (document 35). To guarantee that everything necessary would be ready in the event that Stalin and Churchill agreed with the American plan, Bernays also joined with Hackworth in drafting an "Implementing Instrument" to be signed by the Big Three. Although this document provided a generally accurate reflection of the points contained in the basic memorandum signed by the three secretaries,* it was not seen at this time by any high officials of the U.S. government except Judge Rosenman, a fact that would later have significant consequences (document 36).

The contents of the Three Secretaries Memorandum and the Implementing Instrument were not free from flaws. Legal conservatives could still find much to quarrel with in them. Obvious loose ends also remained, such as uncertainty about whether a judgment was transferable from one court to another, since the tribunal was to be based on an executive agreement rather than an international treaty. But those advocating radical measures and wide-open legal innovations (such as officials in the Treasury), rather than the legal conservatives, were the ones who had the most to complain about (document 37). By and large, in the Washington of early 1945, the documents produced on January 20 and 22 were triumphs of caution and moderation.

Yet a pair of weighty questions related to the work produced in January 1945 remained unanswered: Did the president understand the plan? and Did he support it? On January 19, Secretary of War Stimson had tried to secure answers to these questions during a meeting with Roosevelt at the White House. Stimson produced a verbal synopsis of the plan full of praise for its cleverness and virtue. According to the secretary's diary, the president responded amiably but noncommittally, and Stimson was forced to conclude that in the rush of Roosevelt's departure for the Crimea, it was not clear whether the three secretaries' war crimes policy had actually registered (document 38). The questions about the president's views on the issue were still there after the Stimson-Roosevelt talk ended, and they have continued to hover over the subject of American war crimes policy.

---

*The term *Three Secretaries Memorandum* is used hereafter as a matter of convenience, although technically the attorney general is not a secretary.

DOCUMENT 20

MEMORANDUM BY JOHN J. McCLOY ON JOINT CHIEFS OF STAFF MEMORANDUM 332—APPREHENSION AND DETECTION OF WAR CRIMINALS[1]

November 18, 1944

1. a. This directive should include the substance of paragraph 1 of the Political Directive attached to JCS 1067.[2] The arrest provisions of the Political Directive attached to JCS 1067 are the fundamental basis of U.S. policy in connection with the arrangements leading to prosecution of war crimes and should be included bodily in the provision.

b. It is believed that this directive should provide explicitly for effective steps leading to punishment of those criminal acts committed by enemy nationals against other enemy nationals which are closely analogous to war crimes in nature and for punishment of participants in acts which constitute parts of a general conspiracy involving the commission of a war crime or a series of war crimes. Most of the changes hereafter suggested in this memorandum relate to the inclusion of such other offenses as a basis for the apprehension and detention of the persons suspected of committing them . . .

e. It is believed that the following paragraph 13 should be added to the directive:—

> "13. Within your zone you will take all practicable measures to apply the provisions of this directive to all persons who, as principal or accessory, are charged with or suspected, of the commission since 30 January 1933,[3] of acts,
>
> a. which were preparatory to or in furtherance of the commission of war crimes, or
>
> b. which outrage common justice or involve moral turpitude in connection with the persecution of Germans or non-Germans on racial, religious or political grounds, where the acts were either part of a conspiracy involving the commission of a war crime or war crimes or were violations of local law [and] remained unpunished. . . ."

DOCUMENT 21

JUDGE ADVOCATE GENERAL'S MEMORANDUM FOR THE ASSISTANT SECRETARY OF WAR

SUBJECT: TRIAL OF EUROPEAN WAR CRIMINALS (COMMENTS ON THE BERNAYS PLAN)[1]

November 22, 1944

1. The G-1 plan, first presented at the conference held in your office on 27 September, has been the subject of continuous study and discussion since that time.

2. I agree, first, that there must be a trial of the arch-criminals before an international tribunal, full and complete, with a *verbatim* record of oral evidence and of documents. I feel quite strongly that the world cannot afford to dispose of the war guilt question by compelling the vanquished nations to make an admission under duress, as it did in article 231 of the Versailles Treaty in 1919. There must be convincing proof of guilt, which should be preserved in such form that the record of trial can be widely distributed.[2]

3. The foregoing, the full-dress international trial of the ringleaders, I may call Stage A of the proceedings. All concerned, I think it is fair to say, agree that there must be such a trial. There is likewise agreement as to what I may call the Stage C trials,the individual proceedings against identifiable criminals before the military or civilian courts of the injured nations. As you are aware, there have been a good many conferences recently touching on the proposed trial by U.S. military commission of the Bulgarians who mistreated captured American aviators.[3]

4. My only substantial qualification refers to Stage B, the trial of the individual Nazis not identified as perpetrators of particular crimes, but simply as members of Nazi organizations which have already been in court at stage A.

5. Par. 9*d* of the G-1 paper states, referring to Stage A,

> "d. The judgment should adjudicate:
>
> * * * * * * *[4]
>
> "(2) That every member of the Government and organizations on trial is guilty of the same offense. Such adjudication of guilt would require no proof that the individuals affected participated in any overt act other than membership in the conspiracy
>
> * * * * * * *
>
> "f. Thereafter, every member of the mentioned government organizations would be subject to arrest, trial and punishment in the several courts of the

several United Nations. Proof of membership, without more, would establish guilt of participation in the mentioned conspiracy, and the individual would be punished in the discreation [*sic*] of the court. Proof of the commission of other criminal acts would subject the individual to additional punishment conformably to local law."

6. The only possible difficulty arises from so much of par. 9*f*, just quoted, as proposes to hold the stage B proceedings "in the national courts of the several United Nations". To the extent, of course, that members of the SS, Gestapo, and the like, are tried by French, Dutch, Polish, or Russian courts, for their connection with offenses committed in or against the nationals of France, the Netherlands, Poland, or Russia, the holding of such trials accords with the general principles laid down in the Moscow Statement on Atrocities. Thereafter the legal sufficiency of the proof adduced is a matter of municipal rather than international law, and, in the event of conviction, the accused no longer fall within the protection of the Geneva Convention, but may be executed or held to forced labor, as the case may be, as convicted war criminals.

7. We are concerned primarily with the problem as it affects the United States. It is clear, of course, that the military commissions of the United States, like its courts-martial and its civilian criminal courts, can proceed to judgment of conviction only upon complete proof of the personal guilt of the individuals before them. Each record must be complete in itself. The procedure of the military commission is expeditious, and its rules of evidence are now relaxed; but the basic principle that the accused must be proved guilty on the evidence presented to the tribunal in the particular case still applies.

8. Obviously, if Hans Schultze, an SS man, were a defendant in the Stage A proceeding, the mere fact that he voluntarily joined the SS and swore an oath blindly to obey his leaders, would, even in the absence of further evidence, be sufficient to make him a co-conspirator with the others and subject to the same penalty. The same result would be reached in the federal courts of the United States by a combination of the conspiracy and accessory provisions of the Federal Criminal Code (18 U.S.C., secs. 88,550).

9. Advance the matter by one step, and suppose that Schultze were tried in a Stage B proceeding in a U.S. district court. The judgment in Stage A would not be binding against Schultze, because on this hypothesis he would not have been a party to Stage A. The record in Stage A would be inadmissible hearsay. And Schultze could only be convicted by recalling all the Stage A witnesses. I agree with the G-1 paper that any such procedure would be so cumbrous and time-consuming as to be self-defeating.

10. Before a U.S. military commission, with the rules of evidence relaxed to the point of elimination, the Stage B proceeding would be simpler, because there the record of trial of Stage A would have probative value, and so would

be admissible. But every Stage B trial would require the introduction of that record, which more likely than not, will be of considerable bulk. Therefore, the G-1 paper under consideration proposes a practical short-cut, namely the adoption of a rule of law which would in effect provide that the Stage A record should be considered as being in evidence, or the Stage A judgment as being proved, in all the Stage B proceedings. With this final step taken, there may well be a question whether the Stage B proceedings could be held in either the civil or military courts of the United States unless the judgment at the first trial were either made conclusive as a matter of binding law, or the findings of fact at the first trial were given *prima facie* weight.

11. I agree that, if justice is to be done at all, we must take this final step. It is true that a great many persons will have to be tried, more probably than have ever been tried before; but mass murders have never before been perpetrated on such a large scale either. Certainly we can not afford, by any act or omission of ours, to lend support to the view that crime can be made to pay if it is undertaken with a wide enough scope. Therefore, in order to proceed to the Stage B trials on the footing that Stage A has been established as the law and facts of the case in every Stage B trial, it will be necessary to conduct the Stage B proceedings either (a) in international courts or military commissions, or (b) in the courts of other nations, or (c) to give such force to the Stage A trial as would bind United States courts. This could be done by a treaty provision, which would then become the supreme law of the land; or for military courts, by an executive order under the 38th Article of War[5] making the findings of fact by the Stage A court *prima facie* evidence of such facts in the Stage B proceedings.

12. Although the suggested concept of *res judicata*[6] goes beyond anything now known to our criminal law, I see nothing in it repugnant to natural justice. In civil litigation, parties to causes are bound by judgments obtained against those in privity with them. The class suit is a familiar remedy in Anglo-American equity. The statutes of several states permit unincorporated associations to be sued in actions nominally against an officer thereof, the judgment, however, to be binding against all the members of the association. The modern civil law, I am advised, permits the introduction of certain evidence against some conspirators in trials of other conspirators. And, as I have already pointed out, under the conspiracy and accessory provisions of the U.S. Code, individuals no less remote from the commission of criminal acts than are the Stage B defendants from the Nazi war atrocities can be brought to book for their misdeeds.

13. There, of course, all the co-conspirators must be in court, and we have mass sedition or poultry racket trials, as the case may be. Obviously we cannot try in one proceeding the million odd SS men and Gestapo agents. It would not be practicable to try them individually and to put the Stage A record into

the record of each Stage B trial. But I see nothing inherently unfair or unjust in trying the organization in a proceedings where it is defended and represented by its leaders, and in then making that judgment binding on all who voluntarily become members of the organization. Therefore, subject to the qualifications already noted as to proceeding in United States courts at Stage B, I agree in principle with this part of the proposal also.

14. I suggest, therefore, that the G-1 plan be expanded and revised along the following lines:

a. The *res judicata* principle should be written into the treaty or other agreement which establishes the court for the Stage A trial.

b. The language of the plan should be revised to indicate that the courts in the Stage B proceedings will, in addition to identifying the individuals of the groups and organizations whose criminality will have been adjudicated in Stage A, determine these individuals' respective degrees of guilt, and award appropriate punishments accordingly.

15. I would further suggest that, as soon as the G-1 proposal, duly modified and expanded in the light of this and similar comments, shall have been approved in Washington, it be transmitted to the American delegates to the United Nations War Crimes Commission with directions to present it as the American view. Similar steps should be taken to bring the American plan to the attention of the Russian representatives on the European Advisory Council, as suggested by Ambassador Winant in your office last week.

MYRON C. CRAMER,
Major General,
The Judge Advocate General.

DOCUMENT 22

DRAFT OF

November 27, 1944

(With G-1 corrections)[1]

MEMORANDUM FOR THE PRESIDENT
SUBJECT: TRIAL AND PUNISHMENT OF EUROPEAN WAR CRIMINALS.[2]

We have been giving consideration to ways and means for carrying out the United States policy regarding the trial and punishment of war criminals, as established in your statement on that subject dated October 7, 1942, the

United States Declaration on Persecution of Jews of December 17, 1942, the Concurrent Resolution of the Congress of the United States of March 18, 1943 (57 Stat. 721), the Moscow Statement on Atrocities of November 1943, and your statement on the subject of persecutions dated March 24, 1944.[3]

DIFFICULTIES INHERENT IN SEPARATE TRIALS FOR INDIVIDUAL OFFENSES

Any attempt to reach these crimes on the basis of the separate prosecution of large numbers of individuals will only make good the Nazi assumption that their crimes would go unpunished if they committed them on a sufficiently grandiose scale. The practical difficulties of proceeding on this basis are almost prohibitive. The crimes to be punished have been committed the world over, and have been participated in by thousands upon thousands of offenders. Literally millions of victims and witnesses to these offenses have perished.

As we read the pronouncements mentioned above, they establish the United States policy that we will bring to trial and punishment not only technical violations of the laws and customs of war, but also (1) atrocities committed by the Nazis before there was a state of war, and (2) atrocities committed by them against their own nationals on racial, religious, and political grounds. This raises the further complication that these last two classes of offenses in and of themselves are not cognizable as war crimes in the most limited and technical sense. Moreover, the prosecution of Axis leaders for offenses against their own nationals might be opposed as setting an unacceptable precedent of outside interference in the domestic relationships between a sovereignty and its nationals.

NAZI ATROCITIES, BOTH PRE-WAR AND SINCE, REPRESENT A CRIMINAL CONSPIRACY

The criminality with which the Nazi leaders and groups are charged does not consist of scattered individual outrages such as may occur in any war, but represents the results of a purposeful and systematic conspiracy to achieve domination of other nations and[4] [peoples by deliberate violation of the rules of war as they have been accepted and adhered to by the nations of the world, the violation of treaties and international conventions and customs, and mass extermination of peoples]. The objective in the prosecution of Nazi war crimes should be not only to punish the individual criminals, but also to establish and condemn the basic original purpose underlying the individual outrages.

The writings and statements of the Nazi leaders themselves indicate that, beginning even prior to their assumption of power in Germany, they have been engaged in this conspiracy. The carrying out of the conspiracy demonstrably involved the commission of the atrocities and war crimes which the United Nations have pledged themselves to punish. We believe that further research, which should be undertaken promptly and carried through expeditiously and thoroughly, will develop the full scope of this conspiracy so that it may be proved according to accepted judicial standards before a fair tribunal.

LAW OF CRIMINAL CONSPIRACY APPLICABLE

The well recognized law of criminal conspiracy [makes punishable not only the use of unlawful means to attain lawful ends, but also the use of lawful means to attain unlawful ends].[5] An indictment upon a charge of conspiracy should be returned against the leaders of State, the governmental and party agencies such as the SA, SS and Gestapo, and other individuals and groups who during the time in question have been in control of formalizing and executing Nazi policy. Under such charge there would be admissible in evidence the acts of any of the conspirators done in preparation for, in furtherance of, and in consummation of the conspiracy, regardless of the fact that, separately considered, certain of these acts could not be prosecuted as war crimes in the accepted and most limited definition of that term. The pertinent proof would include, among other things, atrocities committed before there was a state of war, and those committed by the Nazis against their own nationals on racial, religious, and political grounds.

[The indictment could properly include, in addition, conspiracy counts covering the particular unlawful purposes of such organizations as the SS and the Gestapo, and counts charging other particular acts of criminality committed by the respective defendants or groups of defendants. The inclusion of these additional counts would, for the most part, require no additional proof, and at the same time would make it possible to adapt the trial procedures to the facts developed by research as indicated above.][6]

CONSPIRACY CHARGE COULD BE DISPOSED OF IN SINGLE TRIAL

The basic charge of conspiracy and the additional counts in all probability could be disposed of in a single trial of the individuals, agencies, and organizations involved. Certainly no more than a very few trials would be required to dispose of this matter. The United Nations would physically bring to the bar only those individual defendants, considered to be fairly representative of the defendant groups and organizations, as they deem necessary. An adjudication would be sought of the existence, nature, and purposes of the conspiracy, its results, and the identity of the participants in it. The court would prescribe the punishment for those defendants physically before it. The adjudication would, however, determine the facts of the conspiracy and establish them for the purposes of further proceedings against the individuals, groups and organizations dealt with in the judgment and against the members of any such organizations not then physically before the court. After such adjudication, the civil or military courts of the several United Nations (or mixed tribunals of two or more of them) would proceed to identify the additional members of the groups thus adjudicated to have been participants in the conspiracy. These courts would also appraise the degree of participation of each person in the conspiracy, and fix the punishment of each of them in the measure appropriate in the particular case. The procedure proposed could be handled expeditiously enough to insure that justice would not be defeated by delays and complications.

The proceedings will be judicial and not political. They will constitute [an application of legal concepts firmly rooted in our law].[7] Not only will this proposal afford a fair trial to those charged with atrocities, but it can submit to the judgment of an appropriate tribunal the conduct of the Nazis in bringing about and carrying on the war. A condemnation after such a proceeding will meet the judgment of history, so that the Germans will not be able to claim, as they have been claiming with regard to the Versailles Treaty, that an admission of war guilt was exacted from them under duress. It may be noted, in addition, that after the charge is preferred and pending prosecution and punishment those of the criminals who have been or may hereafter be taken prisoners of war will not have any protected status under the Geneva Prisoners of War Convention. They can then be dealt with freed from the restrictions of that Convention.

Recommendation

We recommend that you approve this general method of dealing with the basic war crimes problem.

APPROPRIATE COURTS FOR TRIALS OF CONSPIRACY CRIMES

Two principal types of court could be employed for the trial of conspiracy charges of the character outlined above:[8]

1. Tribunal Created by Treaty. The charges could be tried by an international court created by treaty, which would (a) define the crimes to be tried,

(b) establish the composition and jurisdiction of the court to be established, and (c) make suitable provisions for court procedures, thus insuring the elimination of dilatory and irrelevant tactics without impairing the essentials of due process.

Such a treaty should be simple and should limit the jurisdiction of the court to the trial of the charges specified in this memorandum and nothing else, thus avoiding long-term and unpredictable commitments. This treaty would also determine whether the court shall be created with both military and civilian members or on a purely military basis, appointed in a manner to be stated in the treaty.

Three possible objections to this procedure should be mentioned:

a. There might be concern lest the trial of these offenses should be long drawn out and serve as a sounding board for propaganda on the part of the defendants. This can be avoided by careful research into the facts and clear, fair, well prepared and skillful presentation of those facts before the court.

[b. The negotiations and approval of the suggested treaty might take a substantial period of time and consideration of the treaty by some ratifying bodies might bring suggestions of undesirable reservations. This objection would be largely obviated by restricting the treaty court to a limited jurisdiction as above suggested.][9]

c. If publicity were given to the proposed prosecution, retaliation by the Axis on United Nations prisoners of war and other persons in their custody might occur. This can be avoided by deferring public announcement of the negotiation of the treaty and its presentation for ratification until all United Nations personnel in German custody are safe. However, negotiations could now be undertaken on a confidential basis, as, for example, through the European Advisory Commission.

[***II. Military Courts Created by Executive Agreement or Military Arrangement.*** So far as the offenses to be tried are violations of the laws and customs of war, it is probable that international mixed military tribunals to try them could be created either by executive agreement on a governmental level or by action of military commanders.][10]

We recommend however, since the conspiracy charges to be tried will be of such historical importance and will involve some novel applications of existing principles of law, that the charges should be tried before a court established by a method resting upon the highest sanction provided by the laws of the several interested nations. Trial by such a tribunal would command greater public support among the several United Nations and would receive greater long-term approval. In addition a treaty could make apt provision for trial procedures, which, once ratified, would give them the unquestioned force of law in this and other interested countries.

British View

[The British Government has indicated, in commenting on a Draft Convention for a United Nations War Crimes Court submitted to it by the United Nations War Crimes Commission, that it favors neither the treaty process nor the erection of any international tribunal for the trial of war offenses, other than perhaps mixed military courts.[11]

The War Crimes Commission's proposal, however, is very different from the one presented in this memorandum. For one thing, the convention drafted by the War Crimes Commission would have involved an indefinite, long-term commitment on the part of the contracting powers. It would have established a court of indeterminate duration, sitting in several divisions, for the trial of such war crimes as any of the several nations for any reason did not care to try in their own courts. It made no provision for dealing with conduct not violative of the laws of war in the strict sense. In effect it provided an international tribunal to do work which should properly be remitted to national civil or military courts, and which under the plan proposed herein, will be thus remitted.

Consequently, we do not regard the British objections to the War Crimes Commission's Draft Convention as necessarily precluding assent to the proposal now advanced.][12]

Recommendation

We recommend that you approve the preparation and negotiation of a treaty to create a court of the type and having the limited jurisdiction described above.

OTHER ESTABLISHED PROCEDURES NOT FORECLOSED

The program which we have described is not intended to foreclose other available procedures for dealing with particular offenses. Thus, for example, atrocities against our nationals by identifiable Axis individuals will remain subject to trial by United States military and naval commissions. The military and civilian tribunals of the other United Nations will probably be employed to try other individual crimes, under either international or local law. These procedures present no new problems of policy, and are mentioned only for the sake of completeness. They do not require further action on your part at this time.

POSITION OF THE NAVY DEPARTMENT

The Navy Department has indicated that it has a direct interest only in war crimes in the strict sense, such as are mentioned in the preceding paragraph, and that it disclaims interest in any war atrocities outside that field.[13]

SECRETARY OF STATE SECRETARY OF WAR

DOCUMENT 23

WAR DEPARTMENT
(the Secretary of War to the Secretary of State)[1]
WASHINGTON

November 27, 1944

The Honorable,
The Secretary of State:

The question presented in your letter of November 15, 1944,[2] whether the preparation for and launching of the present war can be considered a war crime, is one upon which the vote of the members of the United Nations War Crimes Commission would be advisory only, and not binding upon their respective governments. Nevertheless, a vote cast by the United States member under your instructions would undoubtedly be referred to and cited in any future consideration of this problem.

Whether the conduct of the Axis powers in this regard can properly be condemned as a war crime is a problem which is not entirely free from difficulty. It is believed that very substantial doubts exist as to the correctness of the negative conclusion on this question reached by the majority of a sub-committee of the Commission appointed to consider this matter.[3] The question involves not only the preparation for and launching of an aggressive war, but also the extent to which the Axis powers planned in advance to conduct their belligerent operations by means and methods in violation of the laws of war, and other considerations which will require careful study before a definitive opinion can be expressed. The problem is thus to some extent also involved in the proposals which are presently pending in your Department and mine, with respect to the basic theory upon which war criminals will be tried.

In the opinion of the War Department, a commitment at this time on the question presented by your letter of November 15 would be premature and might prove to be unfortunate.

In view of the foregoing, it is recommended that the United States member on the War Crimes Commission[4] be instructed that this Government is not at present prepared to express an opinion on this matter, and be directed to request a substantial further postponement in the consideration of this matter. It is further suggested that, in the meantime, the question be made a subject of study in your office and in the office of the Judge Advocate General of the Army, and that further consultation then be had in the light of such studies.

Sincerely yours,

Henry L. Stimson
Secretary of War

(HANDWRITTEN NOTE ADDED BY STIMSON)

I regard this matter as so important,—that I request an opportunity for the expression of my personal views by the Sec'y or in his absence the acting Sec'y.

H.L.S.

DOCUMENT 24

MEMORANDUM ON AGGRESSIVE WAR BY COLONEL WILLIAM CHANLER

(WITH A COVER LETTER FROM HENRY L. STIMSON TO JOHN J. McCLOY)[1]

November 28/30, 1944

WAR DEPARTMENT
Washington

Mr. McCloy[2] November 28, 1944

Dear Jack:

Willie Chanler[3] has sent me, informally and for my personal perusal, a memorandum on the subject of a legal basis for the punishment of Hitler and his associates for their acts of aggression.

It takes up the subject from a new approach—an approach of international law as modified by the Pact of Paris[4] and seeks to demonstrate that these defendants could be charged and convicted for the offense of attempting to overrun and annihilate Germany's peaceful neighbors in violation of treaty obligations and attempting to destroy the peace of the world in an effort to conquer Europe.

While his thesis is, I think, a little in advance of the progress of international thought, it is nevertheless along lines of approach which thoughtful members of the international bar have been putting forward during the past twenty years. Chanler's paper is thought-provoking and well deserves a look-over by you and your committee.[5] While I don't think that the advance has been sufficiently generally recognized to make it safe to place our charges against these men on this basis, nevertheless a chance may come for using some of the arguments he advances and perhaps in making a step forward in international law on this subject.

H.L.S.

DRAFT 30 November 1944

MEMORANDUM:

SUBJECT: CAN HITLER AND THE NAZI LEADERSHIP BE PUNISHED FOR THEIR ACTS OF LAWLESS AGGRESSION, THUS IMPLEMENTING THE KELLOGG PACT AND OUTLAWING WARS OF AGGRESSION?

1. At the time of Hitler's various acts of aggression against his peaceful neighbors, they were universally denounced as lawless by the non-Axis world and it was frequently said that if captured Hitler and his associates would be brought to trial and punished for these acts as common bandits. To thoughtful students of the problem, such a course seemed to present possibilities of real progress along the difficult road toward world peace; for it would establish once and for all the principle for which American statesmen have long striven, that armed aggression is a crime.

2. But now that the time for punishment draws near, this thought seems to have been largely abandoned. In part, this is the natural result of Hitler's barbaric acts of wholesale murder, his destruction of towns, etc. First emphasis is placed on punishing these acts, which, more than anything else have shocked the conscience of mankind. This is as it should be, and the pending proposal to prepare charges in the nature of conspiracy indictments for this purpose appears to present a thoroughly sound method for its accomplishment. But could we not add either as a part of the general conspiracy charge, or as a separate and additional count, a charge that the defendants conspired to

and did direct armed forces unlawfully to enter the borders of peaceful neighboring states and kill all people therein who opposed them?

3. It has been said that there would be no legal basis for such a charge: that it is unprecedented to attempt to hold either the heads of state or the generals of armies criminally guilty for lawful acts of war; that the only basis for their punishment would be to prove that they had violated or were responsible for violation of the laws of war. But such objections are based upon the traditional theory of International Law that war is a legitimate instrument of national policy, a theory which, thanks largely to the efforts of the U.S.A., has now been universally repudiated.

4. As Mr. Stimson, Secretary of War, said in the course of his testimony before the House Committee on Foreign Affairs, on January 16, 1941, in support of the proposed Lend-Lease Bill:

> "This country was one of the authors of one of the greatest changes in International Law that has ever taken place, when it was in 1926 and 1927 and 1928 the initiator of what has been called the 'Pact of Paris' or the Kellogg-Briand Pact."[6]

By that pact, all civilized nations, including Germany, Japan and their satellites, solemnly agreed to "condemn recourse to war for the solution of International controversies, and renounce it as an instrument of national policy in their relations with one another"; and in Article II they further "agree that the settlement or solution of all disputes or conflicts of whatever nature or origin they may be which may arise among them, shall never be sought except by pacific means."

5. The great change in International Law to which Mr. Stimson referred is that one of the legal consequences of that Pact is to deprive a nation which violates it of its traditional rights as a lawful belligerent towards neutrals. In support of this proposition Mr. Stimson cited the resolutions adopted by the International Law Association at its meeting in Budapest on September 10, 1934, reading in part as follows:

> "(2) A signatory State which threatens to resort to armed force for the solution of an international dispute or conflict is guilty of a violation of the Pact.
>
> * * * * * * *[7]
>
> "(4) In the event of a violation of the Pact by a resort to armed force or war by one signatory State against another, the other States may, without thereby committing a breach of the Pact or of any rule of International Law, do all or any of the following things:
>
> "(a) Refuse to admit the exercise by the State violating the Pact of belligerent rights, such as visit and search, blockade, etc.

"(b) Decline to observe towards the State violating the Pact the duties prescribed by International law, apart from the Pact, for a neutral in relation to a belligerent;

"(c) Supply the State attacked with financial or material assistance, including munitions of war;

"(d) Assist with armed forces the State attacked."[8]

6. If the Kellogg Pact, by outlawing war as an instrument of national policy, deprives a violator of that Pact of his rights as a lawful belligerent towards neutrals, surely it must follow that it likewise deprives him of the same protection towards the victims of his aggression. If this is so, then armed forces of a signatory State which enter the territory of a neighboring signatory State and commit depredations therein stand on no better footing than a band of guerillas who under established International Law are not entitled to be treated as lawful belligerents.

7. To give an illustration: when Pancho Villa entered the U.S. unlawfully in 1915–16, he was concededly a bandit. True he did not come as a representative of Mexico; on the contrary, Mexico had repudiated him. Now if Mexico had recognized Villa as one of her generals, and had not repudiated him, under International Law as it then stood his acts would have been lawful acts of war and Villa and his band would have been entitled to all the protection of the laws of war and of course, another consequence would have been that a state of war between the U.S. and Mexico would have existed. But today, under the Kellogg Pact, neither recognition by Mexico, nor even a formal declaration of war would legalize such armed aggression, unless the United States itself had first attacked Mexico. For such a declaration of war would itself be unlawful, and so could not legalize any acts done under it.

8. It thus follows that armed aggression is unlawful and that acts of aggression cannot be defended as lawful acts of war. If this be sound, then all hostile actions of the Axis armies are war crimes and could be punished as such by any Allied military tribunal, whether or not the acts would constitute violations of the laws of war if committed by a lawful belligerent. Thus, a count in the proposed conspiracy indictment charging all acts of the Axis Armies as constituting war crimes would seem logically to be tenable.

9. However, it may be that this is too drastic a step to be taken at the present time. Objection would be raised, for example, that England and France declared war on Germany over the invasion of Poland and that thereafter Germany was lawfully at war with England and France. While these declarations of war are entirely consistent with the theory of the Kellogg Pact, (See Paragraph 4 (d) of the Budapest Resolutions Supra) nevertheless, confusing and unnecessary collateral issues might be raised.

10. It would seem that perhaps the most effective way to raise this issue would be to follow the course laid down in the Moscow Declaration. Let us

assume that, relying upon that declaration, Czechoslovakia or Poland, let us say, or both together, should demand that Hitler and his associates be delivered to them for trial on the charge that they had directed forces under their command to unlawfully enter their territory by force of arms, killing all citizens who stood in their way, etc., in violation of the domestic criminal law of Poland and Czechoslovakia.[9]

11. It must be observed that under this procedure it would not be proposed to punish Hitler and his associates for violation of the Kellogg Pact as such, nor for violation of any principle of International Law. They would be charged with violation of the domestic criminal law of the countries invaded.

12. The War Crimes Commission, or a special tribunal established for such purpose by the United Nations, would then be squarely faced with the question whether or not the Kellogg Pact in fact outlawed a war of aggression. Presumably, the tribunal would hold hearings in the nature of an extradition procedure. The complaining nations would recite the Kellogg Pact, the Munich Pact,[10] the 1934 Ten-Year Guaranty of Peace between Germany and Poland, and would allege a conspiracy to unlawfully enter upon and destroy the existence of Poland and Czechoslovakia and kill any persons therein who might resist, and the actual carrying out of such conspiracy for the purpose of conquering the world, etc.

13. After hearing Hitler's defense which would no doubt be based primarily on the proposition that the acts charged were lawful acts of war, the tribunal could quite properly hold that the defense is not valid because the defendants having violated the Kellogg Pact are not lawful belligerents. To hold otherwise would be to hold the Pact meaningless.

14. What other defense could Hitler present? He would no doubt point out that most of the signatories to the Kellogg Pact, including the United States, either by specific reservation or by collateral formal statements, have taken the position that the Kellogg Pact does not prohibit a defensive war, and would then seek to prove that his aggressions were in fact necessary to the defense of Germany.

15. This would raise a question of fact for the Court to determine and it would seem that if ever a case was presented to a Court in which sufficient facts existed to sustain a charge of aggression, this is it. If properly presented, the Court should have no difficulty in dismissing such a defense as a sham.

So far as Hitler's argument that war was necessary to correct the "Crime of Versailles" and to gain the "Lebensraum",[11] necessary to Germany's existence, the answer is that these are the very issues of "National Policy" which under the Kellogg Pact must be settled by peaceful means. The exception permitting defensive war should be limited to a defense against actual or undeniably imminent armed agression. Otherwise, the pact is meaningless.

16. Thus, we would have a judicial interpretation of the Kellogg Pact to the

effect that any person or group of persons who engage in such a course of conduct as that followed by the Nazis in connection with the present war are violators of the Pact and as such are common criminals, not subject to the protection accorded to a lawful belligerent by International Law. Surely this would be a most beneficial and useful step in the difficult path towards the elimination of war. While it may not of itself deter a future Hitler, it would certainly make it more difficult for him to persuade his people that he was leading them in a lawful and noble enterprise and it would make it much easier to unite the peace-loving nations in opposition to him.

17. But the greatest advantage of the proposal would be that it would get around the great stumbling block which has stayed all previous attempts to outlaw wars of aggression: the difficulty of defining an "aggressor" in a formal treaty. If the definition is broad enough it is always feared that it might prevent a war entered into in good faith purely for the purposes of defense against imminent aggression. As soon as reservations are proposed to meet this difficulty it becomes apparent that any aggressor can easily get around the treaty. But by the procedure here proposed all this would be avoided. There would be no need of entering into any new treaty. We would simply have a judicial determination analogous to a common law precedent to the effect that the facts presented by Hitler's course of conduct constitute a violation of the Kellogg Pact and deprive him and his followers of the protection of International Law.

This would not constitute such a precedent, for example, as to outlaw a war undertaken in good faith for purposes of defense against an enemy threatening armed attack. It would, however, put upon a nation contemplating such a war the burden of being certain that it could establish its good faith before an international tribunal. This should not deter the U.S.A.—it has always been our view that we should not go to war unless actually attacked.[12] Nor should it be unacceptable to France, who originally proposed the Kellogg-Briand Pact, nor to China, nor to any of the smaller nations. The U.S.S.R. led all nations of the world in its efforts to outlaw war during the past 20 years and there is no reason to suppose that its policy has changed. The British Foreign Office might be disturbed by the procedure. By the nature of her far-flung Empire, Great Britain is made acutely conscious of the advantage of the "mailed fist" in its preservation and control. On the other hand, it is very probable that in a public debate the British public would strongly support this proposal, and would not support a government which refused to support a principle outlawing war, on the ground that war might be advantageous to the Empire.

18. An incidental advantage of the proposal is that an indictment of Hitler and his associates on such charges as those here suggested should make their extradition possible from even the most squeamish nation in which they might take refuge.

19. As to procedure: the particular proposal of a demand by Poland or Czechoslovakia is suggested because it seems to present the simplest test case. Unnecessary complicating collateral issues are avoided and the issue is simply and squarely presented. On the other hand, there would probably be serious objection to actually turning over Hitler and the Nazi leaders to Poland or Czechoslovakia for trial and punishment under their domestic criminal law. This could be avoided by providing in the decision that they would not be turned over until after the War Crimes Commission was through with them. They could then be first tried under the general conspiracy indictment.

20. Except for the danger of beclouding the issue with collateral questions, the most satisfactory procedure would be to add a count for unlawfully entering the peaceful neighboring countries, etc., to the pending conspiracy indictment. The danger of beclouding the issue might be avoided by combining the two procedures: First, a decision in a hearing on a demand from Poland or Czechoslovakia. The issue would then become "stare decisis"[13] when the question arose at the general conspiracy trial and collateral complications might thus be avoided.

21. It has also been suggested that such an issue as this should be determined by political action of the United Nations instead of by a judicial proceeding. But this would require formal action, perhaps even on the treaty-making level, and might raise more complications than it avoided. Furthermore, it might not have quite the same effect as a judicial interpretation of the Kellogg Pact. But the question of procedure can no doubt be better solved in the course of the actual drafting. The important thing is to get the principle presented and decided, so that it becomes a recognized precedent in International Law.

22. In conclusion, it must be borne in mind that strong objections will undoubtedly arise from a fear of the possible consequences of the precedent. As suggested above, the British are likely to be the ones most strongly urging this objection. But the short answer is that the more it is urged that such a precedent might be embarrassing in the event that one of the United Nations wanted to go to war in the future, the more obvious it becomes that the precedent will effectively contribute to world peace.

23. So far as legal objections are concerned, the answer is that once it is done, it will *be* International Law, regardless of possible present doubts. If it presents a possibility of contributing to the future peace of the world, legalistic objections should not be permitted to stand in the way.

DOCUMENT 25

MEMORANDUM FOR THE ASSISTANT SECRETARY OF WAR (FROM GENERAL KENNETH C. ROYALL)[1]

December 14, 1944

The following tentative opinions on the trial of German war criminals are based upon a reading of the several documents furnished by your office and upon no other investigation.[2]

1. Military Commission[3]

There should be immediately organized a Commission of five military members, one each to be appointed by the ranking European commander of Russia, England, France, and the United States, and one to be appointed jointly by the ranking European commanders of other Allied countries. The Commission would have the judicial functions suggested below.

Attached to this Commission would be a prosecuting agency with "military legal" personnel sufficient to try cases which come before the Commission and to gather and correlate evidence and otherwise prepare for trial.

The present United Commission for Investigation of War Crimes (UCI)[4] would continue to gather evidence, compile lists of criminals and study procedures and precedents, and would render advice and assistance to the Commission and its prosecuting agency but would have no control over either.

2. German Crimes before Beginning of the War and German Acts in Starting War

None would be punishable except through the civil courts of Germany. The Commission should cooperate with the Allied Commanders in continuing or establishing courts for this purpose, and the German people should be told that the effectiveness of these courts in punishing violations of law would be an indication of the extent to which the nation could be trusted to govern itself.

3. Crimes Committed in Germany during War against German Citizens

The military commanders will repeal by proclamation all amnesties and similar laws and all procedural impediments to trial.

The German courts would be given an opportunity to try these cases. Allied military courts, set up under the Commission primarily for the trial of crimes during occupation, would be given jurisdiction to try these preoccupation cases and would try them, under rules prescribed by the Commission, whenever the commission determined that the German courts were acting slowly or ineffectively. These military courts could assume jurisdiction over cases pending in German courts.

4. Definition of War Crimes

This term would not include any act not recognized by precedent as a crime against the law of war and, specifically, would not include any of the acts mentioned in paragraphs 2 and 3.

5. War Crimes Committed in Germany or Invaded Territories

Except for a designated list of German leaders, all persons committing war crimes in an invaded country could be tried by the Military or civil courts either of the country where the crime was committed or of the country whose nationals were injured by the war crime or by the courts of both. As to war crimes committed in Germany the trial could be either by the occupation courts or the civil or military courts of the injured nation. The Commission would determine any conflicts of custody or jurisdiction.

In exceptional cases the Commission itself could take exclusive jurisdiction in any case where it appeared that the trial procedures did not protect the defendants as they would be protected by a trial before the Commission. The Commission could and would take jurisdiction of any defendant who was a necessary or proper party to any proceeding pending before or contemplated by the Commission.

The prosecuting division of the Commission would assist the other courts in the apprehension and extradition of prisoners, and to the extent reasonably possible, in the gathering of evidence in these trials and also trials before all other courts.

6. Trials by the Commission

The Commission would try the principal leaders of the German Government for the commission of war crimes and for the conspiracy to commit war crimes. The decision in this case would not affect by presumption or otherwise anyone not a party thereto.

As a separate case or as a part of the case the Commission would try certain organizations, such as the Gestapo, and their members for conspiracy to commit war crimes. The members of the organizations would have to be specifically named in the charges but they would be permitted to have only class representation in the trial.

The trial of the leaders and of the organizations would be deferred until after the defeat of both Germany and Japan.

In exceptional cases the Commission could at any time try individual members of the organizations or other persons for the commission of specific war crimes rather than permit such trial by other courts. Conviction or acquittal of a conspiracy charge would not preclude a subsequent trial for the actual commission of a war crime even though such crimes were one of the overt acts of the conspiracy.

7. Evidence and Procedure

The Commission would prescribe its own procedure and its rules of evidence, which would be as liberal as the most liberal rules of the civil or military courts of England, France or the United States.[5]

Consideration should be given to permitting depositions to be offered in evidence, to widening judicial notice of well-known facts, to broadening the scope and effect of circumstantial evidence, to implying consent from the failure to dissent from or prevent illegal action, to admitting more hearsay, to liberalizing proof of documents, to eliminating statutory limitations and other similar provisions. As far as practical these rules should be formulated and announced by the Commission before the commencement of any trial.

These rules would be mandatory on occupation courts and suggestive to other courts which try war crimes.

8. Prisoners of War

All captured Germans or others who are numbered among the leaders of Germany or who are members of the organizations to be tried or against whom there is any appreciable evidence of the commission of war crimes or other crimes, should be kept as prisoners of war until there is an opportunity to try them or until investigation shows that a case cannot be made out against them.

9. Miscellaneous

Rough memoranda relative to other features of the matter have been prepared and are available.[6]

10. Theory and Reasons

Rough memoranda on the theory and reasons for these recommendations are also available.[7] In general it is believed that these recommendations are consistent with history, represent the best policy for the future, and adequately effectuate the declarations heretofore made by the United Nations and by the President of the United States.

KENNETH C. ROYALL
Brigadier General, USA

DOCUMENT 26

MEMORANDUM FOR THE JUDGE ADVOCATE GENERAL

SUBJECT: IS THE PREPARATION AND LAUNCHING OF THE PRESENT WAR A WAR CRIME?[1]

[Shortly before December 18, 1944]

1. By summary sheet dated 24 November 1944, transmitted from the Assistant Chief of Staff, G-1,[2] the opinion of The Judge Advocate General was requested on "whether or not the preparation for and launching of the present war can be considered a war crime." Attached to this sheet was a copy of a letter to the Secretary of War from the Secretary of State, dated 15 November 1944, together with several papers and minutes of the United Nations War Crimes Commission relative to a vote that is to be taken on the above question in the near future by the members of the Commission.[3]

2. From the basic communication and accompanying papers, it appears that a majority of the sub-committee appointed by the Commission to consider the question, answered it in the negative, their position being supported by a note prepared for them by Sir Arnold McNair. A minority report, drawn up by Dr. Ečer, the Czechoslovakian representative, took the opposite position. Further debate thereon was then adjourned to enable the members to receive specific instructions from their governments as to the way they should vote.[4] It is for this purpose that an expression of the views of the War Department is requested.

A more precise statement of what is contemplated by the question here raised would seem to be, whether the acts referred to constitute a *crime under international law*.[5] Application of the term "war crime" to the initiation of war in violation of international law[6] is neither good usage nor justified by the principles ordinarily governing criminal acts committed in the conduct of the war itself. Nor is it believed possible to attribute separate legal significance to the *preparation* of war as distinct from the actual launching thereof, apart from the principle recognized by Sir Arnold McNair that an act of preparation which has the effect of producing a "war crime" after the outbreak of war is itself a war crime or may be assimilated to one.[7] Fundamentally the question involved is whether *resort to an aggressive war* planned in advance to be waged by methods which violate laws governing the conduct of belligerent operations, is *eo ipso*[8] a distinct crime. On the question so phrased this office concurs in the result reached by the majority report. It is, moreover, of the opinion that the views expressed by Sir Arnold McNair, who is one of the most distinguished international lawyers in England, are, in general, an accurate reflection of present international law.

4. Prior to the General Treaty for the Renunciation of War, or "Kellogg-Briand Pact," as it is popularly called, of 27 August 1928,[9] it was a generally accepted principle of international law that every state had a right to resort to war—a right which was inherent in its sovereignty—and which could be exercised whenever and however it saw fit. War was recognized as a legally admissible instrument for attacking and altering the existing rights of States independently of the justness or unjustness of the attempted change.[10]

. . . .[11]

12. In September 1927, the Eighth Assembly [of the League of Nations], on motion of the Polish delegate, voted a resolution to prohibit all wars of aggression. According to the Polish delegate, a declaration establishing that offensive warfare can not serve as a means of settling disputes and should be considered an international crime would exercise a favorable influence upon the opinion of the world. The resolution was in these terms:

> "The Assembly,
>
> . . . .[12]
>
> "Being convinced that a war of aggression can never serve as a means of settling international disputes and is, in consequence, an international crime; * * *
>
> "Declares:
>
> "1. That all wars of aggression are, and shall always be prohibited.

13. Similar in phraseology is the resolution which was adopted by the Sixth Pan American Conference in February 1928, upon the motion of the Mexican delegation:

> "Considering . . .
>
> "That war of aggression constitutes an international crime against the human-species,
>
> "The Sixth International Conference of American States resolves:
>
> "1. All aggression is considered illicit and as such declared prohibited;
>
> "2. The American States will employ all pacific means to settle conflicts which may arise between them."[13]

This resolution created no legal imperative.

Though both of the foregoing declare a war of aggression to be an international crime, neither imposes any sanctions or punishment. The former was not a treaty, which binds the nations ratifying it, but a mere resolution of the Assembly of the League of Nations. The latter, though a treaty, of course bound only the nations which signed and ratified it, but the nations whose misdeeds we are considering were not among them. It is therefore very doubtful whether the resolution and treaty mentioned were intended to give rise to personal punishment of individuals bringing about an aggressive war, or whether the bodies which made them could legally have produced such a result, as to our present enemies, if they had so intended.

15.[14] Finally, in the Anti-War Treaty of Nonaggression and Conciliation concluded on 10 October 1933 between the United States of America and other American Republics, the language of criminal law was omitted altogether. In its stead the contracting parties merely declared that

> "they condemn wars of aggression in their mutual relations or in those with other states, and that the settlement of disputes or controversies of any kind that may arise among them shall be effected only by the pacific means which have the sanction of international law."[15]

16. The capstone of these labors to render war illegal was the Kellogg Pact of 1928, which is binding upon over sixty States, including all the great powers. It consists of a preamble and two articles which are thus worded:

> "Article I. The High Contracting Parties solemnly declare in the name of their respective peoples that they condemn recourse to war for the solution of international controversies, and renounce it as an instrument of national policy in their relations with one another.
>
> "Article II. The High Contracting Parties agree that the settlement or solution of all disputes or conflicts of whatever origin they may be, which may arise among them, shall never be sought except by pacific means."[16]

These articles should be read together with that portion of the preamble in which the signatory States express their conviction that "all changes in their relations with one another should be sought by pacific means and be the result of a peaceful and orderly process, and that any signatory Power which shall hereafter seek to promote its national interests by resort to war should be denied the benefits furnished by this treaty." Volumes have been written about the meaning of these two articles and the preamble itself; about the effect of various reservations which accompanied its negotiation, especially that of the British Government, and of the preliminary documents that bear upon its interpretation; about the relation of the Pact to the Covenant of the League of Nations, and how the obligations concerning recourse to war differed under the two documents; about the extent of the right to go to war in self-defense; and finally, whether renunciation of war as an instrument of *national* policy precluded resorting to war as an instrument of *international* policy.[17] It would serve no useful purpose to develop these matters here. Although the view has been expressed in some quarters that the Pact created no new legal obligations at all for States,[18] authoritative writers have generally rejected the view that the obligation of Article I to "renounce" and "condemn" is not an obligation to refrain from making war. Resort to war is unlawful under the Pact. But although international law is violated thereby, it by no means follows that aggressive war is made a crime. The distinction is important if confusion is to be avoided. The usual consequence of the violation of an international obligation is the duty to make reparation for the damage suffered.[19] What consequences flow from breach of the Kellogg Pact?

14. The first consequence is obvious from that portion of the preamble under which any power which resorts to war to promote its national interests, *is deprived of the benefits of the treaty*. This simply means that the other States are thereupon automatically exempt from these obligations under the pact to the offending state.[20] It is an affirmation of the rule that a treaty broken by one of its parties may be cancelled by the other.[21] As Lauterpacht correctly observes:

> "No other express sanction is provided in the Pact itself or intended by it. In particular, the illegality of the war undertaken in breach of the provisions of the Pact does not automatically deprive the guilty belligerent of the rights of warfare, including those resulting from the law of neutrality. However, although the Pact itself provides for no specific sanction, a breach of its provisions constitutes an international wrong against all its signatories, who thereupon, without electing to go to war, become entitled to such redress, by the way of self-help or otherwise, as the principles of State responsibility warrant. They may resort to reprisals; they acquire the right of intervention; and both as belligerents and neutrals they are entitled to hold the guilty belligerent responsible for the losses sustained as the result of war."[22]

This interpretation is unassailable. There is not the remotest suggestion in the Pact that the authors of a war in violation thereof were to be criminally responsible for their wrong. The language used is the language of compact, not crime; it sounds in contract, not punishment. Indeed, Hyde regards the Kellogg Pact as a "contractual obligation."[23] The language used by Lauterpacht is familiar to anyone conversant with the rules of international responsibility (or "liability"). "Responsibility" is the ordinary result of a violation of International duties. Such violations are unlawful acts; they are "delicts";[24] they will support claim in behalf of the individuals who sustain injuries therefrom. But they are not crimes. The same may be said of the "nonaggression" pacts concluded by Germany with various European powers. Any intention to attach individual criminal responsibility to the persons guilty would have had to be clearly expressed, in the light of the well-established, pre-existing contrary rule. It may not be presumed. But so much uncertainty surrounds the precise meaning of those provisions which were formulated in express terms that it is virtually impossible to conclude that the Kellogg Pact has made an international penal offense of an aggressive war. This result may be most unfortunate; it may be immoral; it may be considered as socially outrageous. But it is the only conclusion compatible with existing principles of positive international law. In this respect, the views of the Commission on Responsibility at the Paris Peace Conference, which dealt with an analogous legal situation in the form of the treaties of 1839 and 1867 guaranteeing the neutrality of Luxembourg and Belgium,[25] would even today be held valid. It may seem somewhat anomalous that the preparation and launching of war with the designed intention of prosecuting it by illegal means of warfare, is not itself a crime. Yet specific acts of warfare were declared to be criminal and prohibited long before serious efforts were made to outlaw war itself. The very term "outlaw" is itself unfortunate, since it suggests "crime", whereas the Kellogg Pact neither intended nor achieved such a result.

15. For these reasons, the position taken by the majority of the sub-committee appointed by the United Nations War Crimes Commission is believed to be legally correct.[26] Nevertheless, there are grounds of impelling weight why the Commission should *not* go on record as having denied the criminality of launching this war. Such a result, if it ever reached the press, would be met with outraged protests by suffering peoples who are not concerned with the legal aspects of what to them has been plain mass murder. The War Crimes Commission would be fatally discredited in the popular mind. It is not inconceivable that such action would be equivalent to signing its own death warrant. But even if the Commission's decision were not made public, the latent risks of prejudicing future criminal proceedings against the culprits can not be disregarded. It could provide all kinds of arguments in defense of the persons accused. On the other hand, if the Commission votes affirmatively on this question, it will find itself in an untenable legal position that an international tribunal may some day tear to pieces. In short, an affirmative vote will discredit the Commission among lawyers; a negative vote will discredit it with the public. The Czechoslovak delegate's desire to have the question considered has placed the Commission in a most unfortunate dilemma.

16. It is therefore believed essential that the whole question be withdrawn from the Commission's consideration, and that no further action be taken by it at the present time. It is a question which can be better disposed of by

appropriate political and legal action outside of the Commission, once the enemy has been defeated.

17. In the memorandum of 24 November, 1944,[27] from the Assistant Secretary of War, which recommended postponement of the vote by the Commission, reference is made to a "conspiracy theory" advocated by G-1, which might afford a basis for rendering the leaders of Germany criminally responsible, not only for the acts of preparing and launching the present war, but for the brutal treatment and persecution of minority groups inside Germany prior to the outbreak of the war. According to this theory, these persecutions would be regarded as part and parcel of a gigantic conspiracy on the part of the German leaders to dominate the world by criminally illegal methods of warfare. Does the theory justify a different conclusion from that reached in the present memorandum on the criminality of the war? The answer is in the negative. There are several difficulties with this conception which are fatal to its acceptance as a sound legal position. To begin with it is in flat contradiction of the established theory that resort to aggressive war is not a crime—until 1928 it was not even *illegal*—and its corollaries. Under existing international law the legality of the war can only be judged with reference to the rules governing resort to war. Use of illegal means to conduct a war is wholly irrelevant and has no effect upon the legality of the war itself. It produces certain other consequences under conventions and customary law; but, even with resort to war rendered illegal by the Kellogg Pact, the intent of a State's leaders to use illegal methods of warfare in violation thereof does not convert the act of resorting to war into a crime. Nor is domination of the world illegal; no rule of international law says that a State can not conspire by illegal means to achieve that end. On the contrary, when such an aggression is successful, international law gives the victor domination and a true legal sovereignty. The greatest conspiracy in the world has nothing to do with the legality of the war, or with the criminal responsibility of its authors. That may be unfortunate, but it is present law. Here the decisive point is whether there is individual criminal responsibility, that is, whether a violation of international law entails a criminal penalty of the person accused. And on the basis of positive law, the answer to this must be in the negative.

18. Moreover, to say that the pre-war persecution of minority groups in Germany was part of a conspiracy to dominate the world by illegal methods of warfare, besides being irrelevant, is historically inaccurate. Anti-semitism was a cardinal point which was relied upon to attract people to Hitler's *domestic* program; and it was also unquestionably employed to gain sympathizers in other parts of the world. Such effects as it had abroad in the present connection were, however, indirect. There unquestionably was a Nazi conspiracy in the decade prior to the war, but it was a *domestic* conspiracy.[28]

Resort to illegal war may have been the necessary consequence of the whole National Socialist Philosophy; but to say that criminal responsibility exists for persecutions committed prior to the war is to depart from the domain of positive international law and to enter the realm of political doctrine. Such an allegation would be immediately met with the defense that the treatment of a nation's own subjects are matters [sic] which fall within the "exclusive domestic jurisdiction" of a State.[29] It is believed that the prestige of the United States would be damaged if it sought to justify *in law* its desire to punish German leaders by reliance upon a *political* doctrine of this kind.[30] On the other hand, if this aspect of the "conspiracy" theory were restricted to preconceived acts of extermination directed against national or minority groups in territories occupied *after the war began*; if, in other words, it were to be argued and could be proved that there was a conspiracy to exterminate enemy nationals by wholesale slaughter and starvation of the civilian population, prepared prior to the war itself by leaders of the Axis, the doctrine would seem to be unobjectionable under present international law . . .[31]

19. These conclusions do not signify that there is no legal procedure which can be adopted to ensure punishment of the authors of the war. Other methods are available, but to discuss them at length is outside the scope of this memorandum. An excellent device, however, and one that appears to be legally unimpeachable, is that developed by Professor Kelsen in an article recently published on "The International Legal Status of Germany to Be Established Immediately upon Termination of the War."[32] Creation of a *condominium*[33] over the occupied area, as he suggests, with real legal sovereignty, would permit the Allies to do that which, as belligerent occupants, they may be precluded from doing by the law of nations . . .

DOCUMENT 27

MEMORANDUM FOR THE ATTORNEY GENERAL (FRANCIS BIDDLE) FROM THE ASSISTANT ATTORNEY GENERAL (HERBERT WECHSLER)[1]

December 29, 1944

I have examined the memorandum prepared in the War Department for submission to the President by the Secretary of State and Secretary of War on the "Trial and Punishment of European War Criminals" which Mr. McCloy forwarded to you with his letter of December 3, 1944.[2] I have also examined various related materials supplied by Mr. Hackworth of the State Department.

I. THE WAR DEPARTMENT PROPOSAL[3]

The thesis of the War Department proposal may be stated to be that it is not sufficient to limit our conception of war crimes to conduct technically violative of the laws and customs of war; that it is necessary to implement the declared policy of this government to punish atrocities committed by the Germans before there was a state of war and atrocities committed by them against their own nationals on racial, religious and political grounds; further, and most important, that the fundamental criminality of the conduct of the German leaders consists of the formulation and systematic execution of a program for achieving world domination through the use of treachery, disregard of treaties, mass exterminations of peoples and other wholesale disregard of the rules of civilized warfare as developed under international law.

The memorandum proposes, therefore, that the German leaders be tried for a "conspiracy to achieve domination of other nations and peoples by deliberate violation of the rules of war as they have been accepted and adhered to by the nations of the world, and violation of treaties and international conventions and customs, and mass extermination of peoples." It is proposed that this charge be tried by an international court created by treaty (apparently of the United Nations) which would not only establish the tribunal but also "define the crimes to be tried" and provide a suitable procedure.

It is contemplated that some unspecified number of German individuals, agencies and organizations will be charged with participation in the basic criminal conspiracy and that there will be brought before the international court a group of individual defendants "considered to be fairly representative of the defendant groups and organizations." An adjudication would be sought of the existence, nature and purposes of the conspiracy and its results, the identity of the participants and the punishment to be administered to those defendants who are physically before the court.

In addition, it is contemplated that the adjudication of the international court would "determine the facts of the conspiracy and establish them for the purposes of further proceedings against the individuals, groups and organizations dealt with in the judgment and against the members of such organizations not then physically before the court." As to defendants not physically before the international court and, evidently, as to persons not named as defendants in the international court proceedings but who nevertheless may be charged with membership in any of the organizations found in the international court proceeding to have been party to the conspiracy, it is contemplated that additional proceedings will be held in the civil or military courts of the several United Nations (or mixed tribunals of two or more of them). These secondary proceedings would, apparently, be sustained by proof that a defendant was a participant in any of the organizations held by the international court to have complicity in the conspiracy. The issue would be limited to a determination of the "degree of participation of each person in the conspiracy" and a fixing of the punishment of each of the participants in such measure as may be deemed appropriate for the particular case.

II. COMMENTS ON THE PROPOSAL

(a) The Nazi Leaders

In proposing that the Nazi leaders be prosecuted for the type of conspiracy described above,it is unclear whether the War Department proposal assumes that such a charge has present legal validity under the laws of war or whether some additional legislative definition of the crime is necessary, in the existing state of international law, if the German leaders are to be brought to account in these terms. The proposal that the treaty define the crimes to be punished is itself ambiguous on this point and requires appropriate clarification.

In developing such clarification, the principal difficulty is the fact that some of the elements of the conspiracy charged, (notably violation of treaties, atrocities committed upon German nationals on racial, religious and political grounds and atrocities committed prior to a state of war) are not embraced within the ordinary concept of crimes punishable as violations of the laws of war. For this reason alone, it is desirable that the treaty definition purport not merely to measure the jurisdiction of the tribunal but also to provide the substantive law under which the prosecutions are to be brought. It may be opposed to this view that any treaty definition which goes beyond the laws of war would have retroactive application in violation of the principle *nulla crimen sine lege*,[4] a principle that the Nazis rejected in Germany but that would ordinarily weigh with us. I think it a sufficient answer that the crime charged involves so many elements of criminality under the accepted laws of war and the penal laws of all civilized states that the incorporation of the additional factors in question does not offer the type of threat to innocence which the prohibition of *ex post facto* laws is designed to prevent. The problem, moreover, is not a legal problem in any genuine sense since under international law the victors may determine the terms of peace.

The problem is, in any event, not crucial since the same result can be achieved by eliminating from the concept of the crime the elements of world domination and treaty violations, stating the definition entirely in terms of (a) violations of the laws of war and (b) violations of the principles of criminal law recognized by all civilized states. This approach would completely eliminate any basis for objection founded upon the principles underlying the maxim *nulla crimen sine lege*. The theory of multiple liability for criminal acts executed pursuant to a common plan presents no comparable problem, being common to all developed penal systems and easily included within the scope of the laws of war.

In connection with multiple liability, it should be noted that some confusion may be engendered by the terminology of the War Department proposal which refers to the basic crime as a "common-law conspiracy," employing that concept as it is known to American law. I should suppose that what is really to be condemned as criminal is not the inchoate crime of conspiracy but rather the actual execution of a criminal plan. The theory of conspiracy affords a proper basis for reaching a large number of people, no one of whom engaged in all of the criminal conduct, but it is an error to designate as conspiracy the crime itself, the more so since the common-law conception of the criminality of an unexecuted plan is not universally accepted in civilized law. The point is rather that multiple liability for a host of completed crimes is established by mutual participation in the execution of the criminal plan. The Nazi leaders are accomplices in completed crime according to concepts of accessorial liability common, I believe, to all civilized legal systems.

If the crime is to be defined in broad terms by treaty the more fundamental question presented is whether the formulation should be in the usual terms of legislative definition or whether the treaty would not itself find the essential facts of the Nazi program and the machinery by which it was put into effect, declare the criminality of that program and of the leaders who participated in its design or execution, remitting to judicial determination only the issue of the personal complicity of the individual leaders and the complicity of additional groups or organizations not specified in the treaty.

Two considerations may be adduced in support of the latter approach:

First: It is exceedingly doubtful whether the semblance of a judicial proceeding could be maintained in a proceeding involving even the minimum number of probable defendants in which the issues were drawn as broadly as the War Department proposal conceives. If the basic facts as to the entire Nazi program and its execution are to be proved in a judicial proceeding in which evidence is to be put forward by witnesses with examination and cross-examination, it is difficult to see how such a mass proceeding could be kept within reasonable limits or how the defendants could be prevented from utilizing the forum to debate the fundamental issues. The first trial envisaged by the War Department proposal—in which the basic facts of the conspiracy are to be established—might well afford precisely the type of forum that would enable the Nazi leaders to project their influence as martyrs into the future of the Reich. Particularly would this be so in so far as the Nazis could contend that any tribunal established by the victors would necessarily be a partial tribunal, incapable of judicious appraisal of the losers' cause.

Second: The more important point is that the fundamental facts with respect to the Nazi program are so notorious in the Allied view that they are not seriously open to disproof. The only genuine issues are, in fact, those which relate to the degree of complicity of particular individuals or groups and the mitigating circumstances, if any, that may exist in a particular case.

For the foregoing reasons, it is my view that the War Department proposal with respect to the punishment of the major Nazi leaders should be modified to provide for a treaty declaration of the essentials of the criminal plan, with judicial findings, limited to individual complicity, mitigating circumstances and penalty determination. If a treaty is practicable at all, as to which a question is raised below, I should suppose that agreement on the essential findings or some approach thereto would be no more difficult than agreement on the proposal that the War Department memorandum puts forth.

(b) Secondary Proceedings

For those persons who are not physically before the court in the basic conspiracy trial but who are nevertheless to be charged with participation in the conspiracy, the War Department proposal contemplates secondary proceedings before civil or military courts of the several United Nations or mixed tribunals of two or more of them. In these proceedings the facts found by the treaty court would be taken as established and the issues limited to that of personal participation and degree of guilt.

In this aspect, the War Department proposal is designed to meet the practical difficulty that would be encountered if it were necessary to prove the basic facts of the conspiracy and the participation in it of particular agencies and organizations over and over again. The difficulty is genuine but I think the solution unwise. If individuals are to be punished because they were active members of the major Nazi organs, the justice of their punishment will gain no added weight from a trial to which they are not real parties and in which they had no opportunity to be heard. Hence, I believe that if punishment is to be based upon this ground it is even more desirable than in the case of the Nazi leaders that the offense be legislatively defined. Such a procedure avoids the pretense of judiciality, deriving its force, as legislation must, from general acceptance of its fairness in light of the accepted facts.

Apart from this consideration, however, I would raise a more fundamental question of policy. I seriously doubt the wisdom of attempting to charge persons who are not included in the category of "higher ups" with complicity in the broad charge of criminality to be leveled at the prime leaders. As to such persons—and there will undoubtedly be hundreds, if not thousands—I should favor attempting to reach and punish them only for particular violations of national laws or the laws and customs of warfare in strictly judicial proceedings either in the courts of the nations in which the offenses were committed or before military tribunals.

I hold this view largely, because, in my opinion, there is a real danger that the force of the broad criminal charge against the leaders may be seriously weakened in the eyes of the world if too many individuals are included in it. I think too that it is desirable so far as possible to reduce the persons who are punished to the level of ordinary criminals and this can be done effectively only by proof of personal participation in specific crimes. This is the sense in which I read the provisions of the Moscow Declaration of November 1, 1943.

If prosecution for specific acts is believed to be impractical in the case of the rank and file members of the principal Nazi organizations, such for example as the Gestapo, there is an alternative course under which a substantial part of the purpose can be achieved. If the occupying military authorities were to issue a decree calling upon all present or former members of designated organizations (S.A., S.S. et cetera) to identify themselves as such, it may be expected that a substantial number of such persons (and presumably the worst) would fail to comply with the decree. This would provide a convenient and wholly defensible basis for summary action by military courts, prescribing the punishment specified in the decree. To the extent, on the other hand, that there was compliance with the decree, the occupying authorities would undoubtedly receive substantial assistance in the investigation of specific crimes.

(c) Miscellaneous Problems

There remain a number of general problems suggested by the memorandum which require some comment.

The memorandum suggests that punishments less than capital may be imposed upon those found guilty of the crimes defined by the treaty. If this contemplates not only the possibility of mitigation in particular cases but also that a class of offenses less than capital might be dealt with by the court, I think it a mistake.

At the same time consideration must be given to the number of capital sentences which, as a practical matter, can be imposed under American or international auspices. It is obviously desirable to gear any proposed international machinery to its capacity for effective operation. To the extent that individuals are brought to justice in the national courts of liberated countries, this problem will be significantly reduced.

I think it also necessary to raise the question whether the treaty approach is a feasible one at all. The British have opposed the United Nations War Crimes Commission's proposal for an international convention to establish a court for the trial of offenses "against the laws and customs of war". The reasons for this opposition, set forth in an aide memoire of October 30, 1944,[5] are (1) that the negotiation and entry into operation of such a convention would require a very long time, (2) that the Soviet Union would have to be brought in from the beginning, and it is not a member of the War Crimes Commission, (3) that the proposal is inconsistent with the Moscow Declaration and in any event unnecessary and (4) that there would be great difficulty, if a convention could be negotiated, in finding suitable personnel for the court, agreeing to procedure and defining rules, evidence, etc.

The War Department memorandum asserts that the British may not extend their opposition to the present proposal because the tribunal here proposed would have a limited life and because the crimes to be dealt with include other than strict violations of the laws of war. I do not follow this reasoning and would expect the British to oppose the present proposal not only for most of the reasons presented in its aide memoire concerning the War Crimes Commission's draft convention but for the additional reason that the present proposal would attempt to reach beyond violations of the laws of war.

Nor does this government have an indication of the position that the Russian Government would take. The Russians, as you know, have not participated in the work of the War Crimes Commission and their participation in the present proposal would, I suppose, be important to its success.

I also point out that the War Department proposal concentrates exclusively on German war criminals. A question exists, therefore, as to whether any undertaking to deal with war crimes' problems should not also embrace Italian, Japanese and perhaps other war criminals.

I have already indicated that the War Department memorandum is vague as to the contemplated parties to the proposed treaty. There is some indication that all of the members of the United Nations will be invited to adhere. I should think they should be so invited and, indeed, one of the most desirable features of the treaty approach would seem to lie in adherence, not only by all members of the United Nations but also by all the neutral countries. Adherence to the treaty by neutrals would obviously facilitate the effort of the principal powers to prevent criminals from frustrating justice by obtaining asylum in neutral territory.

Respectfully,

Herbert Wechsler
Assistant Attorney General

DOCUMENT 28

OFFICE OF THE ATTORNEY GENERAL
WASHINGTON, D.C.

MEMORANDUM RE PUNISHMENT OF CRIMINALS[1]

January 5, 1945

1. I think we should eliminate, at this point at least, any attempt to punish crimes committed *before the war*. We will have our hands full with crimes after the war.

2. It seems to me that crimes against German Nationals within Germany should be separated.

3. Consideration should be given to punishment of Italians and Japanese. Any treaty should be drawn broad enough to include both.

4. Can the objects of a treaty to set up an international court be attained by an international agreement, possibly between the military, approved by the various governments.

5. I think the argument that a conspiracy to do a lawful thing is illegal if the overt acts are unlawful and that a conspiracy to do unlawful acts is a crime irrespective of the overt act, is not applicable. The theory is that the crime can be fixed to mean a conspiracy to dominate the world. I doubt whether such a conspiracy is criminal under international law. Aside from that the theory would involve that any overt act is criminal—in other words any soldier fighting to carry out the conspiracy becomes a criminal by reason of the conspiracy being made criminal. This would entail hopeless confusion.

6. I cannot see how crimes against nationals committed within Germany could be "pertinent proof" of the conspiracy.

7. I think the court should have no discretion on punishment and consider only cases punishable by death.[2] Where would you find enough jails to imprison?

8. It seems to me that a better approach would be to determine whom you wanted to get at and how many before determining the mechanisms of punishment.

9. In what way are *criminal* prisoners of war protected under the Geneva conference as the memorandum seems to indicate.

10. How many are proposed to be tried under this plan, by classification?

11. What is the advantage of a mixed military tribunal?

12. I should think that an international court or mixed military tribunal should be used for the punishment only of the leaders—few in number. Devices should be worked out for the punishment of other criminals by very many courts. Is there any way of establishing a group of mixed military tribunals to punish the large mass of criminals?

DOCUMENT 29

THE WHITE HOUSE
WASHINGTON

PRESIDENTIAL MEMORANDUM FOR THE SECRETARY OF STATE[1]

January 3, 1945

Please send me a brief report on the status of the proceedings before the War Crimes Commission, and particularly the attitude of the U.S. representative[2] on offenses to be brought against Hitler and the chief Nazi war criminals. The charges should include an indictment for waging aggressive warfare, in violation of the Kellogg Pact. Perhaps these and other charges might be joined in a conspiracy indictment.

F.D.R

DOCUMENT 30

WAR DEPARTMENT
WAR DEPARTMENT GENERAL STAFF
PERSONNEL DIVISION G-1
WASHINGTON

MEMORANDUM (BY MAJOR BROWN AND COLONEL BERNAYS, G-1)[1]

January 4, 1945

I

1. The question is presented whether the launching of the present war by the Axis powers is a crime for which the Axis leaders are liable to trial and punishment.

2. a. It is generally agreed that acts committed before the outbreak of war which commanded, or procured, or reasonably and probably involved the commission of so-called war crimes after the outbreak of war, and which were followed by and did result in war crimes after the outbreak of war, are war crimes.

b. It is further commonly agreed that the launching of the war itself by the Axis leaders does not constitute a "*war*[2] crime" in the strict legal sense in which this phrase is used in the literature on the subject, or in official United States policy.

c. For the purpose of this discussion, it may likewise be considered as agreed that at the time of the Versailles Conference, international law held that the launching of an aggressive war was not a crime.

3. The above leaves open the question, however, whether the conduct under consideration nonetheless constitutes a *crime*, and the problem may therefore be stated as follows:

> Does international law today condemn as a crime the launching of the present war, for which its instigators may be tried and punished by an international tribunal?

II

4. International law is based on customary usage and treaties among the several States. These, however, are not the law but only its expression. Together, they disclose the principles of conduct which are from time to time accepted by the States as controlling their relations with one another, but the ultimate foundation of those principles consists of the public concepts of morality and justice in the States concerned. More than any other law, therefore, international law grows and develops with the growth and development of the public conscience upon which it is founded.[3] Whatever was the public view toward aggressive war at the time of the Versailles Conference, it will not be disputed that the launching of a war of aggression today is condemned by the vast majority of mankind as a crime. A formal declaration in treaty form to this effect by the United Nations today would therefore unquestionably rest on solid grounds, and of itself would constitute valid international law.

5. This would be true, even if such a declaration were made today as a new and original matter. It is not necessary to labor that point, however, for there have been, since the Versailles Conference, four formal Governmental declarations on the broadest international basis condemning aggressive war as a crime. These public acts constitute the clearest sanction for the proposition that in the international law of today aggressive war is a crime. The acts referred to were, in chronological order:

a. *The Geneva Protocol.* At the Fifth Assembly of the League of Nations, on 2 October 1924, the Delegates of 48 Governments unanimously accepted the Protocol for the Pacific Settlement of International Disputes (known as the Geneva Protocol), which declared that "a war of aggression constitutes . . .[4] an international crime." While the technical scope of the agency exercised by the several representatives of the 48 Governments concerned is one which may be debated by the legalistically minded, it must be admitted that the Protocol, in the words of an English authority, "is the creation of the governmental will of the vast majority of the civilized states under whose rule mankind today exists".[5] It may be noted that at this date, Germany was not yet a member of the League of Nations nor, of course, did the United States take any official part in the proceedings.

b. *Resolution by the Eighth Assembly of the League of Nations.* On 24 September 1927, at the 18th plenary session of the Eighth Assembly of the League of Nations, the Delegates of 48 States (including Germany and all the world powers save the United States and the Union of Soviet Socialist Republics) unanimously adopted a Resolution stating that a war of aggression constitutes an international crime.

c. *Resolution of the Sixth Pan American Conference*. In Havana, Cuba, in February 1928, the Delegates at the Sixth Pan American Conference, at which all the 21 American Republics were represented, unanimously adopted a resolution prepared by the Commission on Public International Law, stating that "war of aggression constitutes an international crime against the human species." This resolution was introduced by the Mexican Delegation and was immediately accepted by Mr. Hughes on behalf of the Delegation of the United States.

d. *The Kellogg-Briand Pact*. At Paris in 1928, the representatives of over 60 Nations, including all the great powers, signed a pact under which the contracting parties "solemnly declare in the names of their respective peoples that they condemn recourse to war for the solution of international controversies, and renounce it as an instrument of national policy in their relations with one another."

6. The effect of these formal public acts by the Governments concerned in changing international law as it existed prior to that time is summed up in the words of Professor Lauterpacht, a leading British authority on international law, who refers to "the crime of war, as distinguished from war crimes, for which the German Government made itself responsible by resorting to war in violation of its voluntarily undertaken and repeatedly reaffirmed international obligations." Continuing, Professor Lauterpacht states in part as follows:

"****In this matter the position is different from that which obtained in 1914 and which prompted the Commission on Responsibilities set up in 1919 by the Paris Conference to declare that 'by reason of the purely optional character of the Institutions at The Hague for the maintenance of peace (International Commissions of Enquiry, Mediation and Arbitration) a war of aggression may not be considered as an act directly contrary to positive law'. The law of any international society worthy of that name must reject with reprobation the view that between nations there can be no aggression calling for punishment, and it must consider the responsibility for the premeditated violation of the General Treaty for the Renunciation of War as lying within the sphere of criminal law. That responsibility embraces such clearly warlike acts as that perpetrated in the form of the invasion and proclaimed annexation of Czechosolvakia in March, 1939."[6]

To the same general effect is a statement by the present Secretary of War, when Secretary of State, in 1932, that:

"War between nations was renounced by the signatories of the Briand-Kellogg Treaty. This means that it has become illegal throughout practically the entire world. It is no longer to be the subject and source of rights. It is no longer to be the principle about which the duties, the conduct, and the rights of nations

> revolve. It is an illegal thing. Hereafter when two nations engage in armed conflict either one or both of them must be wrongdoers—violators of this general treaty law. We no longer draw a circle about them and treat them with the punctilios of the duelist's code. Instead we denounce them as lawbreakers. By that very act we have made obsolete many precedents and have given the legal profession the task of reexamining many of its codes and treaties."

7. It may further be pointed out that the Soviet view is likewise to the effect that the launching of an aggressive war is today a crime in international law. This is made clear in a book entitled "The Criminal Responsibility of the Hitlerites" by A. H. Trainin, a Soviet professor of law who is a leading member of the Extraordinary State Commission for the Investigation of German Crimes, and who expresses not only his own opinion but also the official attitude of the Soviet Government. At page 40 of this book appears the following statement:[7]

> "****The following classification of international crimes can be worked out:
>
> "*First group*: Interference with peaceful relations between nations:
>
> "1. acts of aggression,
> "2. propaganda aggression,[8]
> "3. conclusion of agreements with aggressive aims,
> "4. violation of treaties which serve the cause of peace,
> "5. provocation designed to disrupt peaceful relations between countries,
> "6. terrorism,
> "7. support of armed bands ('fifth column').
>
> "*Second group*: Offenses connected with war:
>
> "1. offenses against war prisoners, wounded and sick soldiers,
> "2. offenses against the life, health, honor and property of the civil population,
> "3. destruction and looting of material and cultural values."

III

8. The argument which is generally made in opposition to the view that under present international law aggressive war is a crime, is that the Kellogg-Briand Pact, while condemning recourse to war, does not declare that a violation of the treaty constitutes a crime. This argument, however, obviously does not apply to the League of Nations proceedings and to the action taken at the Sixth Pan American Conference, in all of which aggressive war was precisely denounced as a crime.

9. Furthermore, there are many crimes in international law, recognized and established as such and punishable even by death, which are nowhere in any treaty or statute of international application specifically declared to be crimes, and for which criminal sanctions and punishments are nowhere provided. A notable illustration of this fact is found in the treaties which form the entire foundation for the rules of land warfare. These are the Hague Convention No. IV of 1907 with the Regulations annexed as a part thereof, and the Geneva Prisoners of War Convention of 1929. These two Conventions both lay down rules of conduct to be followed by belligerents in the carrying on of military operations, but in neither Convention is a violation of the rules set forth therein declared to be a crime, nor are criminal sanctions or punishment for individual offenders prescribed. Yet is it universally accepted that violations of these Conventions constitute war crimes and that individual offenders may be punished even by death.[9] This being the case with respect to these two Conventions, no valid reason is seen why it is not equally true of the Kellogg-Briand Pact which, it is generally agreed, rendered recourse to an aggressive war by its signatories an illegal act. Individuals who violate this Pact by launching an aggressive war commit no less a criminal act than do individuals who violate the above Conventions by murdering prisoners of war; they simply do it on a greater and more destructive scale. No logical distinction can be established between these Conventions and the Kellogg-Briand Pact and the same results should therefore flow from all of them.

IV

10. Furthermore, the launching of the present war was criminal by reason of the fact that as against certain of the United Nations, it was launched in violation of treaties of friendship and non-aggression, and without any declaration of hostilities as required by Hague Convention No. III of 1907. This Hague Convention, like the others, contains no language declaring a violation of its terms to be a crime, or providing criminal sanctions for such violation. Nonetheless, for the reasons already stated it is not considered that the absence of such language prevents violations of this Convention from being dealt with as crimes under international law.

V

11. It is therefore concluded:

a. That whatever may have been the law at the time of the Versailles Conference, the law of today condemns aggressive war as an international crime, triable and punishable as such.

b. That as against certain of the United Nations, the launching of the present war was a crime because of the manner and circumstances in which it was done.

M. C. Bernays
Lt.Col., G.S.C.

D. W. Brown,
Maj., G.S.C.

DOCUMENT 31

MEMORANDUM FOR THE PRESIDENT:[1]
SUBJECT: TRIAL AND PUNISHMENT OF WAR CRIMINALS

January 13, 1945

We have been giving consideration to ways and means for carrying out the United States policy regarding the trial and punishment of Nazi criminals, as established in your statement on that subject dated October 7, 1942, the United Nations Declaration on Persecution of Jews of December 17, 1942, the Concurrent Resolution of the Congress of the United States of March 18, 1943 (57 Stat. 721), the Moscow Statement on Atrocities of November 1943, and your statement on the subject of persecutions dated March 24, 1944.

An analysis of the problem and recommendations for handling it are set forth below.

I. CRIMINALITY OF THE ENEMY

The Crimes to Be Punished:[2] The criminality of the German leaders and their associates does not consist of scattered individual outrages such as may occur in any war, but represents the result of a systematic enterprise for achieving domination of other nations and other peoples with ruthless disregard for the law of nations, the rules of war and the accepted moral standards of mankind. This has involved preparation, going back as far as 1933, for waging aggressive war, the launching of the war, the violation of treaties and international conventions and customs, deliberate violations of warfare and the mass extermination of peoples.

From the moment of Hitler's appointment as Chancellor of the Reich, there began the policy of making war against opposition elements internally, as part of the program of ultimate conquest by "total war" externally. Separately considered, the liquidation of racial and dissident minorities inside Germany which began in 1933 was the domestic affair of the Reich. Viewed in the light of the intervening years, it is seen that those minorities were only the first "enemy." The second stage in the execution of the plan was the invasion of Austria, Czechoslovakia,[3] Poland, Norway, Denmark, the Lowlands, Russia and other countries, coupled with the unprecedented extermination of civilian populations in those countries. Nazi policy and the actions of the Reich since 1933 have been "totally" geared to the execution of this enterprise with complete disregard for law and morals. Specific atrocities against belligerents in the course of hostilities are merely one aspect of the larger plan.

This is the scope of the criminality to be dealt with and the dimension of the crimes to be reached.

The Criminals to Be Punished: The outstanding offenders are, of course, those leaders of the Nazi party and German Reich who since January 30, 1933, have been in control of formulating and executing Nazi policies. These offenders specifically contemplated the commission of the crimes under discussion, and the program undertaken by them was calculated to bring them about.

In addition, the Nazi leaders created and utilized in the service of their party and the Reich a numerous organization for carrying out the acts of oppression and terrorism which their program involved. Chief among the instrumentalities used by them are the SS, from the personnel of which the Gestapo is constituted, and the SA. These organizations consist of exactingly screened volunteers, pledged to absolute obedience and having as their mission the carrying out of such acts as the following: liquidating internal dissidents; operating concentration camps; carrying out mass arrests, tortures, and exterminations; and committing mass crimes in the execution of large scale repressive operations against enemy civilian populations in the rear of the battlefield. The members of these organizations are also the personnel primarily relied upon to carry on postwar guerilla and underground operations.[4]

II. DIFFICULTIES OF AN EFFECTIVE WAR CRIMES PROGRAM

Difficulties of Identification and Proof: The number and variety of the offenses, the inordinate number of offenders, and the problem of apprehension, trial, and punishment necessarily resulting therefrom, present a situation which is without precedent in the field of criminal justice.

In thousands of cases, it would be impossible to establish the offender's identity or to connect him with the particular act charged. Witnesses will be dead and scattered. The gathering of proof will be laborious and costly, and the mechanical problem involved in uncovering and preparing proof of particular offenses one of appalling dimensions. To the limited extent that individual offenders could be prosecuted under these difficulties, the paper work would be enormous, and liaison and coordination singularly difficult. It is not unlikely, in fact, that the Nazis have been counting on just such considerations, together with delay and war weariness, to protect them against punishment for their crimes if they lost the war.

The first requirement of any program for prosecuting the Nazi war criminals is accordingly, that it shall overcome the above practical difficulties.

Legal Difficulties: In addition to the foregoing practical difficulties, there are difficulties of a legal character in formulating a statement of the crime which is practically adapted to the scope of the criminality involved and which covers all the various types of atrocities which have been committed.

Some of these acts (e.g., the launching of an aggressive war)[5] are not criminal under the municipal law of any of the victim states, but have, since the Versailles Treaty, been declared to be criminal under international law.

Some of the worst outrages were committed by the Nazis against their own nationals, many of them before the war. These, while plainly violations of the accepted moral standards of mankind as expressed in the legal systems of all civilized states, are not technically offenses against international law, and the extent to which they may have been in violation of the German laws as changed by the Nazis is difficult to determine. Moreover, to prosecute the Nazi leaders for these acts as independent crimes would set the precedent of an international right to interfere in the internal affairs of States by sitting in judgment on their conduct toward their own nationals.[6] This would open the door to incalculable consequences and present grave questions of policy.

It is nevertheless the declared policy of the United Nations to insure that these offenses are punished.

Since "war crimes", defined in the most limited and technical sense, might be said to include only those violations of the rules of warfare which are committed in the course of military operations or occupation, it is plain that many of the worst atrocities to be dealt with cannot be reached under this limited concept, but will have to be punished on some other basis. It is also evident that only a negligible minority of the offenders will be reached by attempting to try them on the basis of separate prosecutions for each of their individual offenses. Other methods of procedure must be found.

Any realistic war crimes program, however well adapted to the problems involved, must necessarily contemplate that a substantial number of the criminals will go unpunished. In the interests of postwar security and the rehabilitation of the German people, as well as for the sake of justice, it is essential that, to the largest possible extent, the criminals should be punished in such measure as their offenses deserve—by death, if the facts justify, or by imprisonment at hard labor in the case of lesser offenders. These latter could be employed, for example, in the restoration of devastated areas.

We have, accordingly, undertaken to formulate a program designed to overcome the practical and legal difficulties to which we have referred.

III. RECOMMENDED PROGRAM

We think that a just and practical solution lies in charging the German leaders and the organizations employed by them, such as those referred to above (S.A., S.S., Gestapo), with joint participation in the formulation and execution of a broad criminal plan of aggressive warfare, the commission pursuant to that plan of a multitude of specific violations of the laws of war, and a conspiracy to achieve domination of other nations and peoples by the foregoing unlawful means.

This charge, couched in various counts, would be broad enough to permit full proof of the entire Nazi plan and its execution, including the steps taken before the outbreak of war.

The trial of this charge and the determination of the guilty parties would be carried out in two stages:

The United Nations would, in the first instance, bring to the bar jointly the highest ranking German leaders to a number fairly representative of the groups and organizations charged with complicity in the basic original plan. Adjudication would be sought not only of the guilt of those individuals physically before the bar but also of the complicity of the groups and organizations included within the charge. The tribunal would make findings adjudicating the facts established, including the nature and purposes of the criminal plan, the identity of the groups and organizations guilty of complicity in it, and the acts committed in its execution. The tribunal would also prescribe the punishment of those individual defendants physically before it who are convicted of the offense.

In view of the numerous membership of the organizations that would be charged with complicity, it clearly would be impossible to repeat the proof of the basic criminal plan in the trial of each individual member of the culpable organizations. Accordingly, some procedural mechanism is indispensible in order to permit the members of these organizations to be tried for their participation in the offense, without repeated proof of the facts already established in the first trial. In view of the nature of the charges and the representative character of the defendants who will be physically before the court in the first trial, we think that the findings of the court in that trial may fairly be taken to constitute an adjudication of the criminal character of the groups and organizations binding upon all the members thereof in their subsequent trials.

In such subsequent proceedings, therefore, the only necessary proof of guilt of any particular defendant would be his membership in one of the organizations whose guilt had been adjudicated in the first trial. Such proof would cast upon the defendant the burden of exculpation, as, for example, by establishing that he joined the organization without knowledge of its criminal purposes. In these trials proof would also be taken of the nature and extent of the defendant's individual participation in the crimes adjudicated in the first trial; and the punishment of each defendant would be fixed in a measure appropriate to the facts in his particular case. When, for example, the proof showed no more than minor personal participation, no capital sentence would be imposed and any other penalty would be so adjusted as to reflect fairly the individual's degree of participation in the total criminal plan.

In thus charging the German leaders and the principal groups and organizations which were the instruments for the execution of their illegal purposes with joint responsibility for the crimes committed by the Nazi regime, no novel principle of law is being invoked. The rule of liability involved is common to all penal systems and is included in the general doctrines of the laws of war, namely, that those who participate in the formulation and execution of a criminal plan involving multiple crimes are jointly liable for each of the offenses committed and jointly responsible for the acts of each other. Under such a charge there are admissible in evidence the acts of any of the conspirators done in furtherance of the conspiracy, whether or not these acts were in themselves criminal and subject to separate prosecution as such.

It is apparent, therefore, that the only novel principle involved in the foregoing plan is the procedural one of utilizing in the subsequent proceedings the findings of the tribunal in the first case to the extent indicated above. As we have already stated, in view of the representative character of the principal trial, this procedural mechanism is under the circumstances entirely just; the opportunity afforded each individual defendant to exculpate himself or to mitigate his offense provides all the individual safeguards that substantial justice requires.

IV. RELATIONSHIP OF THIS PROGRAM TO MOSCOW DECLARATION

The Moscow Declaration provides that those German officers and men and members of the Nazi Party who have been responsible for, or who have taken a consenting part in the commission of atrocities, massacres and executions, will be sent back to the countries in which their abominable deeds were done in order that they may be charged and punished according to the laws of these liberated countries and of the free governments which will be created therein. It further provides that the above is without prejudice to the cases of those Nazi criminals whose offenses have no particular geographical localization, and who will be punished by the joint decision of the Governments of the Allies.

The procedure discussed in this memorandum will further the objectives of the Moscow Declaration by simplifying the problem of proof involved in bringing to justice the criminals with whom the Declaration is concerned. The proposed procedure will not preclude trial of individual members of the groups or organizations involved in the conspiracy for particular war crimes or other offenses committed by them insofar as such specific charges can practically be sustained.

V. DEFINITION OF APPLICABLE LAW AND ESTABLISHMENT OF A COMPETENT COURT

There are two alternative methods for determining the applicable law and establishing a competent tribunal under the procedure heretofore set forth. These alternatives are: (a) international action by treaty or convention defining the offenses, sanctioning the procedure and establishing the tribunal by which the basic findings will be made; or (b) utilizing military courts created either by executive agreement or by military arrangement to apply, so far as possible, the laws of war and those principles of international law that might be involved without benefit of treaty declaration.

In view of the general character of the plan we have proposed we believe that the treaty method is very much to be preferred.

The Treaty Method: Whatever the nature or legal basis of the proceedings instituted, it must be expected that the defendants will raise every possible objection both to the substantive law under which they are charged and to the competence of the tribunal. They will, for example, adduce quotations from text writers questioning whether the heads of state may be punished for war crimes and challenging the view that the launching of aggressive war may be punished as crime. They will invoke orders of superior authority as an alleged defense. In addressing their plea to posterity within and without the Reich it is to be assumed that they will attempt by every possible means to challenge the basis in law and justice of the proceedings instituted against them. For this reason, and also because of the legal considerations involved, it is of the highest importance that the prosecution of these war criminals be based upon the firmest possible basis.

To achieve this end, a treaty or convention of the interested United Nations is evidently the most desirable instrument in which to formulate the applicable substantive law and the procedure to be followed as well as to establish the court.

Such a treaty or convention would affirm the criminality of aggressive war. It would recite the applicable principles of the laws of war, affirm the joint responsibility of co-conspirators for participation in such criminal enterprise and declare the appropriate punishment for offenses thus defined. The treaty would further provide for the procedural mechanism outlined above, including the binding effect of the findings of the court in the principal trial. It would establish an international tribunal to adjudicate the basic charge and affirm the competence of military tribunals and national courts to entertain the subsequent proceedings against individual defendants.

A treaty or convention cast in these terms would not only have international status but would also become the law of the land in each of the signatory states. It would thus establish the legal basis of the proposed proceedings upon the most unimpeachable foundation. The justice of its provisions would not be open to significant challenge. Such a treaty would in the most effective sense marshal the sanction of civilized mankind for the proposed proceedings and assure that they will meet the judgment of history.

Procedure Without Treaty: In the event that a treaty should be practically unattainable it would be necessary to proceed in military courts created by executive agreement or by the action of military commanders.

So far as the offenses to be tried are violations of the laws and customs of war, it is probable that international mixed military tribunals could be created to try them either by executive agreement or by military commanders. If what we have described as the basic charge to be directed against the German leaders and their accomplice groups and organizations were to be presented before a military tribunal thus created, we gravely doubt that it would be legally possible to include as a constituent element of the charge the launching of an aggressive war.[7] The elimination of this offense, lying as it does at the root of the other crimes, would in our view represent a serious weakening of the general plan presented herewith. It should be said, moreover, that it is very doubtful whether the adjudication in the first trial could be made binding in subsequent trials, as proposed in this memorandum, without amendatory legislation in the United States, and possibly in other countries as well.

We are mindful that the treaty method involves disadvantages. Procuring an agreement upon the terms of the treaty would probably involve considerable negotiation. In addition, the project might provide extended parliamentary proceedings, resulting perhaps in undesirable changes and limitations in the terms of the treaty in those countries in which legislative approval is required. It is apparent, however, that substantial difficulties are presented in furthering the program we believe to be desirable unless the treaty method is employed.

Accordingly, we recommend that if it is possible to do so the treaty method be employed.

VI. RECOMMENDATIONS

We recommend:

1. That you approve the program for dealing with the basic war crimes problem as described in this memorandum.
2. That you approve the setting up of an appropriate agency to undertake promptly and carry out thoroughly and expeditiously the research necessary to establish the proof in support of the proposed indictment.
3. That you approve the preparation and negotiation of a treaty to create a court of the type and jurisdiction described above.

DOCUMENT 32

QUESTIONS POSED BY MAJOR GENERAL WEIR FOR PRESENTATION TO EDMUND M. MORGAN, ACTING DEAN, HARVARD LAW SCHOOL, AND FORMER LIEUTENANT COLONEL, JUDGE ADVOCATE GENERAL'S DEPARTMENT, U.S.A.:[1]

January 12, 1945

1. May you rationally use a conspiracy theory of prosecution of the principal leaders of Germany to dominate other peoples by acts violative of the laws and customs of war?
2. If that premise is sound, may you prove as a part of the chain of the conspiracy the persecutions of dissident groups of their own nationals committed prior to the beginning of the war on racial, political, and religious grounds?

Morgan:

The first question posed is in effect whether the principal leaders of Germany may be charged with and convicted of conspiracy to violate the laws and customs of war. It is phrased in terms of conspiracy to dominate other peoples by acts violative of the rules of war. I take it, that this means to acquire and control territory and peoples by conquest and in the process to violate the rules of war.

The question seems to me to be purely academic. Had the German leaders conducted this war according to the rules of civilized warfare, I venture to say that there would have been no thought of charging them with conspiracy to violate the rules of war. To test the case, let us suppose (1) that these leaders planned (a) to assert a wholly fictitious act of war by Belgium, (b) to wage war against Belgium, and (c) to put to death all prisoners of war and all Belgian civilians who did not promptly swear allegiance to Germany; (2) that they (a) widely advertised their assertion that Belgium had committed the act of war, (b) mobilized their armed forces, and (c) prepared lethal chambers for the execution of prisoners of war and non-complying civilians; but (3) that they went no further, and after an interval withdrew the assertion and demobilized their forces. There would not be the slightest doubt that they would have conspired to dominate Belgium by acts violative of the laws and customs of war; but would anyone seriously contend that they would be personally guilty of, and punishable for, an offense against the law of nations, against international law, or against the laws and customs of war? If no such offense was recognized prior to the commission of these acts, would it be rational, to say nothing of consonant with Anglo-American legal thought, to create the offense *ex post facto*? In my opinion, to ask these questions is to answer them in the negative.

But these German leaders, whether or not they originally planned the execution of their designs by acts violative of the laws and customs of civilized warfare, certainly committed such acts. For these, whether planned in advance, ordered or ratified, I think they can rationally be held responsible by properly constituted military tribunals or by a tribunal erected pursuant to international agreement. They are as guilty as principals as are the subordinates who carried into effect their obviously illegal plans or orders.

Consequently I can see no occasion and no justification for a charge of conspiracy to commit these acts violative of the laws and customs of war as distinguished from the commission of the acts. I might be willing to concede that on common law analogies a conspiracy to commit these outrages might rationally be made an international crime; but the proposition is so highly questionable and so novel to international law that it should be entertained only in the most necessitous circumstances.

The second question discloses the reasons for desiring a charge of conspiracy. It contemplates punishment not for acts violative of the rules of war, but for acts committed before the war, acts which had to do solely with German nationals on German territory. No one would dream of calling this conduct a violation of the rules and customs of war. At most, it was conduct in preparation of the nation for prosecution of a future war. There is, I venture to assert, no recognized tenet of international law which gives to one nation the right to prevent or punish what it considers barbarous and criminal persecution by another nation of citizens of that other nation. The question contemplates that this is now to be made *ex post facto* an international offense for which officials are to be held personally responsible criminally. Certainly no military tribunal set up by other nations could have jurisdiction to try such an offense under any existing system of military law. Such jurisdiction would have to be conferred by international agreement, or arbitrarily assumed.

If the international crime of conspiracy to dominate by acts violative of the rules of war is created, could these acts by Germany against her own nationals be rationally considered as themselves punishable? A negative answer seems imperative. The conspiracy theory is too thin a veneer to hide the real purpose, namely, the creation of a hereto unknown international offense by individuals, *ex post facto*.

If the question relates merely to evidence of the conspiracy, that is, if a charge of conspiracy is made and proof of it is necessary, then evidence of all relevant conduct of the alleged conspirators is admissible. Where enough evidence is received to make a finding of conspiracy justifiable, evidence of the conduct of one conspirator is admissible against all the others. On this theory evidence of such conduct against dissident German nationals would be receivable; but it would, in my opinion, be highly inadvisable to receive it in detail, for its probative value would be slight because (a) there is so much more direct evidence available and (b) the direct evidence of commission of acts violative of the rules of war will be so much more persuasive. This evidence of slight probative value will consume an enormous amount of time. Evidence of refutation will be offered by way of denial and explanation. The offenders could drag out this inquiry almost indefinitely.

In short, the whole theory of prosecuting for conspiracy seems to me not only unwise but unjustifiable. Of course, the victors have power to work their will, but if they violate basic principles of Anglo-American law, they cannot expect the reasoned approval of civilized communities.

/s/ E. M. MORGAN

DOCUMENT 33

MEMORANDUM FOR THE PRESIDENT
SUBJECT: TRIAL AND PUNISHMENT OF EUROPEAN WAR CRIMINALS[1]

January 18, 1945

I

FUNDAMENTAL POLICY

We have been giving consideration to the problem of carrying into effect the policy of the United States regarding the trial and punishment of European war criminals as established in your statement dated 7 October 1942, the Concurrent Resolution of the Congress of the United States of 18 March 1943 (57 Stat. 721), the Moscow Statement on Atrocities of November 1943, and your statement on the subject of persecutions dated 24 March 1944. Our analysis of the problem and our recommendations are set forth below.

II

CRIMINALITY OF THE ENEMY

The Crimes to Be Punished. The criminality of the enemy consists not only of scattered individual outrages and the barbarous treatment and murder of prisoners of war[2] such as may occur in any war, but also of a systematic and planned reign of terror in the occupied countries of Europe characterized by imprisonments, mass expulsion, execution of hostages, mass murders, starvation of civilians, the wholesale looting of public and private property unparalleled in history, in the utter and ruthless disregard of the laws and customs of warfare and the accepted moral standards of mankind. The enemy's criminality extends not only to these acts of barbarism but also to the treacherous launching of war against Belgium, Holland, Norway and other countries of Europe without ultimatum or declaration of war, in violation of the Third Hague Convention of 18 October 1907. Their premeditated design to conduct military operation by methods which outrage the principles of international law and the moral and civilized standards of humanity are manifested not only by their acts of barbarism but by their flagrant disregard of solemnly entered obligations under the Locarno Treaty, the Kellogg-Briand Pact, and nonaggression pacts concluded with various countries in Europe.

The Criminals to Be Punished. The outstanding offenders are, of course, the prime leaders of Germany and Italy[3] who are responsible for the commission of the crimes under discussion and for the program by which they were undertaken. In a lesser degree of responsibility are the subordinate leaders and officers who counseled, aided, and abetted the program and the execution of specific offenses and finally, the soldiers and civilians who have personally committed specific atrocities: murder, rape and other war crimes.

III

DIFFICULTIES OF AN EFFECTIVE WAR CRIMES PROGRAM

Difficulties of Identification and of Proof. The names of the prime leaders of Germany and Italy are well known and the proof of their guilt will not offer great difficulties.[4] The principal problem will be that of apprehension. However, these crimes have been committed upon such a large scale that the problem of identification, apprehension, trial and punishment of the actual perpetrators of the crimes present [*sic*] a situation without parallel in the administration of criminal justice. In many cases it will be impossible to establish the offender's identity or connection with a particular crime. In many instances the witnesses will be dead, otherwise incapacitated, and scattered. Each of the United Nations, however, are presently engaged in investigating the crimes committed against their nationals and in perpetuating the evidence against the day when the offenders will be brought to the bar of justice to answer for their acts.

IV

RECOMMENDED PROGRAM

Political vs. Judicial Disposition. There are two methods which may be used in the disposition of the enemy war criminals. One is a political disposition without any trial or hearing. Punishment could be death, imprisonment at hard labor, or banishment as was done in the case of Napoleon. This action could be taken by agreement between the heads of states. We do not favor this method. While the advantages of this method are that a sure and swift disposition would be made of the criminals, it is an arbitrary action violative of Anglo-American systems of justice. The other method is the judicial method. By this method each accused would be called before a tribunal where a record of the trial of the offenses would be made; the accused could be represented by counsel and would have an opportunity to be heard in his own behalf. We favor this method, and we believe that history will approve of this disposition of the war criminals. Under this method there will be made a record of the evidence, and this record will be available for all mankind to study in future years.

The Tribunals Which May Be Used. For the trial of the prime leaders whose offenses have no geographical limits, there are two methods available. One would be by an International Court established under the authority of a treaty between the United Nations. The other method would be by an International Military Commission or Court to be appointed by the Supreme Military Authority in the field. By a treaty the jurisdiction, competence, and procedure of the court would be established. The disadvantages of a treaty court are numerous and we think outweigh the advantages.[5] The difficulties in the negotiation of such a treaty are patent. The reservations which may be attached to the treaty upon ratification might seriously challenge the competence of any court established thereunder. A treaty court is unnecessary. We favor the trial of the prime leaders by international military commission or court. Such a system will not require enabling legislation in the form of a treaty or otherwise to establish it. For the trial of other than the prime leaders and in furtherance of the Moscow Declaration, those lesser offenders whose offenses have geographical limits would be tried either by the national courts of the country concerned or by their own military courts or, if desired by that country, by international military courts.

V

THEORY OF PROCEDURE

Prime Leaders. Our theory for the prosecution of the prime leaders is that they should be charged as principals for violations of the laws of war:

1. For the mass murder and extermination of civilians in occupied countries;
2. For the mass deportation of individuals from occupied countries and their use as slave labor within Germany, and their use in the building of German fortifications behind the front lines;
3. For the unlawful and willful destruction of towns and villages such as Lidice;[6]
4. For the unlawful and willful destruction and looting of public and private property;
5. For the denationalization of illegally annexed territories and the impressment of the nationals thereof into the German military service;
6. For the treacherous waging of war without ultimatum or declaration of war against Holland, Belgium, Norway, and other countries in violation of the Third Hague Convention of 1907;[7]
7. For the uncontrolled rapes committed against women of occupied

countries and the impressment of women of occupied territories into brothels for German soldiers.[8]

8. For the wholesale removal of materials and resources of the occupied countries with a view to destroying the political economy of those countries;

9. For the murders and other mass atrocities committed against prisoners of war within Germany and within occupied countries;

10. For the deliberate starvation, torture, and inhuman treatment of civilians in occupied countries, especially Poland, Bulgaria, and Greece;

11. For the deliberate planning and systematic operation of a reign of terror in the occupied countries;

12. For the violation of the fundamental rights of inhabitants of the occupied territories in disregard of the Fourth Hague Convention of 1907[9] and of general international law;

13. For the unlawful and deliberate execution of civilian hostages;

14. For conspiracy to commit the crimes mentioned;

15. For failure to take measures both for the punishment of the offenders and for the prevention of other cases after having had knowledge of the commission of specific atrocities and other offenses.

Subordinate Leaders and Officers. Those subordinate leaders and officers who counseled, aided, and abetted in the program or who are guilty of the execution of specific offenses would be tried for their participation in both the planning and the execution of the offenses.

Soldiers and Civilians. Soldiers and civilians who have personally committed specific atrocities such as murder, rape and other war crimes will be tried for their crimes.

In the trial of the prime leaders and other war criminals evidence of acts committed prior to the beginning of the war will be admissible for the purpose of proving plan, motive and intent to commit specific war crimes. The admissibility of evidence of acts prior to the war will depend upon the relevency of the particular act as tending to show plan, scheme, and design systematically to commit war crimes. Research into the Nazi and Fascist ideology is being conducted with a view to determine at what point prior to the war their plans began to be developed.

VI

RUSSIAN ATTITUDE

The Russian attitude, so far as is presently known, on the prosecution of the war criminals is contained in the statement of M. Molotov under date of 14 October 1942[10] to the effect that the Soviet Union is ready to support all practical measures on the part of the Allied and friendly governments in seeking out, handing over, bringing to court and passing sentence on the Hitlerites and their accomplices guilty of the organization, promotion, and perpetuation of crimes in occupied territory. It is further stated that the Soviet Government considers it essential to deliver without delay to a *special international tribunal*, and to punish according to all the severity of the criminal code, any of the leaders of Fascist Germany who in the course of the war have fallen into the hands of states fighting against Hitlerite Germany.

VII

BRITISH ATTITUDE

The British attitude in regard to dealing with war crimes is indicated in the Aide Mémoire of the British Embassy to the Secretary of State dated 30 October 1944. The British in effect endorsed[11] the recommendation of the United Nations War Crimes Commission that military tribunals be employed for the trial of specific defendants on the grounds that such tribunals (1) could be established promptly from qualified available personnel; (2) would be a cooperative activity between the Supreme Commanders of the United States, the United Kingdom, and the Soviet Union, and other commanders who may participate; (3) and would be useful for the trial of war crime offenders against the nationals of two or more of the United Nations. The British Government inquired whether the United States Government would be willing to take parallel action in indorsing this recommendation of the War Crimes Commission. The British Government, however, disapproved the recommendation of the United Nations War Crimes Commission that there be established by treaty a United Nations War Crimes Court. The reasons given for this disapproval were as follows:

1. The long period of time required to negotiate the proposed treaty,—estimated to be at least one year;
2. Russia is not a participant in the United Nations Commission which proposes to have charge of the treaty negotiations and of the operation of the court;
3. Some of the smaller civil law countries among the United Nations would introduce difficulties and complexities into the operation of the plan;
4. A treaty court appears to be unnecessary;
5. A treaty court would raise great difficulties in finding suitable personnel and in agreeing upon procedure.

RECOMMENDATIONS

1. We recommend that the disposition of Axis war criminals be made by judicial rather than political procedures; that trials be held by the established types of national or military courts but that the trial of the prime leaders be held by international military court to be appointed by heads of state or by the supreme military authority in the field.

3.[12] We recommend that war criminals be charged with war crimes, including conspiracies to commit war crimes,[13] as defined and established by international law.

DOCUMENT 34

IMMEDIATE RECOMMENDATION TO THE PRESIDENT FOR HIS COMING CONFERENCE (YALTA)

DICTATED BY JOSEPH E. DAVIES[1]

January 18, 1945

The idea of this proposal is that it measurably complies with the points of view of both the British and Soviet Government [*sic*], and, while setting the matter in principles, leaves time to work out details for further procedures by the Foreign Offices of the conferees and with the representatives of the other United Nations, if necessary to take any action.

Propose:

1. That the "War Criminals" of Germany, both great and small, have been guilty of the most heinous and horrible "Crimes", which have violated the conscience of humanity, and have also violated the customs and laws of War.

2. That all of these "Criminals," whether immediate perpetrators or responsible therefore as accessories, must be visited with suitable punishment by established judicial Tribunals; that this must be speedy and through organized channels of justice.

3. That typical such Crimes are Mass Executions, Mass Atrocities, Extermination Camps, Murdering of Hostages, Reprisal Destruction of Villages, and others too numerous to mention.

4. That the Chiefs of States now in Conference have already given directives to their Military Commanders and their Foreign Offices and other officials, to prepare a list of such "War Criminals," and recommenda-

tions as to the manner in which Hitler and his associates in crime may be most speedily brought before a Tribunal wherein suitable Justice may be administered, not as legalized vengeance, but as an act of suitable retribution, and as a deterrent to future similar crime. That this is in process.[2]

The foregoing could be made as a formal Declaration. That would settle the matter that arch-political and all of them "War Criminals" [*sic*] are going to be tried and shot, and put an end to this clamor which is not justified, that any of the Governments advocate that Hitler and his leaders be not punished. It would then leave the opportunity still open for the procedure to be worked out, and a list compiled and preparation made for the best means of bringing about this and other objectives. After the next Conference we will all be in a better position to know exactly what is possible to accomplish.

It will be of far greater value to posterity and to the future rule of Law in the creation of a Peace Structure, if there be unity as between the Big Three in this matter. It would also be far preferable for the sake of the judgment of posterity, if it is at all possible, to secure the punishments of "War Criminals" on specific crimes now, and leave for the Peace Treaties and the subsequent development of the Peace Structure, to declare by specific Convention that waging Total War, Launching Aggression, and Crimes Against Humanity,[3] are specific International Crimes, and provide punishment therefore. If such a course is developed and followed, there can be no possible criticism now or a hundred years from now. On the contrary, the verdict of history will acclaim the adherence to formalized Justice, which characterized the leaders of this War.

The procedure would permit of discussion and negotiation of ways and means for bringing about a common purpose through the negotiations and discussions upon the lower levels. A plan could be worked out conjunctively through negotiations after the general idea is agreed upon.

Because of the existence of Courts, already existing, and machinery now being employed, I feel confident that a detailed plan can be worked out satisfactorily to the Soviets and to the British Foreign Offices, if we can have time to work out details which will effect that their objectives in the main,[4] and will also command the approval of the present and the future historian.

. . . .[5]

V. COMMON OBJECTIVES

There can, however, be no disagreement upon the following:

1. All agree that all who committed crimes under the customs, usages and laws of war, whether as principal or as accessory before or after the fact, should be speedily and surely punished, and without delay.

2. That the arch-criminals—Hitler and his policy-making associates, the high-ranking members of the Army, the Gestapo and the Nazi Party, under the law of all civilized countries, including Germany, are guilty of violations of "War Crimes" which are clearly identified as such in International Law. They are guilty as accessories. They can be punished by proceedings of Military Tribunals under existing law.
3. Existing agencies are sufficient to punish practically all offenders, great and small, without resort to the enactment of retroactive Criminal Legislation defining Crimes and proscribing Punishment.
4. All of those heinous "War Crimes", clearly recognized as such in International Law, to wit: Mass Executions, Mass Atrocities, Extermination Camps, Murdering of Hostages, Reprisal Destruction of Villages, and the innumerable forms of horror employed by the German Army, are subject in the first instance, under the Moscow Agreement, to punishment when the offenders are brought back to the place where they have been committed. This also applies to any and all chiefs of State or Political Administrators, who were responsible for the orders and the policy which was adopted, resulting in these "Crimes", whether the orders were signed prior to the War or after hostilities.
5. All of these offences were also "Crimes" defined by the Domestic Laws of the States in which they were perpetrated and can be tried by the Domestic Courts. They can even be tried in Germany under Domestic Law, enforced by Military Tribunals during the period of Occupancy, where the Local Tribunals cannot be trusted to so do.
6. All of these "Crimes" can also be tried speedily and expeditiously by the High Military Courts either jointly or severally, in the areas in which they function.
7. The leaders of the victor nations and Chief Executives of the victor States can now direct the Military Commanders to punish speedily, through proper Military Tribunal, all such Criminals.
8. The Chiefs of State of the United Nations can make a list of such Political Criminals, heads of the vanquished States, and set forth the "War Crimes" of which they have been guilty, and require the Military Tribunals to proceed effectively and speedily to their punishment.
9. Under such a proceeding there can be no possible criticism that the principles of organized justice have been violated. International Law clearly gives that right to the victors.
10. If, at the next Conference to be held, this procedure were to be agreed upon, there could be no possible criticism from either posterity or from the present that the punishment of War Criminals was "legalized vengeance" or any violation of those principles of Law which the centuries have developed for the protection of any man, from being tried for a crime where neither the crime or its punishment had been

previously defined. The ancient Roman maxim, "nulla crimen et nulla poena sine lege" (Neither crime nor punishment without law), has been the basic protection for the oppressed for 2000 years and more.

11. If a United Nations Crimes Court were to be established at all, its jurisdiction and power should be exercised upon what is clearly an existing Crime in International Law. It should not be employed to enforce a law or punish a Crime which had to be created, and punishment defined after the criminal act had been perpetrated. This is particularly so because there is no need for it. Sixty thousand and more Criminals of high and low degree could be conclusively proven to be guilty of indisputable Crimes against the Laws of War, which are punishable by death.

VI. CONSPIRACY NOT TECHNICALLY A "WAR CRIME"

There is great diversity of opinion as to whether launching this War or so-called "Crimes against Humanity" can be considered to be International "War Crimes." The only "War Crimes" known and accepted as such are "Piracy" and the "Unlawful Use of Submarines", proscribed by Convention. "Conspiracy" is not "malum in se."[6] It is specifically "malum prohibitum". Personally, I think that it would require a considerably [*sic*] torturing of the Law to hold that "Conspiracy" could be created into a "War Crime" by an "ex post facto" Treaty definition.

VII. CONCLUSIONS

If the impending Conference finds that it is advisable in the building up of the precedent, and to establish rules for the future through such an International Tribunal, my suggestion would be that it be done by a directive from the three Chiefs of State to their Military Commanders, to organize such a Joint Tribunal, to bring to trial a list of Political Offenders, who are to be tried upon a series of indictments for clearly defined, explicit "Crimes," which are indisputably not only "Crimes against Humanity" but "Crimes against Specific Law." If such a Court, consisting largely of civilians, were to hold a drum-head Court Martial, receive and consider the indictment, supported by documentary proof of incontrovertible character, and would then give an opportunity for the collective accused to be heard, and the hearing not to exceed two days, why judgment should not be rendered and sentence imposed; and if then, that Court would render its judgments only upon

"Crimes" specifically defined and recognized to be "Crimes" as of this date, and by "obiter dicta"[7] recommend and declare that other "Crimes against Humanity" not yet legally defined, such as Total War, Aggression, Conspiracy, and the like, should be defined[8] proscribed as "International Crimes", with suitable punishment attached for the future, there could never arise, either now or for posterity, any criticism that the spirit of Justice, Law, and Order, which we proclaim this War is being fought to establish, were [*sic*] violated by a disregard of one of the fundamental civil liberties that should apply to all Criminals, whether common or political.

DOCUMENT 35

MEMORANDUM FOR THE PRESIDENT[1]

SUBJECT: TRIAL AND PUNISHMENT OF NAZI WAR CRIMINALS

January 22, 1945

This memorandum deals with ways and means for carrying out the policy regarding the trial and punishment of Nazi criminals, as established in the statements on that subject which are annexed.[2]

I. THE MOSCOW DECLARATION

In the Moscow Declaration[3] the United Kingdom, the United States, and the Soviet Union took note of the atrocities perpetrated by the Germans and laid down the policy: (1) that those German officers and men who have been responsible for or have taken a consenting part in these atrocities "will be sent back to the countries in which their abominable deeds were done in order that they may be judged and punished according to the laws of these liberated countries and of the free governments which will be created therein": and (2) that the above decision "is without prejudice to the case of the major criminals, whose offenses have no particular geographical localization and who will be punished by the joint decision of the Governments of the Allies."

II. THE UNITED NATIONS WAR CRIMES COMMISSION

The United Nations War Crimes Commission is located in London, and consists of representatives of some fifteen of the United Nations. The Soviet Union is not a member.[4]

This Commission has been charged with the collection of lists of the criminals referred to, the recording of the available supporting proof, and the making of recommendations as to the tribunals to try and the procedure for trying such criminals. The Commission has no investigative or prosecuting authority to try offenders of any kind.

The War Crimes Commission receives its lists of war criminals from the investigating authorities, if any, set up by the respective United Nations. The first unofficial meeting of the Commission was held in London on October 26, 1943, and the first official meeting was held there on January 18, 1944. Up to this time, the cases of approximately 1,000 offenders have been docketed with the Commission. The labors of the Commission have not resulted in any governmental agreement as to the tribunals to try or the procedures for trying war criminals.

The Commission has been widely and publicly criticized for the paucity of the results of its work. In recent months its activities have been marked by dissensions. The British representative, who was also Chairman of the Commission, and the Norwegian member, have resigned.[5]

III. SCOPE AND DIMENSIONS OF THE WAR CRIMES PROBLEM

The Crimes to Be Punished.[6] The criminality of the German leaders and their associates does not consist solely of individual outrages, but represents the result of a systematic and planned reign of terror within Germany, in the satellite Axis countries, and in the occupied countries of Europe. This conduct goes back at least as far as 1933, when Hitler was first appointed Chancellor of the Reich. It has been marked by mass murders, imprisonments, expulsions and deportations of populations; the starvation, torture and inhuman treatment of civilians; the wholesale looting of public and private property on a scale unparalleled in history; and, after initiation of "total" war, its prosecution with utter ruthless disregard for the laws and customs of war.

We are satisfied that these atrocities were perpetrated in pursuance of a premeditated criminal plan or enterprise which either contemplated or necessarily involved their commission.

The Criminals to Be Punished. The outstanding offenders are, of course, those leaders of the Nazi Party and German Reich who since January 30, 1933, have been in control of formulating and executing Nazi policies.

In addition, the Nazi leaders created and utilized a numerous organization for carrying out the acts of oppression and terrorism which their program involved. Chief among the instrumentalities used by them are the SS, from the personnel of which the Gestapo is constituted, and the SA. These organizations consist of exactingly screened volunteers who are pledged to absolute obedience. The members of these organizations are also the personnel primarily relied upon to carry on postwar guerilla [*sic*] and underground operations.

IV. DIFFICULTIES OF AN EFFECTIVE WAR CRIMES PROGRAM

Difficulties of Identification and Proof. The names of the chief German leaders are well known, and the proof of their guilt will not offer great difficulties. However, the crimes to be punished have been committed upon such a large scale that the problem of identification, trial and punishment of their perpetrators presents a situation without parallel in the administration of criminal justice. In thousands of cases, it will be impossible to establish the offender's identity or to connect him with the particular act charged. Witnesses will be dead, otherwise incapacitated and scattered. The gathering of proof will be laborious and costly, and the mechanical problems involved in uncovering and preparing proof of particular offenses one of appalling dimensions. It is evident that only a negligible minority of the offenders will be reached by attempting to try them on the basis of separate prosecutions for their individual offenses. It is not unlikely, in fact, that the Nazis have been counting on just such considerations, together with delay and war weariness, to protect them against punishment for their crimes if they lost the war.

Legal Difficulties. The attempt to punish the Nazi leaders and their associates for all of the atrocities committed by them also involves serious legal difficulties. Many of these atrocities, as noted in your statement on the subject of persecution dated 24 March 1944,[7] were "*begun by the Nazis in the days of peace*[8] and multiplied by them a hundred times in time of war." These prewar atrocities are neither "war crimes" in the technical sense, nor offenses against international law; and the extent to which they may have been in violation of German law, as changed by the Nazis, is doubtful. Nevertheless, the declared policy of the United Nations is that these crimes, too, shall be punished; and the interests of postwar security and a necessary rehabilitation of German peoples, as well as the demands of justice, require that this be done.

V. RECOMMENDED PROGRAM

After Germany's unconditional surrender the United Nations could, if they elected, put to death the most notorious Nazi criminals, such as Hitler or Himmler, without trial or hearing. We do not favor this method. While it has the advantages of a sure and swift disposition, it would be violative of the most fundamental principles of justice, common to all the United Nations. This would encourage the Germans to turn these criminals into martyrs, and, in any event, only a few individuals could be reached in this way.

We think that the just and effective solution lies in the use of the judicial method. Condemnation of these criminals after a trial, moreover, would command maximum public support in our own times and receive the respect of history. The use of the judicial method will, in addition, make available for all mankind to study in future years an authentic record of Nazi crimes and criminality.

We recommend the following:

The German leaders and the organizations employed by them, such as those referred to above (SA, SS, Gestapo), should be charged both with the commission of their atrocious crimes, and also with joint participation in a broad criminal enterprise which included and intended these crimes, or was reasonably calculated to bring them about. The allegation of the criminal enterprise would be so couched as to permit full proof of the entire Nazi plan from its inception and the means used in its furtherance and execution, including the prewar atrocities and those committed against their own nationals, neutrals, and stateless persons, as well as the waging of an illegal war of aggression with ruthless disregard for international law and the rules of war. Such a charge would be firmly founded upon the rule of liability, common to all penal systems and included in the general doctrines of the laws of war, that those who participate in the formulation and execution of a criminal plan involving multiple crimes are jointly liable for each of the offenses committed and jointly responsible for the acts of each other. Under such a charge there are admissible in evidence the acts of any of the conspirators done in furtherance of the conspiracy, whether or not these acts were in themselves criminal and subject to separate prosecution as such.

The trial of this charge and the determination of the guilty parties would be carried out in two stages:

The United Nations would, in the first instance, bring before an international tribunal created by Executive Agreement, the highest ranking German leaders to a number fairly representative of the groups and organizations charged with complicity in the basic criminal plan. Adjudication would be sought not only of the guilt of those individuals physically before the court, but also of the complicity of the members of the organizations included within the charge. The court would make findings adjudicating the facts established, including the nature and purposes of the criminal plan, the identity of the groups and organizations guilty of complicity in it, and the acts committed in its execution. The court would also sentence those individual defendants physically before it who are convicted.

The above would complete the mission of this international tribunal.

Thereafter, there would be brought before occupation courts individuals [not sent back for trial under the provisions of the Moscow Declaration, and][9] members of the organizations who are charged [~~only~~][10] with complicity through such membership, [but] [~~and~~] against whom there is [~~no proof~~] [not sufficient proof] of specific atrocities. In view of the nature of the charges and the representative character of the defendants who were before the court in the first trial, the findings of that court [should] [~~may~~] justly be taken to constitute a general adjudication of the criminal character of the groups and organizations referred to, binding upon all the members thereof in their subsequent trials in occupation courts. In these subsequent trials, therefore, the only necessary proof of guilt of any particular defendant would be his membership in one of these organizations. Proof would also be taken of the nature and extent of the individual's participation. The punishment of each defendant would be made appropriate to the facts of his particular case. In appropriate cases, the penalty might be imprisonment at hard labor [instead of the death penalty] and the offenders could be worked in restoring devastated areas.

Individual defendants who can be connected with specific atrocities will be tried and punished in the national courts of the countries concerned, as contemplated in the Moscow Declaration.

VI. NATURE AND COMPOSITION OF TRIBUNALS

We favor the trial of the prime leaders by an international military commission or [military] court, established by Executive Agreement of the heads of State of the interested United Nations. This would require no enabling legislation [or treaty]. If deemed preferable the tribunal could be established by action of the Supreme Authority [(Control Council for Germany)].[11]

The court might consist of seven members, one each to be appointed by the British Commonwealth, the United States, the Soviet Union and France, and three to be appointed by agreement among the other United Nations who become parties to the proposed procedure.

The court may consist of civilian or military personnel, or both. We would prefer a court of military personnel, as being less likely to give undue weight to techical contentions and legalistic arguments.

The subsequent trials would be had [*sic*], as noted, in occupation courts; or in the national courts of the country concerned or in their own military courts; or, if desired, by international military courts.

VII. PREPARATION OF CASE

A successful prosecution [of the basic charge] will manifestly depend upon early, careful, and thorough compilation of the necessary evidence. This is particularly important with regard to so much of the case as involves the basic criminal plan. Success will depend, further, upon cooperative action in this regard among the interested United Nations, and the early establishment of a competent executive and technical staff to carry out the project.

In our opinion, the United Nations War Crimes Commission cannot be satisfactorily employed for this purpose, and having performed its mission, may now be dissolved.

We recommend that there be set up [a full time] [~~an~~][12] executive group consisting of one [military] representative each of the British Commonwealth, the United States, the Soviet Union, and France. This group should have under it an adequate staff of attorneys and research personnel to search out the available data, analyze them, prepare the charges to conform to the proof, and arrange the evidence for presentation to the international military tribunal.

VIII. SOVIET ATTITUDE

The Soviet attitude, we believe, is indicated in the Note of M. Molotov attached hereto.[13] The position taken therein is that the Soviet Union is ready to support all practical measures on the part of the Allied and friendly governments in bringing the Hitlerites and their accomplices to justice, and favors their trial before "the courts of the special international tribunal" and their punishment in accordance with applicable criminal law.

IX. BRITISH ATTITUDE

In an *Aide-Mémoire* from the British Embassy to the Department of State dated October 30, 1944, the British Foreign Office indicates that it is prepared to agree and to cooperate in establishing Mixed Military Tribunals to deal with cases which for one reason or another could not be tried in national courts. This would appear, according to the *Aide-Mémoire*, to include those cases where a person is accused of having committed war crimes against the nationals of several of the United Nations.

DOCUMENT 36

PUNISHMENT OF WAR CRIMINALS[1] IMPLEMENTING INSTRUMENT

January 20, 1945

The United Nations have on various occasions expressed their abhorrence for the unspeakable crimes and atrocities of which the German leaders and their associates are guilty, and have pledged themselves that those responsible for such crimes and atrocities shall not escape retribution.

The United Kingdom, the United States, and the Soviet Union in the Declaration issued at Moscow November 1, 1943 stated:

(1) That those German officers and men who have been responsible for or have taken a consenting part in these atrocities "will be sent back to the countries in which their abominable deeds were done in order that they may be judged and punished according to the laws of these liberated countries and of the free governments which will be created therein"; and

(2) that the above declaration was "without prejudice to the case of the major criminals, whose offenses have no particular geographical localization and who will be punished by the joint declaration of the Governments of the Allies."

The criminality of the German leaders and their associates does not consist solely of individual outrages, but represents the result of a systematic and planned reign of terror within Germany and within the area occupied by German military forces, in connection with which the crimes and atrocities referred to were committed. We are satisfied that these crimes and atrocities were perpetrated pursuant to a premeditated criminal plan.

For the carrying out of the acts of oppression and terrorism which their program involved, the Nazi leaders and their associates created and utilized a numerous organization, chief among which are the SS, the Gestapo, and the SA.

Having in view the foregoing, and in order to press on with the necessary practical measures to bring to justice the criminals referred to, the President of the United States of America, the Prime Minister of Great Britain, and the Premier of the Soviet Union have agreed upon the following:

I

The German leaders and their associates, and the organizations employed by them, such as those referred to above, will be charged with both the commission of their atrocious crimes, and also with joint participation in a broad criminal enterprise which included and intended these crimes, or was reasonably calculated to bring them about. The allegation of the criminal enterprise will be so couched as to permit full proof of the entire Nazi plan from its inception and the means used in its furtherance and execution, including the pre-war atrocities and those committed against their own nationals, neutrals, and stateless persons, as well as the waging of an illegal war of aggression with ruthless disregard for international law and the rules of war. There will be invoked the rule of liability, common to all penal systems and included in the general doctrines of the laws of war, that those who participate in the formulation and execution of a criminal plan involving multiple crimes are jointly liable for each of the offenses committed and jointly responsible for the acts of each other. In support of this charge there will be admitted in evidence the acts of any of the conspirators done in furtherance of the conspiracy, whether or not these acts were in themselves criminal and subject to separate prosecution as such.

II

The trial of the charge described in Article I and the determination of the guilty parties will be carried out in two stages:

(a) There will be brought before an international tribunal to be created the highest ranking German leaders to a number fairly representative of the groups and organizations charged with complicity in the basic criminal plan. Adjudication will be sought not only of the guilt of those individuals physically before the tribunal, but also of the complicity of the members of the organizations included within the charge. The tribunal will make findings adjudicating the facts established, including the nature and purposes of the criminal plan, the identity of the groups and organizations guilty of complicity in it, and the acts committed in its execution. The tribunal will sentence those individual defendants physically before it who are convicted.

The above will complete the mission of this international tribunal.

(b) Thereafter, other individuals charged with specific atrocities and members of the organizations who are charged with complicity through such membership in the basic criminal plan but against whom there is not sufficient proof of specific atrocities shall, unless held for trial by one of the United Nations or sent back for trial under the provisions of the Moscow Declaration, be brought before occupation or other appropriate tribunals. The findings of the tribunal in the trial provided for in paragraph (a) of this Article will be taken to constitute a general adjudication of the criminal character of the groups and organizations referred to, binding upon all the members thereof in their subsequent trials in occupation tribunals or in other tribunals established under this instrument. In these subsequent trials the only necessary proof of guilt of any particular defendant, as regards the charge of complicity, will be his membership in one of those organizations. Proof will also be taken of the nature and extent of the individual's participation.

(c) The defendant in each case shall, upon conviction, suffer death or such other punishment as the tribunal may direct, depending upon the gravity of the offense and the degree of culpability of the defendant.

III

The tribunal for the trial of the basic crime referred to in Article II (a) shall consist of seven members, to be appointed as follows: one each by the British Commonwealth, the United States, the Soviet Union, and France, and three by agreement among the other United Nations who become parties to this instrument.

The members of the tribunal may be civilian or military as the appointing authority in each case may prefer.

IV

(a) There shall be created a full time executive group consisting of one military representative each of the British Commonwealth, the United States, the Soviet Union, and France. This group shall be assisted by an adequate staff of attorneys and research personnel to compile and analyze data, prepare the charges to conform to the proof and arrange the evidence for presentation to the international tribunal.

(b) The presentation of the case before the international tribunal shall be made by persons designated by the British Commonwealth, the United States, the Soviet Union, and France, each of these countries being entitled to designate one person, who may be its member of the executive group referred to in paragraph (a) of this Article.

V

(a) The emoluments and expenses of those members of the tribunal provided for in Article III, designated by the British Commonwealth, the United States, the Soviet Union, and France, and of the executive group provided for in Article IV (a), shall be borne by the respective Governments just mentioned.

(b) The emoluments and expenses of the other three members of the tribunal shall be borne by the Governments of the other United Nations parties to this instrument.

(c) The emoluments and expenses of the staff assisting the executive group, and of secretarial staffs for the tribunal and the executive group, and incidental expenses, such as rent, heat, light, stationery and printing, shall be borne by the parties to this instrument in equal shares.

VI

All members of the United Nations shall be invited by the Government of the United Kingdom, acting on behalf of the other signatories hereto, to adhere to this instrument. Such adherence shall in each case be notified to the Government of the United Kingdom which shall promptly inform the other parties to this instrument.

Done at ____________________ this the ____________________ day of ____________________, 1945.

DOCUMENT 37

MEMORANDUM (FROM THE DEPARTMENT OF THE TREASURY)[1]

RE: THE WAR DEPARTMENT MEMORANDUM CONCERNING THE PUNISHMENT OF WAR CRIMINALS

January 19, 1945

With respect to the attached draft of a memorandum for the President, concerning the trial and punishment of European war criminals, we in the Treasury have the following comments to make:

(1) We think that the most fundamental issue which the President should focus on immediately is the procedure to be followed which will give the fullest possible effect to the following provision in the Moscow statement on atrocities of November 1943:

> "At the time of the granting of any armistice to any government which may be set up in Germany, those German officers and men and members of the Nazi party who have been responsible for, or have taken a consenting part in the above atrocities, massacres and executions, will be sent back to the countries in which their abominable deeds were done in order that they may be judged and punished according to the laws of these liberated countries and of the free governments which will be created therein."

It is our view that, in accordance with the principle laid down by this provision, the Allied military authorities should hand over upon demand, without any examination of any nature whatsoever of the merits, all Germans requested by any of the United Nations. These Germans would be returned to the country demanding them where they would be tried and disposed of according to the laws and procedures of that country.

Specifically, it could be provided that upon a request filed with the appropriate authorities by a representative of any of the United Nations, any person[2] who was stated in such request to be charged by such United Nation with an offense against its laws or its nationals, or under the laws of war, should immediately be delivered up to the designated authorities of such country. Such request should be promptly and summarily complied with upon the apprehension of the person named in the request. If the same person is requested by the representatives of more than one country, such person should be delivered up to the country charging him with the offense which, in the judgment of the appropriate authorities, is most serious. Compliance with any request, however, should not be held up on the grounds that other requests for the same person may be anticipated. A time limit should be set, say six months, during which the country to which the person is delivered must convict him or else return him for delivery to such other country as may desire to try such person.

As provided in the Moscow Declaration this provision would not apply to the case of the major criminals, whose offenses have no particular geographical localization.

From the standpoint of keeping faith with our allies as well as with our own people, we feel that it is most important that no attempt be made to cut away at the principle of the Moscow Declaration by provisions such as those requiring that a formal extradition procedure be followed, that *prima facie* evidence as to the guilt of the person be established, etc. The extradition procedure should be administered in the most simple and expeditious manner, the only question being one of identifying the individual or group of individuals requested.

(2) Whatever procedure is adopted to deal with the war criminals who are not turned over to the various United Nations, this procedure should not involve any agreement in the form of a treaty, as is suggested in the War Department memorandum. We are of the opinion that any attempt to deal with this problem through a treaty is totally unnecessary and could only lead to endless frustrating delays and disagreements; and that if the problem is handled in this way we might have even a worse fiasco than we had after the last World War.[3] If it is felt for any reason that some sort of a formal agreement between the United Nations is necessary with respect to some aspects of this problem, an executive agreement entered into between the nations concerned can be just as effective as a formal treaty.

(3) With respect to those criminals who are not requested by any of the

United Nations for trial in their own country, the important thing in our mind is that these people be tried by military tribunal under the most simple and expeditious procedure that can be devised. Our fear with respect to a conspiracy trial such as suggested in the War Department memorandum is that, unless the greatest effort is made to avoid legalistic red tape, it may become simply another glorified "sedition trial".[4]

If it is possible to have such a trial which would carry with it the dignity of recognized judicial procedures, but which at the same time would be unencumbered by the technical delays and defenses which even under our own system frequently impede the execution of essential justice, then, in our opinion, the suggestion that there be such a trial has some merit. Such a trial might serve to demonstrate to the world that we as civilized nations are able to bring to justice by regular legal methods those who have committed unspeakable crimes against humanity and might accordingly increase respect for ourselves and for law and order. But if criminals known to the whole world by their acts are permitted to delay punishment by reliance on technical legal rules, we would earn the enmity and disrespect of world opinion. The question, therefore, is whether a procedure can be devised which will afford the defendants some of the privileges afforded to defendants under our normal criminal procedures and which will not at the same time impede the punishment of those already convicted at the bar of world opinion. If it is possible to devise such a procedure, it will certainly be necessary that it assure such things as the following:

(a) That the pleas of sovereign immunity, superior orders, and insanity be eliminated as automatic defenses.

(b) That the crimes for which punishment is sought be so specifically defined that the defendants will not be able to argue collateral and irrelevant issues. For example, Hitler and the other leaders should not be permitted to reargue the theories expounded in "Mein Kampf" and other expositions of Nazi dogma. They should be confined to specific factual issues, such as, did the German army invade Poland, Czechoslovakia, etc. and did German civilians and military personnel pursue certain courses of action in those countries and in Germany itself.

(c) The opportunity of the criminals to speak in their own behalf should also be strictly limited as to time.

(d) The representatives of the Allied governments should be completely unrestricted by rules of evidence and other technicalities in presenting their case against the defendants.

————————————[5]

The War Department memorandum provides that once the judgment in the conspiracy charge is obtained, the civil and military courts of the several United Nations will proceed to try the members of the organizations which were adjudicated to have been participants in the conspiracy and that these trials would ascertain the nature and extent of their participation and fix the punishment of *each* participant in a measure appropriate in the particular case.

We feel that if there is to be a conspiracy trial along the lines suggested that the judgment in this trial should be conclusive as to the guilt of those persons who fall within those groups which are adjudged to have taken part in the conspiracy. Thus, if Organization X is adjudged to have participated in the conspiracy, the only questions remaining would be the following, which could be handled summarily:

(a) The identification of the individual members of Organization X.

(b) The determination that all members of Organization X should receive as a minimum a certain type of punishment, with graduations depending upon the position of responsibility held by such individuals in the organization.

(4) Whatever procedure is worked out must cover the punishment of crimes committed by Germans against Germans and persons of other Axis nationalities. If the conspiracy charge is used, it should cover, for example, the murder of Jews and other minority groups of Axis nationality.

* * * * * * *[6]

Above all, it is most important that in dealing with this problem we recognize the fundamental fact that international law must be dynamic, not static. Unless it grows as the problems which the world faces grow, it will die. The respect which the people of the world will have for international law is in direct proportion to its ability to meet their needs. The one way of assuring that the trial and punishment of war criminals will produce a cynical public opinion would be to attempt to apply past practices and procedurs growing out of the relatively puny wars of history to the present gigantic struggle for survival.

International law envisions the handling of novel situations according to the rule of reason. When confronted by problems which can not adequately be dealt with in accordance with historical precedents, we must approach them with boldness, courage and the determination to advance the science of international law by making the necessary decisions in a manner consistent with the ethical, moral and humane principles recognized by civilized men. The responsibility of the United Nations in this unprecedented situation is a heavy one. It must not be discharged with primary emphasis on the technical construction of obsolete rules of conduct, but, on the contrary, it must be discharged with due regard to achieving the goals for which this war is being fought. There are no rules of international law which present legal obstacles to obtaining these goals.

DOCUMENT 38

DIARY ENTRY OF HENRY L. STIMSON (DESCRIBING A TALK WITH THE PRESIDENT)[1]

January 19, 1945

I then talked with him about the work which has been done by our Committee in the War Department in connection with the Attorney General's Office and Joe Davies and Judge Rosenman[2] culminating in their meeting of yesterday of which I wrote in yesterday's diary.[3] I told him of my own view of the importance as a matter of record of having a state trial with records and one that would bring out and show the full nature of the Nazi conspiracy or evil plan to wage a war of terrorism of the European world involving totalitarian war and breaches of the laws of war. I also pointed out to him the advantage which such a system would have over so-called political action which I heard the British are advocating and I said that our method was in accord with the views of Russia. He assented to what I said but in the hurry of the situation I am not sure whether it registered.

PHASE III

III

Documents

February to August 1945

III

Introduction

February to August 1945

After all the work and effort that had gone into preparing the Cabinet-level policy papers in January 1945, the results of Yalta were a disappointment to the proponents of the conspiracy/criminal-organization plan. Not only did the Big Three fail even to consider the proposal, but Mr. Roosevelt returned to Washington in late February without having given anyone a clear indication whether or not he was inclined to support it. In March 1945, therefore, the plan bobbed along as the probable or presumptive American war crimes policy, but without the final certification of presidential approval.

The supporters of the conspiracy/criminal-organization approach were nonetheless able easily to sidestep another effort of General Royall to replace the plan with a more conventional, and limited, trial system (document 39), and they also mastered a new attempt by Morgenthau and his staff to impose harsher occupation procedures on Germany. The new statement on occupation policy for Germany signed by the top U.S. planners and initialed by the President on March 23 not only declared that the Nazi leaders would be tried rather than simply shot, but also stated that the trial defendants would include those who had "participated in planning or carrying out Nazi enterprises involving or resulting in atrocities or war crimes" (document 40). This was again not a direct endorsement of the conspiracy/criminal-organization plan by the president, but the emphasis on planning and participation seemed to tip in that direction.

Yet, as had occurred in December 1944—January 1945 when the Malmedy massacre and the Yalta planning had pushed Washington policymakers into action, so again outside events spurred the plan in March and April. With Anglo-American armies across the Rhine in force and the end of the Third Reich "approaching on a galloping horse," to use Henry Stimson's phrase, the planners had obviously run out of time. Therefore, when an opportunity to get things moving again presented itself in late March in the form of a British invitation for an American delegation to come to London to discuss matters concerning war crimes, U.S. officials jumped at the opportunity. The British government was apprehensive about what it had concluded was a rising Washington mood in favor of legally radical trial plans for the Nazi leaders rather than the safe summary execution scheme agreed to at Quebec. London hoped to ease the Americans back into a program under which the UNWCC would be sidetracked, Hitler and his aides would simply be shot, and all other war criminals would be given regular military trials. In furtherance of this objective, the British wished to lure to London for discussions men whom they considered cautious and conservative, and they therefore asked specifically that Hackworth and General Weir should represent the United States. The British Foreign Office did not realize who was actually setting the pace in Washington, nor did it grasp that by this time both Hackworth and Weir had been co-opted by the proponents of the conspiracy/criminal-organization plan.

For their part, American officials were almost completely in the dark about British hopes and intentions. The chief concern of McCloy and his associates was to use the offer from London to produce renewed action on planning war crimes policy. Overcoming some personality conflicts and jurisdictional backbiting, by April 2 Washington authorities had selected a three-man team led by Judge Rosenman and including General Weir and Colonel Cutter. A week previously, General Weir had reaffirmed the reality and orthodoxy of his recent conversion in a memorandum recommending that a mission be sent to London to urge creation of a conspiracy/criminal-organization trial system that would use simplified evidentiary procedures and would even employ court-appointed masters, or "commissioners," to gather summaries of evidence (document 41). Since Cutter and Rosenman were among the most devoted advocates of the kind of trial system that General Weir had just come to espouse, little question should have arisen about this delegation's loyalty to the plan. The State Department, nonetheless, prepared a briefing paper instructing the group to advance the proposal contained in the Three Secretaries Memorandum (document 35) as if it were the policy of the United States government. The delegation was cautioned, however, that in the opinion of Hackworth, the Three Secretaries Memorandum should be treated as if it were a classified document and should not be shown to the British (document 42).

The inexperienced Rosenman delegation was therefore sent off to London with little choice but to use the implementing instrument (document 36) as the basis of its approach to the British, although this document had presumably never been seen or approved by any top American official except Rosenman himself. These circumstances were an open invitation for the members of the group to improvise as they saw fit, and in spite of a telegram of April 4 from Ambassador Davies to Rosenman urging moderation and caution (document 43), changes were made in the implementing instrument almost immediately (document 44).

Once the Americans met their British counterparts, pressure to revise the basic U.S. plan and to shift its focus increased. Following a low-level diplomatic skirmish on April 4, Rosenman and his associates met with a more prestigious group of United Kingdom officials, led by Lord Chancellor Sir John Simon, the next day. The lord chancellor succeeded in taking the initiative away from the Americans, who were not given an opportunity to explain their conspiracy/criminal-organization scheme before Simon rushed forward and proposed an "arraignment plan" as a compromise between the British desire for summary execution and the American predilection for a trial (document 45). Instead of calling Simon up short, Rosenman chose instead to let the "arraignment" proposal stand as a possible means of dealing with the leaders of the Third Reich and advanced the conspiracy/criminal-organization plan as a suitable device for taking care of the middle-level Nazi culprits, including members of organizations, who might be difficult to convict of traditional war crimes.

This exchange laid the groundwork for much confusion and difficulty. Since the British did not see even a summary of the complete American plan, they were unable to comprehend the basic thrust of American policy on war crimes prosecution. On the other hand, although Sir John told the Americans that his arraignment proposal had not been approved by the War Cabinet, Rosenman and his colleagues assumed that while they were trying to secure Washington's concurrence, Simon would be able to obtain "in principle" acceptance of the idea in London. Therefore, some members of the two delegations immediately set to work tugging at the arraignment idea, with the British trying to make it appear as much as possible like summary execution and the Americans attempting to dress it up to approximate a trial. Colonel Cutter even went so far as to redraft the implementing instrument to embody a summary of the arraignment proposal (document 46).

In the meantime, Judge Rosenman informed Washington of Simon's recommendation and added that with some modifications, it might be a satisfactory way of dealing with the top Nazi leaders (document 47). For five days Rosenman and his colleagues waited impatiently for the verdicts of Washington officialdom and the British War Cabinet. Then on April 12, the world fell in on the American delegation. On that day, in Warm Springs, Georgia, President Roosevelt suddenly died, bringing the American governmental system to a shuddering halt and cutting short the speculations on war crimes policy of American officials in both Washington and London. On the same day, at Whitehall, the War Cabinet decided that the arraignment proposal, with its attempted compromise between trial and summary execution, had managed to combine the worst of both worlds, and flatly rejected the idea. Although the British government sweetened the pill by looking sympathetically on the use of the American conspiracy/criminal-organization approach against middle-level malefactors, London had definitely moved in the direction of political execution of the top Nazi leaders.

The Rosenman mission had failed in its effort to get the British to accept the complete American plan or to find a viable basis for compromise. The judge therefore immediately left to attend President Roosevelt's funeral in Washington, nursing a sense of frustrated confusion laced with suspicion that he might have been the victim of some dark deception by Simon and his associates. On the heels of Rosenman's departure, John J. McCloy passed through London on his return from a continental tour of inspection, and he, too, briefly tried his hand at testing the temper of the British authorities on war crimes policy. But Simon and the other officials with whom McCloy spoke, now thoroughly chastened by the War Cabinet action of April 12, abruptly dismissed any idea of trial or arraignment, and insisted that Hitler and a handful of his closest collaborators be politically liquidated (document 48).

Thus, when McCloy and Cutter returned to Washington near the end of the third week of April, they were able to provide strong confirmation for Rosenman's conclusion that there was no prospect of rapid success in additional bilateral discussion of war crimes policy with the British. This was especially important because a radical change had occurred in the mood of official Washington and in the attitude of the war crimes policy planners during the week after President Roosevelt's death. Harry Truman had revealed himself to be a man of quick and firm decision, little inclined to the artful, evasive tactics of his predecessor. As soon as Judge Rosenman and Secretary Stimson supplied him with a copy of the Three Secretaries Memorandum and told him of the Anglo-American conflict over whether to use trial or summary execution to get rid of the Nazi leaders, the new President decided that there must be a trial and that the basic American policy position was sound. Emboldened by the strong presidential mandate that had so long eluded them, the American planners then raced forward on a number of fronts.

On April 20, McCloy and his assistants produced an impassioned memorandum defending the trial approach and scoring the British for supporting summary execution (document 49). During a meeting held in McCloy's office on the same day, which resembled a summit conference of war crimes policy planners, it was emphasized that the British were isolated. The Soviet Union had indicated its support for some kind of war crimes judicial procedure on a number of occasions, and in the course of his recent stay in Paris, McCloy had been told by Charles de Gaulle that he, too, favored a trial. Therefore, the way seemed clear for the Americans, first to create a war crimes policy organization, then to refine their proposal, and finally to make use of the first available four-power meeting to compel the British to yield on the trial issue and to accept the American plan.

After a week of soundings and consultations, the president—apparently again prompted and guided by Stimson and Rosenman—quietly inquired if Supreme Court Justice Robert H. Jackson would be willing to head an American war crimes prosecution agency. On April 29, Jackson signaled his agreement, and two days later Mr. Truman issued an executive order creating the prosecution organization and designating Jackson as "Chief of Counsel for the Prosecution of Axis Criminality." Even before this appointment was made, the president had directed that Judge Rosenman should assume the task of sparkplugging an effort at the San Francisco United Nations Conference to convince America's major allies that the Nazi leaders should be tried before an international military tribunal on the basis of the conspiracy/criminal-organization plan. Henry Stimson had then unobtrusively moved in and secured Truman's agreement for McCloy to accompany Rosenman to San Francisco to strengthen the American delegation and to make certain that it was not outwitted or overpowered by the British.

By the end of April, therefore, the double-winged American war crimes organizational structure had come into existence, at a time when the Third Reich was collapsing, the concentration camps had been overrun, and Goebbels and Hitler reportedly had just committed suicide in Berlin. Consequently, American idealistic fervor was burning at a white heat. The Washington planners were determined to vindicate the Allied cause and to punish the Nazi culprits, but they believed that to do this properly they had to convince their allies, especially the British, that only the American plan could do the job. Colonel Cutter was thus set to work preparing a memorandum, drafted on April 25 and revised five days later, setting out Washington's favorite arguments in support of its proposal. Although filled with moral idealism and intended to confound London's summary-execution position, Cutter's memorandum did contain a few passing references to arraignment as a palliative to the British (document 50).

During the same period, Cutter also produced a draft executive agreement to be laid before the Allied delegations at San Francisco. In preparing this document—an outgrowth of the old and oft-revised implementing instrument—the colonel again put in some arraignment references, together with a sampling of other features drawn from earlier formulations of the plan (document 51). But while Cutter's memorandum managed to slip past unchallenged and was presented to the Allies in its original form, the draft executive agreement ran into trouble. In one of his first acts as chief of counsel, Justice Jackson insisted that the executive agreement be completely rewritten (document 52), and on May 2, in a fiesta of revision, the document was redrafted no less than four times. Jackson, Bernays, Wechsler, Cutter, and Rosenman all had a hand in producing these changes (documents 53 and 54). Together with many alterations of detail, the revisions eliminated every trace of the arraignment compromise. In consequence, one of the documents presented to the Allies in San Francisco retained allusions to arraignment (document 50), while the other did not (document 52). A second notable consequence of the May 2 revisions was the inclusion, at Justice Jackson's behest, of strongly worded clauses authorizing that the Nazis be charged and punished for the crime of aggressive war. The third significant shift in emphasis concerned the legal basis on which the charges relating to prewar atrocities and crimes against enemy nationals should rest. In the original Bernays plan and every subsequent redraft, the chief device employed was the conspiracy, or criminal-enterprise, approach. However, in all four of the May 2 revisions, the conspiracy/criminal-organization theory was played down in favor of charging the Nazi leaders with violations not only of international law, but of the domestic laws of all the Axis countries, their satellites, and of all the United Nations. This not only introduced a shockingly innovative and wide-open legal device, it also made it more difficult for Allied governments to grasp the basic legal approach that had shaped the evolution of American planning of war crimes policy.

When, on May 3, the American delegation finally presented its much revised executive agreement and memorandum to the Allied representatives in San Francisco, the long-expected clash with the British did not materialize. Foreign Secretary Anthony Eden had already taken precautionary measures and had asked for War Cabinet instructions on what he should do in the event that the three other Allied nations supported trial rather than summary execution. The Cabinet had thereupon reversed itself and told Eden that if he was faced with a solid protrial block, he should yield in principle, while placing the burden of preparing a workable trial plan on the Americans. What neither the Cabinet nor Eden had forseen was that the United States believed it had developed not only a plan for an effective judicial system but a trial structure that constituted the very best means of disposing of Hitler's paladins and cleansing Nazi Germany.

Consequently, when the British yielded in principle on May 3, the way seemed clear for an Allied examination, and perhaps rapid acceptance, of the American proposal. In the days that followed, legal specialists of the four powers met and discussed various features of the plan while the French, Soviet, and British delegations awaited authorization from their home governments to accept it. After a week, Rosenman grew tried of this delay, however, and returned to Washington. The American war crimes planners who remained in San Francisco—Wechsler, Cutter, and McCloy—spent another week tentatively redrafting various sections of the executive agreement to meet Allied suggestions and to try out new features developed by the Americans themselves. By the time this group left San Francisco in mid-May, none of the Allied governments had officially approved the plan, and so one last phase of redrafting and revising took place in Washington in mid-May.

On May 16, Colonel Cutter completed another revision of the executive agreement, embodying the changes that had been developed in San Francisco (document 55). This provided the basis for a critique (perhaps produced by Hackworth and Wechsler) completed and circulated on May 19. The critique (document 56) was important primarily because it suggested employing in the executive agreement a definition of international law that would give the court great latitude in finding the Nazis guilty of international crimes. The definition in question had first appeared in the Fourth Hague Convention of 1907 to help guide courts confronting the task of dealing with complaints about the use of new weapons not covered by existing rules of land warfare. Due to the hypothetical and uncertain nature of the problems to which it was intended to apply, the language employed in the Fourth Hague Convention was especially broad. It suggested that, along with other indicators, courts should look to "the laws of humanity and the dictates of the public conscience" for guidance when faced with technical innovations in the instruments of war. However, if such a recommendation was to be elevated to a general definition of the elements of international law, a court such as that envisioned in the American executive agreement would be empowered to find that virtually any act was a violation of prevailing international law.

The final revision of the executive agreement, prepared by Jackson and his staff on May 19, not only took over the elastic declaration of the nature of international law from the critique, but also employed—sometimes expanding and sometimes narrowing—a number of other provisions from earlier drafts to tip the scales heavily in favor of the prosecution (document 57). The conspiracy/common-enterprise features that had been muted in the paper presented to the Allies in San Francisco (document 54) were restored to their central position in the document of May 19. Charges of aggression and prewar atrocities were also specifically enumerated once more. Although substantially restricted, so that it held the Nazis liable only for violations of the domestic statutes of the countries where their acts were committed, this culminating form of the executive agreement also allowed for prosecution of leaders of the Third Reich for breaching the domestic laws of other nations.

All in all, the executive agreement of May 19 went further in creating a court intended to convict than did any of the earlier formulations of the plan. The new Jackson team seems to have been more possessed by self-righteousness and moral fervor than had the men who earlier gathered around McCloy and Rosenman, but the latter group, too, had started to move in the direction of a crusade even before Jackson appeared on the scene. But it would be a distortion merely to note this characteristic of the document of May 19. Jackson and his staff had also raised the level of legal draughtsmanship, and the new executive agreement was more tightly and precisely composed than any of its predecessors. In addition, among the new faces brought in by the justice were such men as Colonel Telford Taylor, who, although they did not play a part in this drafting, would soon leave their mark by asking tough, direct questions (document 58).

The combination of moral purpose, clear vision, and technical competence that pervaded the executive agreement of May 19 was a major factor in the American government's ultimate success in securing Allied acceptance of the basic elements of the U.S. plan. Although there are many gaps in our current knowledge of what went on at the four-power London conference on war crimes policy that lasted from June to August 1945, it is obvious that it was not all smooth sailing for the Americans. Allied representatives objected to features of the U.S. proposal and were frequently put off by what they saw as an arbitrary and domineering American manner—starting with the fact that Jackson's people dropped the new form of the executive agreement on them just before the conference opened. That in the end the Americans pretty much had their way was surely more of a tribute to their great power and the merits of the trial system they proposed than it was to any skills that they showed in diplomacy.

The final London Agreement and Charter, formally approved by the four powers on August 8, laid down the system on which a tribunal would conduct the trial at Nuremberg of the surviving leaders of the Third Reich and of a group of Nazi "criminal" organizations. In the trial, the defendants could be charged with traditional war crimes, "crimes against humanity," and "crimes against peace." They would further be subject to prosecution for having participated in the "formulation or execution of a common plan or conspiracy" to commit any of these criminal acts (document 59). Despite changes of language and tone, the American war crimes planners had reached their main goal. The last great Allied encounter with Nazism would occur in a court of law, and this "Great Assize" would be carried out on the basis of the ideas that had been set forth and developed in Washington between September 1944 and June 1945.

DOCUMENT 39

MEMORANDUM FOR THE ASSISTANT SECRETARY OF WAR[1] (FROM BRIGADIER GENERAL KENNETH C. ROYALL)[2]

March 21, 1945

1. Since no definite action has been taken on the recommendations of the State, War and Justice Departments for the trial of Axis war criminals and since these recommendations, if approved, would probably require one or more treaties or conventions[3] for the establishment of the non-military International Tribunal suggested therein, it would seem that the War Department should promptly formulate a military plan for dealing with war criminals, particularly in Germany.

2. It is recommended that the Secretary of War, with the approval of the President, authorize the Commanding General of ETO[4] to establish a War Crimes Division in the European Theater, the Chief of which Division would be a member of the ETO staff . . .

3. It is further recommended that the War Crimes Division, in cooperation with similar organizations of other United Nations, establish a Joint War Crimes Organization to handle the apprehension, prosecution, trial and punishment of those war criminals which are not tried by the individual Nations.

4. This joint Organization would organize a United Nations Military Commission for the trial of such war criminals. Such trials would be without prejudice to any future judicial or political trials which might be provided for by an armistice or by a treaty or convention. The crimes to be tried by the Commission and the procedure to be followed would be in accordance with the memorandum of 14 December 1944.[5] The Commission would not try any offense of starting the war or any offense committed before the beginning of the war.

. . . .

6. It is further recommended that the Joint War Crimes Organization:

a. Arrange to amend the Rules of Land Warfare of the United States and of England, and possibly of other countries, to the extent necessary to clarify the offenses to be charged and to deny the defenses of "sovereignty" or "acts of State" and to deny or materially modify the defense of "superior orders."[6]

b. Immediately prepare proposed armistice terms (1) recognizing the validity and jurisdiction of a United Nations Military Commission and possibly certain of the rules of and crimes cognizable by the Commission and (2) denying immunity to Hitler and the other German leaders . . .

DOCUMENT 40

FROM SUMMARY OF U.S. POLICY RELATING TO GERMANY IN THE INITIAL POSTDEFEAT PERIOD[1]

March 23, 1945

War criminals and those who have participated in planning or carrying out Nazi enterprises involving or resulting in atrocities or war crimes, shall be arrested, brought to trial and punished. Nazi leaders and influential Nazi supporters and any other persons dangerous to the occupation or its objectives, shall be arrested and interned.

DOCUMENT 41

MEMORANDUM
SUBJECT: WAR CRIMES CONFERENCE (THESE ARE GENERAL WEIR'S ROUGH IDEAS)[1]

March 27, 1945

1. The time has come, I believe, when there should be called an international conference on the trial of the war criminals . . .

2. The state of our thinking has pretty well coalesced into a definite plan or theory and we should bring our theory and thinking to a combined meeting of representatives of the United States, United Kingdom, Soviet Russia and France . . .

. . . . [2]

4. As to size and composition of the military court to be used for the trial of Hitler et al, we are all in accord; that is, the court should consist of seven members—one each from the United States, United Kingdom, Soviet Russia and France, with the remaining three to be chosen by agreement of the other countries. This latter place may present some difficulty in reaching agreement. It may be desirable to limit the court membership to the "Big Four"

countries and increase representation to two or three which would make the court panel eight or twelve . . .

5. If there is to be a speedy trial the usual and normal procedures will have to be greatly simplified. Otherwise such a trial by reason of the gigantic ramifications would stretch out in time and space almost without end.

6. Preconceived ideas and theories of criminal procedure will have to give way to more workable rules to be made for the trial of the war crimes cases. I can not conceive of any rule that will extend to the accused the protection which the common-law has peculiarly developed through the years in the Anglo-American countries. The European continental legal systems have not gone as far as the common-law.[3] The accused is entitled to examine the evidence and an opportunity to be heard. The presumption of innocence should not apply nor should the rule against compulsory incrimination. The prosecution should be permitted to call the accused as a witness and examine him as one of its principal witnesses.

7. The rules of evidence as we know them do not exist in the continental countries. The judge in such countries may receive into evidence anything which to him has probative value in reference to the particular case. Such should be the rule in the war crimes trials. It will be practically an impossibility for the court in the trial of the major cases to bring to it the witnesses from all over Europe and elsewhere. Neither would it be practical for the court to move with the accused, the prosecution staff, and its impedimenta to various places to hear different phases of the case. To simplify this I propose to borrow from equity procedure which offers a workable, rational and fair plan. I would designate commissioners or masters who would report to the court a finding of facts covering the particular country or zone assigned to them.[4] It would be impractical and unnecessary for the accused to be present while the commissioner was conducting his hearing. The commissioner's report would constitute the evidence covering his particular zone. Additional or supporting evidence as may be desired by the prosecution staff, could of course, be submitted.

8. The adoption of the commissioner system would have the added advantage of going a long way to satisfy the smaller countries which would not be represented in the membership of the Court itself, for under this system the commissioners would be from the country or zone involved; and would be appointed by the government concerned.

9. The rule as to "superior orders" should be that the accused may show that his acts were committed pursuant to orders which he received from superior authority, but such fact will not excuse from responsibility but goes only to the quantum of punishment[5] which the court may impose under the circumstances of the case. The defense of superior orders is not greatly

different from turning state's evidence and should be treated in about the same manner. I have the idea that such defense will likely be widely used especially by the lesser individuals. So much the better as such evidence will prove out of the mouths of such accused the guilt and responsibility of the leaders of the criminal plan.

10. The responsibility of heads of state and other officials for acts done in their official capacities should be determined to be personal and not recognized as a defense.

11. Agreement should be reached by the countries concerned for the execution of sentence imposed—where confinement would be served, etc. My own views are that confinement imposed by special international or occupation courts should be served under the jurisdiction of the occupational authorities; and that the prisoners may be utilized wherever desired.

DOCUMENT 42

FROM STATE DEPARTMENT PROGRAM OF DISCUSSION WITH JUDGE ROSENMAN[1]

April 2, 1945

3. Stage 2 proceedings—

Organizations found to have participated in the common enterprise would be determined in the first stage. Members would be subject to penalty.

a. upon identification as members

b. upon their failing to prove (i) that their membership was involuntary; or (ii) that their participation was nominal only.

Involuntary servitude or rehabilitation work would be normal punishment for membership more than nominal. Proof of explicit consent to, direction of, or participation in any atrocity would be required for capital punishment. Trials at this state would be in the nature of orders to show cause and verification of identity.[2]

DOCUMENT 43

FROM CABLE, AMBASSADOR DAVIES TO JUDGE ROSENMAN[1]

April 4, 1945

I am strongly impressed that there now exists specific law, domestic and international, as well as available judicial machinery entirely adequate to provide and assure speedy and just punishment for outlaws and criminals, whether principals or accessories; and that therefore just punishment can be administered through legalized channels and within recognized principles of law which civilization has evolved as chief bulwark for protection of the individual against either tyranny or injustice STOP Under vigorous application of present existing law no guilty person can escape STOP To resort to additional retroactive criminal legislation might now appease some who have suffered but would ultimately be condemned by more sober judgment and succeeding generations who would see in it a violation of the principles for which we fought STOP The ideals for which our men have died should not be tarnished by even the shadow of a suspicion that we have stooped to Nazi methods or have tortured legal principle in order to wreak formalized vengeance rather than to administer dispassionate justice under law STOP.

DOCUMENT 44

REVISIONS BY COLONEL CUTTER OF THE "IMPLEMENTING INSTRUMENT" (OF JANUARY 20, 1945)[1]

April 3, 1945

III

The tribunal for the trial of the basic crime referred to in Article II(a) shall be a military tribunal which shall consist of five to seven members, to be appointed as follows: one each by the British Commonwealth, the United States, the Soviet Union, and France, and one to three members to be chosen by agreement of the four members of the tribunal, first selected as above provided, from a panel consisting of one person each nominated by each of the other United Nations who may become parties to this instrument.

The members of the tribunal shall be military personnel of the nations of which they respectively are citizens.

IV

In order to accomplish the swift trial and punishment of those guilty of war crimes and other atrocities, the tribunal mentioned in Article II, the national courts of the United Nations, and the appropriate military and occupation courts, all shall adopt and apply, to the greatest extent possible, expeditious, fair non-technical procedures. Such procedures, in a manner consistent with the other provisions of this agreement should:

(a) Provide each accused with notice of the charges against him and an opportunity to be heard reasonably on such charges.

(b) permit the court to admit any evidence which it considers would have probative value.

(c) Except as the court in its discretion shall deem appropriate in particular cases, exclude any defense based upon the fact that the accused acted under orders of a superior officer or pursuant to state or national policy or upon the fact that the accused is or was the head or purported head or other principal official of a state, and[2]

(d) confine trials strictly to an expeditious hearing of the issues raised by the charges.

V

(a) There shall be created at the earliest possible moment a full time executive group consisting of one military representative each of the British Commonwealth, the United States, the Soviet Union, and France. So far as the operations of this executive group are carried out within Germany or Austria, such operations shall be subject to the administrative direction of the Control Council for Germany or for Austria, as the case may be.[3] This group shall be assisted by an adequate staff of attorneys and research personnel to compile and analyze data, prepare the charges in the principal case or cases to conform to the proof and arrange the evidence for presentation to the international tribunal.

(b) The presentation of the principal case or cases before the international tribunal shall be made by persons designated by the British Commonwealth, the United States, the Soviet Union, and France, each of these countries being entitled to designate one person, who may be its member of the executive group referred to in paragraph (a) of this Article.[4]

(c) The full time executive group shall also be charged with:

(1) the preparation of plans for, and general supervision of, the prosecu-

tion of individuals to be charged with specific war crimes and atrocities and with complicity (as mentioned in Article II, paragraph (c) above) in the basic criminal plan through membership in one of the organizations hereinbefore mentioned, not only in the national courts of the United Nations but also before occupation or other appropriate tribunals.

(2) the organization, through military or civil agencies of the several parties to this Agreement, of prosecuting organizations to prepare and present charges and to conduct trials.

(3) the planning and making of arrangements for the detection, apprehension, extradition, transfer, trial and punishment of persons charged with war crimes and atrocities or with participation in the basic criminal plan.

(4) the planning and putting into effect of suitable, expeditious, non-technical procedures for the swift but fair trial and punishment of war criminals in a manner consistent with the provisions of this Agreement and designed to bring to certain and prompt justice those guilty of war crimes and atrocities.

(5) the recommendation to the appropriate governmental authorities of agreements and measures supplemental to or in addition to this Agreement, necessary or appropriate to accomplish the objectives of this Agreement, and

(6) the maintenance of liaison among and with the appropriate military and civil agencies, authorities and commissions of or representing any of the United Nations which are or may be charged with responsibility for any matters dealt with in this Agreement . . .

DOCUMENT 45

MEMORANDUM TO JUDGE ROSENMAN FROM LORD SIMON (LORD CHANCELLOR)[1]

April 6, 1945

HOUSE OF LORDS

SECRET

Dear Judge Rosenman, 6th April 1945

I promised to send you in writing an outline of the method of dealing with Hitler, Mussolini and other arch-criminals which I described to you at our meeting on Thursday. The method is designed to furnish an appropriate mode of dealing with these master criminals in a way which avoids summary execution without trial, on the one hand, and a long-drawn out process with endless witnesses as to details who would have to be cross-examined with all the paraphernalia of an immense State trial, on the other.

My proposal is that the Allies should draw up what I would call a "*document of arraignment*" in somewhat general terms and that an inter-allied judicial tribunal (which might, however, include some members who were not professional judges) should be appointed to report upon the truth of this Arraignment after Hitler and Co. had been brought before the tribunal and given the opportunity to challenge the truth of its contents, if they could. The function of the court would be, after giving Hitler and Co. the opportunity of being heard, and, if they liked, of producing documents and witnesses, to report to the Allies whether the Arraignment or any part of it had been disproved. It would then be for the Allies themselves (as indeed the Moscow Declaration announced) to determine what the punishment should be.

I feel most strongly that no tribunal of a judicial character can be left with the responsibility of deciding the sentence, but that is a very different thing from saying that a specially constituted tribunal could not pronounce impartially and judicially as to whether the Arraignment is disproved. If the actual choice of sentence is left to a body of judges they must, of course, act on their own judgment without any prompting from Executives—Our Anglo-American traditions make this the very corner-stone of criminal justice, and I would never consent to allow British judges to mount the Bench for the purpose of carrying out the orders of any Government or combination of Governments. My plan avoids this and puts the ultimate responsibility of deciding what is to be done with Hitler and Co. where it must rest, i.e. upon the Allies themselves, for the ultimate fate of Hitler may influence the history of the world for a hundred years. At the same time, I think that by calling on Hitler and Co. to challenge and disprove, if they can, a carefully drawn document of Arraignment, we would secure the substance of trial before sentence.

The document of Arraignment, as I conceive it, would set out the real offence which these major criminals are felt, throughout the free world, to have committed. The offence charged would be, in substance, the Nazi policy which has been pursued of world conquest and the methods employed to achieve it. Mussolini's active share to promote this policy would, of course, also be alleged in his case. One count in the Arraignment would be the abominable treatment of Jews in Germany and elsewhere. I would propose that the Arraignment should be supported by the principal documents, such as passages from "Mein Kampf," or Hitler's speeches, but the whole point of the proceedings would be that these wicked men would be arraigned by reference to broad descriptions of what they have done (as the whole world knows), and that they would be left to meet this arraignment, or any part of it, if they could. The sort of document I have in mind (which would, of course, have to be most carefully settled between the principal Allies) would leave them no loophole.

I would beg to call attention to the following considerations which appear to me strongly to support this plan.

(a) Such a trial would not be a trial for "war crimes" in the technical sense known to international law. There would be no discussion as to whether what the Arraignment charged was recognised as a crime by the law of nations or by any other law. The issue would simply be, can Hitler prove to an impartial tribunal that the statements alleged are not true.

(b) The plan would have the enormous advantage of including within the scope of the charges Nazi infamies such as the treatment, torture, and attempted annihilation of the Jews. Hitler would not be able to say that it is no offense under international law for a ruler to maltreat his own subjects.[2] The question would simply be whether in the light of the documents appended to the Arraignment he can satisfy the court that he did not deliberately adopt and promote these infamies.

(c) It may be that Hitler and Co., when presented with the charges, would deny the jurisdiction of the court and refuse to take any part in the proceedings. I see no reason why the Allies should feel any difficulty in that event. He will have been charged on lines which are known to the whole world to be true, and he would have decided not to challenge the charges. The fact that an independent inter-allied tribunal was prepared to hear him, if he had anything to say, would justify to history his subsequent doom.

(d) On the other hand, he may challenge the Arraignment volubly and at length and repeat some of his almost interminable speeches. If the facts alleged are carefully chosen, this will not in the end affect the approval which the world would give to a judicial pronouncement. Anyhow, you cannot claim to deal with the man judicially if you do not offer to hear what he has to say, so far as it is relevant to the charges made.

(e) I venture to press for favourable consideration of the above scheme for another reason. History is easy to get distorted, and I think it would be of great advantage if by the co-operation of the Foreign Offices of the principal Allies a document of this sort was drawn up with considerable, but not excessive, documentation, putting on record for all time the grounds upon which we dealt with a man who has proved himself to be nothing but *hostis humani generis*.[3]

I have been very much impressed by the news I have received partly through Lord Halifax, of Mr. Stimson's strong feeling that there ought to be a judicial proceeding before execution. But I have also been very worried by the prospect of a trial which might be drawn out almost indefinitely, in which all sorts of things might be raised and discussed—whether legal or historical—

leading to controversy and debate in the world at large, with a reaction which we can hardly calculate. I hope very much that you will feel the force of what I have written, for I regard it as the first condition for the successful handling of this most difficult matter that there should be agreement between your authorities and our own.

I ought to add that, while I am taking upon myself to send you this description of the plan, I am not writing with the authority of the War Cabinet, though I know that the members of the Government whom I have consulted view the suggestion with favour.

I think the number of individuals who should be dealt with under this plan would be quite limited. They would be the people whom the public know as being the principal leaders in plotting and planning world supremacy, to be attained by these villainous methods. As regards the intermediate class represented by the chiefs and members of the Gestapo and S.S.,[4] I appreciate the value of your suggestion based on an allegation of conspiracy in a common criminal endeavor. You are sending me a document which sets out this scheme in more detail, and I look forward to studying it. But I would most strongly urge that a limited number of men at the top whom the public know to be the chief architects of the war, such as Hitler, Himmler, Mussolini, Goering, Ribbentrop, Goebbels, ought to be dealt with [by] a special method which will set out their real crime before the world, and not merely as leading specimens of a very much larger group.

(With kind regards)
(Yours sincerely)

(Sgd) SIMON

The Honourable
Judge Rosenman.

DOCUMENT 46

REVISION OF PORTIONS OF THE "IMPLEMENTING INSTRUMENT"[1]

April 10, 1945

1. The full time executive group mentioned in Article ___[2] below shall prepare a document of arraignment setting forth the offences which the United Nations allege that Hitler, Mussolini, Goebbels, Himmler, Ribbentrop, Goering and certain few others of the principal Nazi and Fascist leaders

have committed or have caused or permitted to be committed. The document of arraignment shall set forth clearly and in adequate detail the principal facts of the great Nazi criminal enterprise from its inception through the whole of its attempted execution, including among other things—

a. The program of persecutions of minority groups in Germany and the occupied countries, conducted with a view to suppressing opposition to the Nazi regime and destroying or weakening certain racial strains;

b. The encouragement of internal disorders in countries bordering upon Germany with a view to overthrowing their political and economic structures and making them subservient to Germany and easy prey for the Nazi invader;[3]

c. The invasion by force, or threat of force, of neighboring countries in violation of international customs and guarantees.

d. The initiation and waging of a ruthless war of aggression in deliberate and calculated disregard and violation of treaties and international commitments to which Germany and Italy were parties;

e. The cruel and relentless oppression of the nationals in territories occupied by the Germans in violation of international conventions and practices and in gross disregard of the laws and customs of war, including, among other things, the enslavement of subject peoples, the confiscation and looting of private property, the unreasonably stern administration of military occupation, the murder, rape, and despoilment of the citizenry, the deportation of the inhabitants, the grossly unreasonable and excessive punishment of innocent victims for the acts of others for which these victims were in no way responsible, and the extermination of minorities in these occupied areas in pursuance of an absurd, cruel, bestial philosophy of race supremacy which characterizes its protagonists as uncivilized and perverted.

2. The document of arraignment shall be supported by carefully prepared, accurate and authentic reports, original documents, records, affidavits and statements of the particular facts and circumstances alleged therein, with a view to setting forth, in the form of a complete *dossier* of indisputable documents, a comprehensive analysis and proof of the totality of the criminal and uncivilized acts for which the freedom loving nations of the world are in duty bound to call upon the principal Nazi aggressors to make an accounting.

3. An international Allied military court of five members shall be appointed by the Control Council for Germany, for the purpose of examining the document of arraignment, giving notice thereof to the persons accused therein, affording them an opportunity to be heard personally and by counsel with respect to the facts charged therein, and receiving such evidence, making such inquiry and holding such hearings as to the Court may seem proper and relevant. Each member of the Control Council shall designate one member of

the Court and the Control Council, acting as a group, by unanimous action, shall designate a fifth member of the Court from among the officers of the armed forces of a United Nation which is not represented on the Control Council for Germany. The military court may sit in any zone in Germany, Austria or Italy or in the territory of any one of the United Nations which shall adhere to this agreement, with the consent of any such nation. It shall have within Germany, Austria and Italy the power to summon witnesses and to compel their attendance, to require the production of documents, to administer oaths, to appoint special masters and other officers, to hold hearings, to make or cause to be made investigations as to the facts set forth in the document of arraignment and generally to exercise plenary judicial authority with respect to its subject matter, in a manner consistent with the provisions of this agreement.

4. The Court shall proceed with its duties expeditiously and without delay with a view to completing its examination into the matters alleged in the document of arraignment at the earliest possible practicable moment after its appointment. It shall serve, so far as such service can be effected, upon each of the individuals named in the document of arraignment three copies thereof, translated into their native language, at least 15 days prior to the date set for hearing upon the document. The individuals so arraigned shall be required to admit or to deny the several facts set forth in the document of arraignment and be given reasonable opportunity in open court to answer or controvert the facts alleged in the document, to offer evidence relevant to the facts charged in the document, and to be heard in person and by counsel. The Court may receive any evidence which it considers to have probative value and to be relevant. Upon the completion of its hearings it shall indicate by appropriate written findings whether and to what extent it determines the facts set forth in the document of arraignment to be true after giving due weight to the documents submitted in support thereof, which may be taken into consideration as evidence; in the light of any testimony or explanation offered by the persons accused in the document of arraignment; and upon the basis of any facts of which the Court in its discretion may choose to take judicial notice. The facts alleged in the document of arraignment, if verified under oath, upon information and belief, by the four principal members of the Executive Group hereinafter mentioned, shall be taken to be true *prima facie*, and no further evidence in support of their truth shall be required unless the Court shall otherwise direct. The Court shall also determine whether and to what extent the facts alleged and found to be true warrant the punishment of the persons named in the document and may sentence such persons to death or such other punishment as the Court may deem proper, subject only to the written approval of the Control Council for Germany which may approve, reduce,

increase, or otherwise alter such sentences or any of them. Such sentences, when and as approved, and as and if modified, shall be carried out in accordance with the written instructions of the Control Council. The Control Council shall act only by unanimous vote of its members.

DOCUMENT 47

COLONEL R. A. CUTTER TO JOHN J. McCLOY[1]

April 7, 1945

. . . .[2]

Judge Rosenman generally likes the British proposal, subject to three comments.

(1) He feels a military court and not a civil court should try the six or seven principal leaders.

(2) The court should pass sentence and determine punishment, although possibly subject to later approval by the four EAC[3] Governments through the Control Council (Germany).

(3) There must be adequate documentation of the arraignment instrument, so that to prove the accused guilty, no oral testimony will be necessary.

He also feels that approval of this arrangement should not be given unless, for the trial of others than the 6 or 7 top people, the British approve the common enterprise theory.

DOCUMENT 48

THE ARGUMENT FOR SUMMARY PROCESS AGAINST HITLER AND CO.[1]

PREPARED BY THE LORD CHANCELLOR (SIMON)

April 16, 1945

1. H.M.G. assume that it is beyond question that Hitler and a number of arch-criminals associated with him (including Mussolini) must, so far as they fall into Allied hands, suffer the penalty of death for their conduct leading up to the war and for the wickedness which they have either themselves perpe-

trated or have authorised in the conduct of the war. It would be manifestly impossible to punish war criminals of a lower grade by a capital sentence pronounced by a Military Court unless the ringleaders are dealt with with equal severity. This is really involved in the concluding sentence of the Moscow Declaration on this subject, which reserves for the arch-criminals whose offences have no special localisation treatment to be determined in due course by the Allies.

2. It being conceded that these leaders must suffer death, the question arises whether they should be tried by some form of tribunal claiming to exercise judicial functions, or whether the decision taken by the Allies should be reached and enforced without the machinery of a trial. H.M.G. thoroughly appreciate the arguments which have been advanced in favour of some form of preliminary trial. But H.M.G. are also deeply impressed with the dangers and difficulties of this course, and they wish to put before their principal Allies, in a connected form, the arguments which have led them to think that execution without trial is the preferable course.

3. The central consideration for deciding this difficult choice must, in H.M.G.'s view, be reached by asking—what is the real charge which Allied people and the world as a whole make against Hitler? It is the totality of his offences against the international standard which civilized countries try to observe which makes him the guilty man that he is. If he were to be indicted for these offences in the manner that is necessary for reasons of justice in a criminal court, and if his fate is[2] to be determined on the conclusion reached by the tribunal as to the truth of this bundle of charges and the adequacy of the proof, it seems impossible to conceive that the trial would not be exceedingly long and elaborate. He, of course, must have in such a trial all the rights properly conceded to an accused person. He must be defended, if he wishes, by counsel, and he must be allowed to call any relevant evidence. According to British ideas, at any rate, his defence could not be forcibly shut down or limited because it involves great expenditure of time. There is nothing upon which British opinion is more sensitive in the realm of criminal procedure than the suspicion that an accused person on trial—whatever the depths of his crime—has been denied his full defence.

4. There is a further consideration which, in the view of H.M.G. needs to be very carefully weighed. If the method of public trial were adopted, the comment must be expected from the very start to be that the whole thing is a "put-up job" designed by the Allies to justify a punishment they have already resolved on. Hitler and his advisers—if they decide to take part and to challenge what is alleged—may be expected to be very much alive to any opportunity of turning the tables. Public opinion as the trial goes on is likely to weary at the length of the process. It is difficult to think that anybody would in the course of time look on Hitler as an injured man, but it is by no means

unlikely that a long trial will result in a change of public feeling as to the justification of trying Hitler at all. Will not some people begin to say "The man should be shot out of hand"? And if in the complicated and novel procedure which such a trial is bound to adopt—for Russian, American and British ideas must in some way be amalgamated[3]—the defence secured some unexpected point, is there not a danger of the trial being denounced as a farce?

5. There is a further point. Reference has been made above to Hitler's conduct leading up to the war as one of the crimes on which the Allies would rely. There should be included in this the unprovoked attacks which, since the original declaration of war, he has made on various countries. These are not war crimes in the ordinary sense, nor is it at all clear that they can properly be described as crimes under international law. These would, however, necessarily have to be part of the charge and if the tribunal had—as presumably they would have—to proceed according to international law, an argument, which might be a formidable argument, would be open to the accused that this part of the indictment should be struck out. It may well be thought by some that these acts ought to be regarded as crimes under international law. Under the procedure of trial this would be a matter for the tribunal, and would at any rate give the accused the opportunity of basing arguments on what has happened in the past and what has been done by various countries in declaring war which resulted in acquiring new territory, which certainly were not regarded at the time as crimes against international law.

6. H.M.G. earnestly hope that their Allies will consider the arguments set out above for they are most anxious that a very early agreement should be reached as to the method of dealing with Hitler and his chief associates, and that the method should be one in which the principal Allies concur. It would in any case be valuable if a document could now be drawn up giving the reasoned basis for the punishment of the men concerned.[4] It may be worth consideration whether such a document could not be served upon each of these men (the list will have be to agreed) as soon as possible after his capture. He should then be told that if he wishes to make any answer he must do so in writing within, say, 14 days, and that his answer will be submitted to the Government in whose charge he was, and that the principal Allies would thereafter promulgate their decision upon his case. This suggested procedure would not be, of course, in the nature of a trial and would not involve the attempt to set up a judicial tribunal, but it would give the accused the opportunity of putting forward what he wished to say, and might conceivably, in some cases, influence the decision.

S.

DOCUMENT 49

THE PUNISHMENT OF THOSE GUILTY OF WAR CRIMES AND ATROCITIES IS FOR CRIMINAL VIOLATION OF INTERNATIONAL LAW:[1]

(Prepared In Assistant Secretary Of War's Office)

April 20, 1945

The Allied promises to bring the major Axis leaders to justice rests squarely on the ground that these leaders have been responsible for crimes, acts which violate generally accepted standards of the conduct of nations—not only during the war but in preparing for it and starting it. Those standards are defined partly by custom; partly by treaties; but, in any event, they constitute law, the violation of which is regarded by the world as criminal.

Punishment for Crime Should Only Follow a Judicial Trial:

No principle of justice is so fundamental in most men's minds as the rule that punishment will be inflicted by judicial action and only for a violation of existing law which sets a standard of conduct. Judicial punishment is imposed only after notice to the accused of the charges against him, establishment of the facts upon which the charges rest, and an opportunity to defend against the charges, preferably with the advice of counsel. The form in which proof is presented varies from nation to nation. So does the extent of the opportunity to defend, the nature of the hearing, and the incidence of the burden of proof. This principle is applied in greater or less degree by all nations, and historically its recognition is the first step in the approach to the democratic standard of liberty under law.

Political Disposition Involves Resort to Primitive Practices:

Accordingly, there normally would be no doubt that even the worst of the Axis leaders, falling into Allied custody, would be entitled to be put upon his trial, if charged with offenses under the laws and customs of war. Any other method of punishment involves resort to primitive practices of murdering helpless prisoners. It is a reverting to the bare concept of might based on force. There is no real middle ground. In Caesar's day the enemy were treated as enemies, i.e. slaughtered out of hand if they were not enslaved. In Napoleonic times there was banishment and imprisonment by what was called political action—now, if political action is taken, we would impose death—surely this is retrogression rather than progress. Even in Napoleon's day such political action was applauded only in England. Napoleon's case, however, provides no real precedent except as a method of getting a threat to the peace of the world to a place where he could cause no trouble. It was not, and was not regarded as the punishment of a man for crimes he had committed.[2]

Punishment of War Criminals Is Designed as a Deterrent and to Raise International Standards of Conduct:

Punishment of war criminals is justified primarily by its deterrent effect, by the impetus which it gives to improved standards of international conduct and, if the theory of punishment is broad enough, by the implicit condemnation of ruthlessness and excessive force as instruments of attaining national ends. The satisfaction of instincts of revenge and retribution for the sake of retribution are obviously no sound basis of punishment. If punishment is to lead to progress, it must be carried out in a manner which world opinion will regard as progressive and as consistent with the fundamental morality of the Allied cause. A purely political disposition of the Axis leaders without trial, however disguised, will be regarded eventually, and probably immediately, as a descent to the methods of the Axis itself. It will retard progress towards a new concept of international obligations simply because those who have sought in this war to preserve democracy will have made their most spectacular dealing with the vanquished, a negation of democratic principles of justice. They will have adopted methods repugnant alike to Anglo-American and Continental traditions.

The Method of Punishment Adopted Must Not Detract from the Moral Force Behind the Allied Cause:

The preservation of the moral force behind the Allied cause is important. That force, born from the exigencies of self defence, has brought freedom-loving peoples together and can keep them together. If we lose it in the matter of punishing war criminals, we sacrifice a part of something very precious. Only the most imperative reasons could conceivably justify such action.

The Verdict of History upon the Fairness of the Disposition of War Criminals Has Practical Significance:

A further highly important reason for adopting a fair judicial method of bringing war criminals to justice is that such methods are more likely than any others to commend themselves to the judgment of history. What future generations think of Allied action on war criminals may have a profound effect upon the preservation of peace in years to come. That action certainly will set the tone of the Allied occupation of Germany by showing that a government of laws and not of men has begun. A political disposition of the Axis leaders, on the other hand, would look like, and would be, a continuation of totalitarian practices. One has only to remember the confusing propaganda interpretations of the Versailles Treaty to realize what might be[3] the disastrous results of action dictated by politics and not by[4] fundamental principles of law and justice. If our actions are soundly conceived, however, we have before us an opportunity to mark up an important step in the obtaining [of] future world security[5]—a step which may in effect be of even greater significance than what may evolve from Dumbarton Oaks.[6] Punishment following a judicial determination, in which a number of nations participate, to the effect that the alleged violations of international law have occurred, will certainly induce future government leaders to think before they act in similar fashion.

Arguments Advanced against Trails for the Axis Arch-Criminals:

The arguments advanced against some proper trial for the Axis leaders seem to come to this—*First*, that the trial might be one, lasting almost indefinitely, in which all sorts of irrelevant matters might be discussed, producing a fertile field for controversy and possibly leading to adverse world reactions; *second*, that attempts to restrict the trial to a reasonable length and to matters which are relevant might lead to a trial which is a mere travesty upon Anglo-American ideals of judicial inquiry. The fear really is that the trial will be either (1) a prolonged "State" trial, unsatisfactory to the Allies and providing Hitler and his associates[7] with an effective sounding board for propaganda and an easy road to martyrdom, or (2) an inadequate substitute for our traditional procedures which the world will brand as an attempted fraud.

Both these objections are mere arguments against the ability of Allied legal brains to produce a fair, expeditious, reasonable procedure to meet the novel situation which is presented. As a problem of pure procedure it obviously can be solved. If a proper procedure is devised, an Allied military tribunal can administer it with fairness, dignity and swiftness and give in substance and not merely in form, a trial and decision as impartial as it lies within the ability of humans to provide. There are few issues of fact which cannot be tried in a reasonable time and, if the military judges properly control the trial, the accused should receive a fair hearing without unduly prolonged discussion of wholly irrelevant matters. The advantages of the trial over political action are so fundamental that we should not allow the bug-a-boos of possible embarrassments to hinder us from establishing the principle. More is involved than convenience and avoiding the chance of Nazi propaganda and countercharges.

It should not shock anyone that a trial before an Allied military tribunal should have some aspects drawn from the Continental and Slavic systems. The United States and the United Kingdom cannot insist on the full, rigid application of Anglo-American procedures, the rules of evidence, the privilege against self incrimination and similar matters. These are not inherent parts of other systems of criminal practice and there is no need for leaning over backward to give the Axis leaders the benefit of protective principles, not afforded by German law, even prior to Axis distortion of German justice. They need only have a fair trial—and procedures should properly partake of elements of Russian and French legal customs. Of course, the accused while in custody should not be subjected to duress or to any essentially unfair or unreasonable inquisition.[8]

A final objection is raised that there can be no real trial when the real offense for which Hitler and the other Axis leaders are being tried, is the totality of what they have done to the world since 1933. It is true that all that the Axis has done should be brought into the grounds of punishment. The offenses charged should include the preparation for war, the prewar atrocities and the launching of aggressive war in violation of Germany's treaty obligations as well as the ruthless conduct of war in violation of international law and custom. The very breadth of the offense, however, is not in itself argument against judicial action. It is a most important reason for a trial, for it is highly desirable that there be established and declared by actual decision, after adequate hearing and determination of the facts, the principles of international law applicable to the broad, vicious Nazi enterprise. In texture and application, this law will be novel because the scope of the Nazi activity has been broad and ruthless without precedent. The basic principles to be applied, however, are not novel and all that is needed is a wise application of those principles on a sufficiently comprehensive scale to meet the situation. International law must develop to meet the needs of the times just as the common law has grown, not by enunciating new principles but by adapting old ones. By including within the general area of punishable international crimes the violation of compacts, there will be world judicial condemnation of depredations so great and so violent that international security cannot exist if they should be permitted to continue unchecked. The law should be supple enough to cope with the totality of the offense and though the most solid basis for prosecution under existing law relates to the violations of actual and recognized rules of war, the full offense covers so obviously areas wider than this limited field that it is natural and proper in this day and age that we must deal with those too.

DOCUMENT 50

MEMORANDUM OF PROPOSALS FOR THE PROSECUTION AND PUNISHMENT OF CERTAIN WAR CRIMINALS AND OTHER OFFENDERS[1]

April 25–30, 1945

I. The Moscow Declaration Did Not Cover the Whole Problem of the Trial and Punishment of War Criminals.

In the statement jointly issued by President Roosevelt, Premier Stalin and Prime Minister Churchill on 1 November 1943, usually referred to as the Moscow Declaration, it was announced that those members of the Hitlerite forces who have been responsible for, or have taken a consenting part in, atrocities and war crimes in territory occupied by the Axis forces, would be sent back to the countries in which their abominable deeds were done in order that they may be judged according to the laws of those countries. It is assumed for the purposes of this memorandum that the four principal Allies will cooperate in carrying out this policy set out in the Moscow Declaration and also that the several Allies will cooperate fully in arranging for the trial and punishment by the United Nation concerned (or before an Allied military tribunal) of those Hitlerite nationals who have committed war offenses anywhere against the civilians or soldiers of any United Nation.

No policy, however, was fixed in the Moscow Declaration covering

a. the punishment of the major war criminals, whose offenses have no particular geographical localization, beyond the announcement that they would be punished by joint decision of the Governments of the Allies; or

b. the methods of punishment of those members of the principal Nazi organizations, [such as] the Gestapo and S.S., who [voluntarily] engaged in carrying out the ruthless policies of the Nazi regime but who cannot readily be ~~identified with particular war crimes~~ [proved to have participated personally in the execution of specific atrocities].

II. Summary of Proposals

This memorandum proposes that the following policy be adopted by the Governments of the United States, the Soviet Union, and the United Kingdom, and the Provisional Government of France for the trial of

a. the major Nazi leaders ~~for their instigation of~~ [and their principal accomplices in] the broad program of war crimes and atrocities which have characterized the Nazi regime since 1933 and

b. the principal Nazi organizations and their members, through whom the most bestial of the Nazi cruelties have been put into effect.

Considerations Taken into Account in Framing the Proposals

The proposals now advanced give recognition to the following facts:

a. That the criminality of the German leaders and their associates does not consist solely of individual outrages, but represents the result of a systematic and planned reign of terror within Germany and within the areas occupied by German military forces, in connection with which the crimes and atrocities referred to were committed;

b. that these crimes and atrocities were perpetrated pursuant to a premeditated criminal plan;

c. that for the carrying out of the acts of oppression and terrorism which their program involved, the Nazi leaders and their associates created and utilized a numerous organization, chief among which are the S.S., and the Gestapo, and

d. that there is necessity for establishing practical measures for bringing these criminals, their principal organizations, and their active leaders and members to justice on a basis ~~which establishes the guilt of the Hitlerites not only~~ [takes adequate account not only] (1) for [of] those offenses committed [within and] outside Germany, during the war or against the citizens of the United Nations, but also (2) ~~for~~ [of] those atrocities, both before and after 1939, committed against [members of] Axis minorities.

Proposed Policy

1. The Axis leaders should be tried before Allied military tribunals composed of officers of the four principal Allies. Their guilt and punishment should be determined by *judicial* action of a military tribunal and not by political action of the Allied Governments. (See discussion below Part IV . . .)[2]

2. Either in separate trials, or at the same time the leaders of the principal Hitlerite organizations (e.g., the Gestapo and the S.S.) and the organizations themselves should be tried before an Allied military tribunal. This tribunal should determine [both the guilt of the individual leaders and] the extent of the participation of each of these organizations and its members in the great Nazi criminal enterprise, of which the crimes and atrocities which have shocked the world were [an integral part or at least] the natural and probable consequence. (See discussion below Part III, Section B . . .)[3]

3. The extent of the guilt of the individual members of the Hitlerite organizations, which may be found to have participated in the Nazi enterprise, should be determined and the individual members should be punished in a manner based upon the extent of their guilt. (See discussion below, Part III, Section C . . .)[4]

4. An Allied executive group, composed of representatives of the four principal Allies, should be established to prepare the charges against the Hitlerite leaders and the organizations, to collect and present the evidence in support of those charges and to conduct their prosecution. (See discussion below, Part V.)

The proposals now advanced contemplate that the four principal allies will enter into an executive or military agreement embodying the foregoing policies, to which the other United Nations will be invited to adhere after the agreement has been negotiated and signed. Prior participation by the other United Nations in the negotiation of the agreement is probably not appropriate because the agreement will be largely a matter affecting the four nations engaged in the occupation of Germany and because of the necessity for speed in reaching agreement.

III. The Trial and Punishment of the Hitlerite Leaders and the Major Hitlerite Organizations Should Be Based upon Their Voluntary Participation in a Common [Criminal] Enterprise of Which the Axis Atrocities and ~~War Crimes Were [an Integral Part (or at Least)~~[5] and] the Probable Consequence.

A. Method of Determining Guilt.

After Germany's defeat or unconditional surrender, the Allies by joint action, pursuant to treaty or otherwise, could probably agree to put to death the most notorious Nazi criminals without trial. Such action, however, would be violative of concepts of justice, which the freedom loving United Nations accept and, on that account, would be distasteful and inappropriate. For reasons more fully stated in Part IV of this memorandum, it is felt that all reasonable efforts should be made to avoid such a purely political disposition of the Nazi leaders. Instead, it should be possible to determine upon a suitable judicial process more in accord with the common traditions of the principal United Nations.

It is believed that a military tribunal is the appropriate type of court for this judicial action for the following reasons:

a. The ~~principal~~ offenses of the Axis leaders and their organizations which will be the subject of judicial inquiry will be [largely] war crimes properly cognizable by a military tribunal. ~~The other offenses to be tried are closely related to the strictly military offenses.~~

b. The trials will take place as a part in connection with a military occupation of Germany and Austria.

c. The crimes to be punished are atrocities which should be dealt with by the swift justice of a military tribunal created by simple military or executive agreement. The prosecutions should not be subject to the delays inherent ~~either~~ in the formal setting up of an international treaty court[.] ~~or in remitting the cases to any national civil court.~~

B. Nature of the Charges to be Made.

For the systematic and planned policy of oppression and aggression both within Germany and against Germany's neighbors, the Nazi leaders and the whole membership of the principal Nazi organizations share responsibility. The leaders and their organization must be made to pay the penalties which international law and the laws and customs of war exact for war crimes and atrocities [contemplated by their program and perpetrated in its execution.] ~~of the type which were the natural and probable consequence of such a program.~~ It should be remembered that in this program members of the S.S. and the Gestapo, as volunteers pledged to absolute obedience, joined, with their leaders.

Accordingly, the Government of the United States advances for consideration a plan which in no way would interfere with the punishment of individual Hitlerites at the scene of their crimes for specific atrocities which they have committed. Neither would it interfere with separate trials of the principal Nazi leaders before Allied military tribunals if that is considered desirable. Indeed such separate trials might have substantial advantage in that they can be conducted quickly and without awaiting final disposition of the trial of the charges of the common criminal enterprise of the whole Hitler[6] hierarchy of criminals. The plan proposed, however, would ensure the punishment of the Nazi leaders and the active members of the principal Nazi organizations for the program in which they have played the major part.

The German leaders and their associates and the organizations employed by them should be charged with the commission of their atrocious crimes, and also with joint participation in a broad criminal enterprise which included and intended these crimes, or was reasonably calculated ~~or likely~~ to bring them about. The allegation of the criminal enterprise should be so couched as to permit full proof of the entire Nazi plan from its inception and the means used in its furtherance and execution, including the pre-war atrocities and those committed against their own nationals, neutrals, and stateless persons, as well as the waging of an illegal war of aggression with ruthless disregard for international law and the rules of war. There should be invoked the rule of liability, common to most penal systems and included in the general doctrine of the laws of war, that those who participate in the formulation and execution of a criminal plan involving multiple crimes are jointly liable for each of the offenses committed and jointly responsible for the acts of each other. In support of this charge there should be admitted in evidence the acts of any of the conspirators done in furtherance of the conspiracy,[7] whether or not these acts were in themselves criminal and subject to separate prosecution as such.

C. TRIAL OF THE CHARGES.

The trial of the charges described in the preceding paragraph should be carried out in two stages:

> a. *Stage 1*—There should be brought before an international military tribunal the highest ranking German leaders to a number fairly representative of the groups and organizations charged with complicity in the basic criminal plan. (As stated above, this need not preclude separate prior trial of particular German leaders if that is deemed desirable.) Adjudication should be sought not only of the guilt of those individuals physically before the tribunal, but also of the complicity of the members of the organizations included within the charge. The tribunal should make findings adjudicating the facts established, including the nature and purposes of the criminal plan, the identity of the groups and organizations guilty, of complicity in it, and the acts committed in its execution. The tribunal should sentence those individual defendants physically before it who are convicted.

The above, which might take place in one or more trials, should complete the mission of this international tribunal.

> b. *Stage 2*—~~Thereafter, other individuals charged with specific atrocities and members of the organizations who are charged with complicity through such membership in the basic criminal plan but against whom there is not sufficient proof of specific atrocities should, unless held for trial by one of the United Nations or sent back for trial under the provisions of the Moscow Declaration, be brought before occupation or other appropriate tribunals. The findings of the tribunal in the~~ [Without prejudice to the trial of individuals charged with specific atrocities before any suitable tribunal, the members of the organizations who are charged with complicity through such membership in the basic criminal plan but against whom there is not sufficient proof of personal participation in specific atrocities should be brought before occupation or other appropriate tri-

bunals. The findings of the tribunal in the][8] trial provided for in paragraph *a* above should be taken to constitute a general adjudication of the criminal character of the groups and organizations referred to, binding upon all the members thereof in their subsequent trials in occupation tribunals or in other tribunals established under this instrument. In these subsequent trials the only necessary proof of guilt of any particular defendant, as regards the charge of complicity, should be his membership in one of those organizations. Proof should also be taken of the nature and extent of the individual's participation.

c. The defendant in each case should, upon conviction, suffer death or such other punishment as the tribunal may direct, depending upon the gravity of the offense and the degree of culpability of the defendant. In general, except upon proof of very substantial individual participation in specific atrocities, the less prominent defendants might well be sentenced to perform useful reparational labor, etc., rather than to capital punishment.

D. Procedures.

Any military or executive agreement should include an undertaking to adopt and apply comprehensively in the trial of war criminals, to the greatest extent practicable, expeditious, fair, non-technical procedures which would (in a manner consistent with the purposes of the agreement):

a. provide each accused with notice of the charges against him and an opportunity to be heard reasonably on such charges;

b. permit the court to admit any evidence which it considers would have probative value;

c. except as the court in its discretion shall deem appropriate in particular cases, exclude any defense based upon the fact that the accused acted under orders of a superior officer or pursuant to state or national policy;

d. exclude any defense based upon the fact that the accused is or was the head or purported head or other principal official of a state; and

e. confine trials strictly to an expeditious hearing of the issues raised by the charges.

IV. The Guilt and Punishment of the Hitlerite Leaders Should Be Determined Judicially before an Allied Military Tribunal and Not by Purely Political Action:[9]

It may be argued that the Axis leaders should be dealt with politically rather than judicially and that, without trial, by joint action of the Allies they should be put to death upon capture. The United States is vigorously opposed to any such political disposition. Because great importance is attached to judicial action, the arguments in favor of a swift but fair trial of the Hitlerite criminals, are set out below in considerable detail:

A. The Punishment of Those Guilty of War Crimes and Atrocities Is for Criminal Violation of International Law:

The Allied promises to bring the major Axis leaders to justice rest squarely on the ground that these leaders have been responsible for crimes [—] acts which violate generally accepted standards of the conduct of [individuals and] nations [—] not only during the war but in preparing for it and starting it. ~~These~~ [The violation of these] ~~standards are defined partly by custom, partly by treaties, but, in any event, they constitute law, the violation of which~~ is regarded by the world as criminal.

B. Punishment for Crime Should Only Follow a Judicial Trial:

No principle of justice is so fundamental in most men's minds as the rule that punishment will be inflicted by judicial action. Judicial punishment is imposed only after notice to the accused of the charges against him, establishment of the facts upon which the charges rest, and an opportunity to defend against the charges with the advice of counsel. The form in which proof is presented varies from nation to nation. So does the precise extent of the opportunity to defend, the nature of the hearing, and the incidence of the burden of proof. This principle is applied in greater or less degree by all nations, and historically its recognition is the first step in the approach to the democratic standard of liberty under law.

C. ~~Political Disposition Involves Resort to Primitive Practices:~~

~~Accordingly, there normally would be no doubt that even the worst of the Axis leaders, falling into Allied custody, would be entitled to be put upon his trial, if charged with offenses under the laws and customs of war. Any other method of punishment involves resort to primitive practices of might based on force. There is no real middle ground. In Caesar's day the enemy were treated as enemies; i.e., slaughtered out of hand if they were not enslaved. In Napoleonic times there was banishment and imprisonment by what was called political action,—now, if political action is taken, we would impose death—surely this is retrogression rather than progress. Even in Napoleon's day such political action was little applauded. Napoleon's case, however, provides no real precedent except as a method of getting a man who was a threat to the peace of the world to a place where he could cause no trouble. It was not, and was not regarded as, the punishment of a man for crimes he had committed.~~

~~D~~. [C] Punishment of War Criminals Is Designed as a Deterrent and to Raise International Standards of Conduct:

Punishment of war criminals should be motivated primarily by its deterrent effect, by the impetus which it gives to improved standards of international conduct and, if the theory of punishment is broad enough, by the implicit condemnation of ruthlessness and unlawful force as instruments of attaining national ends. The satisfaction of instincts of revenge and retribution for the sake of retribution are obviously the least sound basis of punishment. If punishment is to lead to progress, it must be carried out in a manner which world opinion will regard as progressive and as consistent with the fundamental morality of the Allied cause.[10] A purely political disposition of the Axis leaders without trial, however disguised, ~~will~~ [may] be regarded eventually, and probably immediately, as ~~a descent to~~ [adoption of] the methods of the Axis itself. It will retard progress towards a new concept of international obligations simply because those who have sought in this war to preserve democracy will have made their most spectacular dealing with the vanquished a negation of democratic principles of justice. They will have adopted methods repugnant alike to Anglo-American and Continental traditions.

E.[11] The Method of Punishment Adopted Must Not Detract from the Moral Force behind the Allied Cause:

The preservation of the moral force behind the Allied cause is important. That force, born from the exigencies of self defense, has brought freedom-loving peoples together and can keep them together. If we lose it in the matter of punishing war criminals, we sacrifice a part of something very precious. Only the most imperative reasons could conceivably justify such action.

F. The Verdict of History upon the Fairness of the Disposition of War Criminals Has Practical Significance:

A further highly important reason for adopting a fair judicial method of bringing war criminals to justice is that such methods are more likely than any others to commend themselves to the judgment of history. What future generations think of Allied action on war criminals may have a profound effect upon the preservation of peace in years to come. That action certainly will set the tone of the Allied occupation of Germany by showing that a government of laws and not of men has begun. A political disposition of the Axis leaders, on the other hand, would look like, and would be, a continuation of totalitarian practices. One has only to remember the confusing propaganda interpretations of the Versailles Treaty to realize what might be the disastrous results of action dictated by politics and not by fundamental principles of law and justice. If Allied actions are soundly conceived, however, there exists an opportunity to mark up an important step in the obtaining of future world security. Punishment following a judicial determination, in which a number of nations participate, to the effect that the alleged violations of international law have occurred, will certainly induce future government leaders to think before they act in similar fashion. It will serve also to bring home the truth to those Germans who remain incredulous about the infamies of the Nazi regime.[12]

G. The Arguments Advanced against Trials for the Axis Arch-Criminals Are Not Persuasive:

The arguments which may be advanced against some proper trial for the Axis leaders must come to this—First, that the trial might be one, lasting almost indefinitely, in which all sorts of irrelevant matters might be discussed, producing a fertile field for controversy and possibly leading to adverse world reactions; second, that attempts to restrict the trial to a reasonable length and to matters which are relevant might lead to a trial which is a mere travesty upon Allied ideals of judicial inquiry. The fear really is that the trial will be either (1) a prolonged "State" trial, unsatisfactory to the Allies and providing Hitler and his associates with an effective sounding board for propaganda and an easy road to martyrdom, or (2) an inadequate substitute for our traditional procedures which the world will brand as an attempted fraud.

Both these objections are mere arguments against the ability of Allied legal brains to produce a fair, expeditious, reasonable procedure to meet the novel situation which is presented. As a problem of pure procedure it obviously can be solved. If a proper procedure is devised, an Allied military tribunal can administer it with fairness, dignity and swiftness and give, in substance and not merely in form, a trial and decision as impartial as it lies within the ability of humans to provide. There are few issues of fact which cannot be tried in a reasonable time, and, if the military judges properly control the trial, the accused should receive a fair hearing without unduly prolonged discussion of wholly irrelevant matters. The advantages of the trial method over political action are so fundamental that we should not allow the bug-a-boos of possible embarrassments to hinder us from establishing the principle. More is involved than convenience and avoiding the chance of Nazi propaganda and countercharges.

It should not shock anyone that a trial before an Allied military tribunal should have some aspects based upon common law traditions and some drawn from the Continental and Slavic systems.[13] For example, the United States and the United Kingdom cannot insist on the full, rigid application of Anglo-American procedures, the rules of evidence, the privilege against self incrimination and similar matters. These are not inherent parts of other systems of criminal practice and there is no need for leaning over backward to give the Axis leaders the benefit of protective principles, not afforded by German law, even prior to Axis distortion of German justice. The Hitlerites need only have a fair trial. Similarly, those raised in the Russian and Continental systems of law cannot properly object to having the methods of trial influenced by common law principles to some extent. The trial should be an Allied venture, reflecting the influence of the systems of justice in force in all four of the principal Allied nations. Of course, the accused while in custody should not be subjected to duress or to any essentially unfair or unreasonable inquisition and the trial in all respects should be conducted justly and impartially.[14]

A final objection may be raised that there can be no real trial when the real offense, for which Hitler and the other Axis leaders are being tried, is the totality of what they have done to the world since 1933. It is true that all that the Axis has done should be brought into the grounds of punishment. The offenses charged should include the preparation for war, the prewar atrocities and the launching of aggressive war in violation of Germany's treaty obligations as well as the ruthless conduct of war in violation of international law and custom.

Principal emphasis, doubtless, will be placed in the trial upon those patent violations of the customs of war which most shock the Allies (e.g., murder of prisoners of war, abuse of populations in occupied territories, deportation of Allied peoples for use as slave labor, etc.)[15] Nevertheless, these offences were only a part of the whole ghastly Hitlerite enterprise, ~~of which these offenses were the inevitable consequence.~~ The[se] particular atrocities color the ~~Hitlerite~~ enterprise and make the whole ~~enterprise~~ [of it] so clearly a criminal ~~violation of international law,~~ that the whole enterprise should be included in the charges and revealed in the trial.

The very breadth of the offense, however, is not in itself an argument against judicial action. It is a most important reason for a trial, for it is highly desirable that there be established and declared by actual decision, after adequate hearing and determination of the facts, the principles of international law applicable to the broad, vicious Nazi enterprise. ~~In texture and~~ [The] application [of] this law ~~will~~ [may] be novel because the scope of the Nazi activity has been broad and ruthless without precedent. The basic principles to be applied, however, are not novel and all that is needed is a wise application of those principles on a sufficiently comprehensive scale to meet the situation. International law must develop to meet the needs of the times just as the common law has grown, not by enunciating new principles but by adapting old ones. By including within the general area of punishable international crimes the violation of compacts, there will be world judicial condemnation of depredations so great and so violent that international security cannot exist if they should be permitted to continue unchecked. The law should be supple enough to cope with the totality of the offense and though the most solid basis for prosecution under existing law relates to the violations of actual and recognized rules of war, the full offense covers so obviously areas wider than this limited field that it is natural and proper in this day and age that we must deal with those too.

V. There Is Immediate Need of an Allied Executive Prosecuting and Planning Organization to Deal with the Principal War Crimes Trials and Related Problems:

1. In the trial of the Hitlerite leaders no charges which cannot be proved should be presented and the theory of prosecution should rest upon ascertainable facts. The actual trial of cases must be planned and conducted by persons familiar with the techniques of the expeditious presentation of intricate causes. Accordingly, there should be created to take charge of preparations for the major trials, an Allied executive or planning group consisting of one representative each of the United States, the Soviet Union, the British Commonwealth and France. This group should be assisted by an adequate staff of attorneys and research personnel to compile and analyze data, prepare the charges in the principal case or cases to conform to the proof and arrange the evidence for presentation to the international military tribunal.

So far as the operations of this executive group are carried out within Germany or Austria, such operations might appropriately be subject to the Administrative direction of the Control Council for Germany or for Austria, as the case may be.

2. The presentation of the principal case or cases before the international tribunal should be made by persons designated by the United States, the Soviet Union, the British Commonwealth and France, each of these countries being entitled to designate one person, who might be its member of the executive group referred to in the preceding paragraph.

3. The full time executive group might also be charged with:

a. the recommendation to the appropriate governmental authorities of agreements and measures supplemental to or in addition to the agreement, necessary or appropriate to accomplish its objectives, and

b. the maintenance of liaison among and with the appropriate military and civil agencies, authorities and commissions of or representing any of the United Nations which are or may be charged with responsibility for any matters dealt with in the agreement.

4. *Expenses*—Any military or executive agreement should make suitable provision for the payment of the expenses of the prosecution and the executive group.

DOCUMENT 51

PUNISHMENT OF WAR CRIMINALS[1]

REDRAFT BY COLONEL CUTTER

April 28, 1945

The United Nations have on various occasions expressed their abhorrence for the unspeakable crimes and atrocities of which the German leaders and their associates are guilty, and have pledged themselves that those responsible for such crimes and atrocities shall not escape punishment.

The United Kingdom, the United States, and the Soviet Union in the Declaration issued at Moscow November 1, 1943 stated:

(1) that those German officers and men who have been responsible for or have taken a consenting part in these atrocities "will be sent back to the countries in which their abominable deeds were done in order that they may be judged and punished according to the laws of these liberated countries and of the free governments which will be created therein"; and
(2) that the above declaration was "without prejudice to the case of the major criminals, whose offenses have no particular geographical localization and who will be punished by the joint declaration of the Governments of the Allies."

The criminality of the German leaders and their associates does not consist solely of individual outrages, but represents the result of a systematic and planned reign of terror within Germany and within the areas occupied by German military forces, in connection with which the crimes and atrocities referred to were committed. It is apparent that these crimes and atrocities were perpetrated pursuant to a premeditated criminal plan.

For the carrying out of the acts of oppression and terrorism which their program involved, the Nazi leaders and their associates created and utilized a numerous organization, chief among which are the SS and the Gestapo.

Having in view the foregoing, and in order to press on with the necessary practical measures to bring to justice the criminals referred to, the governments of the Union of Socialist Soviet Republics, the United States of America, the United Kingdom of Great Britain and Northern Ireland, and the Provisional Government of the French Republic, acting by their respective duly authorized representatives, have agreed upon the following:

I

ARRAIGNMENT AND TRIAL OF PRINCIPAL AXIS LEADERS

1. The executive group mentioned in Article IV below, subject to the approval of the Governments represented on the group, shall prepare a document of arraignment (hereafter called the arraignment)[2] setting forth the offenses which the United Nations allege that Hitler, Mussolini, Goebbels, Himmler, Ribbentrop, Goering, and possibly a certain few others of the principal Nazi and Fascist leaders have committed, caused or permitted. The arraignment shall set forth in adequate detail the principal facts of the great Nazi criminal enterprise from its inception through the whole of its attempted execution, including among other things—

a. The program of persecutions of minority groups in Germany and the occupied countries;

b. The encouragement of internal disorders in countries bordering upon Germany with a view to making them easy prey for the Nazi invader.

c. The treacherous invasion by force, or threat of force, of neighboring countries in violation of international customs and treaties;

d. The initiation and waging of a ruthless war of aggression in deliberate and calculated disregard and violation of treaties and international law;

e. The murder and deliberate mistreatment of prisoners of war and displaced persons;

f. The cruel and relentless oppression of the nationals of territories occupied by the Germans in violation of international conventions and practices and in gross disregard of the laws and customs of war, including, among other things, the initiation of a reign of terror, the enslavement of subject peoples, the unlawful confiscation and looting of private and public property, the unreasonable administration of military occupation, the wanton destruction of towns and villages, the murder, rape and despoilment of the inhabitants, the deportation of peoples, the unreasonable and excessive punishment of individuals for the acts of others for which they were in no way responsible, and the ruthless program of mass extermination in these occupied areas.

2. Each phase of the arraignment shall be supported by reports of investigations, authentic original documents, records, photographs, affidavits and accurate statements of the particular facts and circumstances alleged therein, with a view to setting forth, in the form of a complete *dossier* of reliable documents, a comprehensive analysis and proof of the totality of the criminal and uncivilized acts for which the freedom loving nations of the world are in duty bound to call upon the principal Nazi aggressors to make an accounting and to bring them to trial.

3. An Allied military court of four members shall be appointed by the Control Council for Germany, for the purpose of examining the arraignment, causing written notice thereof to be given to the persons accused therein, and presiding at the trial of such accused persons at which they shall be given fair opportunity to be heard personally and by counsel with respect to the facts charged therein. Each member of the Control Council shall designate one member of the Court.[3] The military court may sit in any zone in Germany, Austria or Italy or in the territory of any one of the United Nations which shall adhere to this agreement, with the consent of any such nation. It shall have within Germany, Austria and Italy (and elsewhere to the extent permitted by the laws of the territory in question) the power to summon witnesses and to compel their attendance, to require the production of documents, to administer oaths, to appoint special masters and other officers, to hold hearings, to make or cause to be made investigations as to the facts set forth in the arraignment and generally to exercise plenary judicial authority with respect to its subject matter, in a manner consistent with the provisions of this agreement.

4. The Court shall proceed with its duties expeditiously with a view to completing at the earliest practicable moment the trial of the accused persons upon the charges set out in the arraignment. So far as such service can be effected, it shall serve three copies of the arraignment, and its supporting documents, at least 20 days prior to the date set for hearing upon the arraignment, upon each of the individuals named therein. Such copies shall be translated into the native language of the persons named. The accused persons shall be required to admit or to deny in writing the several facts set forth in the document of arraignment within 15 days after service of the arraignment upon them and to state the names and addresses of any witnesses whom they wish to call in their defense and the substance of the testimony which each shall present.[4] The Court shall then fix a reasonable limit of time within which the several persons arraigned may attempt in open court to controvert, and offer relevant evidence with respect to, the facts charged in the document and be heard in person and by counsel. The Court shall have full power to determine what evidence has probative value and is relevant, and, among other evidence, may give weight, as it may deem proper, to (a) the documents submitted in support of the arraignment; (b) any facts of which the Court in its discretion may decide to take judicial notice. The Court shall determine whether and to what extent the facts warrant the punishment of the persons named in the arraignment and may recommend to the Control Council such sentences as it may deem proper, subject only to the written approval of the Control Council for Germany which may approve, reduce, or otherwise alter such sentences or any of them. Such sentences, when and as

approved, shall be carried into execution in accordance with the written orders of the Control Council.

II

CHARGES AGAINST CERTAIN NAZI ORGANIZATIONS AND THEIR MEMBERS

The German leaders (but without prejudice to the trial of the arraignment of any of them in accordance with Article I) and associates, and the organizations employed by them, such as those referred to in the preamble of this Agreement, will be charged with the commission of their atrocious crimes, and also with joint participation in a broad criminal enterprise which included and intended these crimes, or was reasonably calculated or likely to bring them about. The allegation of the criminal enterprise will be so couched as to permit full proof of the entire Nazi plan from its inception and the means used in its furtherance and execution, including the pre-war atrocities and those committed against their own nationals, neutrals, and stateless persons, as well as the waging of an illegal war of aggression with ruthless disregard for international law and the rules of war. There will be invoked the rule of liability, common to all penal systems and included in the general doctrines of the laws of war, that those who participate in the formulation and execution of a criminal plan involving multiple crimes are jointly liable for each of the offenses committed and jointly responsible for the acts of each other. In support of this charge there will be admitted in evidence the acts of any of the conspirators done in furtherance of the conspiracy, whether or not these acts were in themselves criminal and subject to separate prosecution as such.

III

TRIAL OF ORGANIZATIONS AND THEIR MEMBERS

The trial of the charge described in Article II and the determination of the guilty parties shall be carried out in two stages:

(a) Stage 1—There will be brought before an international tribunal to be created high ranking German leaders, other than those already arraigned and punished, in the manner provided in Article I, to a number fairly representative of the groups and organizations charged with complicity in the basic criminal plan. Adjudication will be sought not only of the guilt of those individuals physically before the tribunal, but also of the complicity of the members of the organizations included within the charge. The tribunal will make findings adjudicating the facts established, including the nature and purposes of the criminal plan, the identity of the groups and organizations guilty of complicity in it, and the acts committed in its execution. The tribunal will sentence those individual defendants physically before it who are convicted.

The above, which may take place in one or more trials, will complete the mission of this international tribunal.

(b) Stage 2—Thereafter there will be brought before occupation or other appropriate tribunals:

(1) other individuals charged with specific atrocities, unless held for trial by one of the United Nations or sent back for trial under the provisions of the Moscow Declaration; and

(2) persons, against whom there is not sufficient proof of specific atrocities, who are members of those organizations (or sections of organizations) which have been adjudicated to be criminal in the Stage 1 proceedings, and who through such membership are charged with complicity in the basic criminal plan.

The findings of the tribunal in the trial provided for in paragraph (a) of this Article III will be taken to constitute a general adjudication of the criminal character of the groups and organizations referred to in such findings, binding upon all the members thereof in their subsequent trials in occupation tribunals or in other tribunals established under this instrument. In these subsequent trials the only necessary proof of guilt of any particular defendant, as regards the charge of complicity, will be his membership in one of those organizations. Proof will also be taken of the nature and extent of the individual's participation.

(c) The defendant in each case shall, upon conviction, suffer death or such punishment as the tribunal may direct, depending upon the gravity of the offense, the degree of culpability of the defendant.

IV

TRIBUNAL FOR TRIAL OF NAZI ORGANIZATIONS AND THEIR MEMBERS

The tribunal for the trial of the individuals and organizations charged with the basic crime referred to in Articles II and III (a) shall be a military tribunal which shall consist of four members, to be appointed as follows: one each by the representatives on the Control Council for Germany of the Soviet Union, the United States, the British Commonwealth and France.[5]

The members of the tribunal shall be military personnel of the nations of which they respectively are citizens.

V

CERTAIN PROCEDURAL MATTERS

In order to accomplish the swift trial and punishment of those guilty of the war crimes and other atrocities dealt with in this Agreement, the tribunals mentioned in Articles I and III, and the appropriate military and occupation courts, all shall adopt and apply, to the greatest extent possible, expeditious, fair, non-technical procedures. Such procedures, in a manner consistent with the other provisions of this agreement should:

(a) provide each accused with notice of the charges against him and an opportunity to be heard reasonably on such charges;

(b) permit the court to admit any evidence which it considers would have probative value;

(c) except as the court in its discretion shall deem appropriate in particular cases, exclude any defense based upon the fact that the accused acted under orders of a superior officer or pursuant to state or national policy.

(d) exclude any defense based upon the fact that the accused is or was the head or purported head or other principal official of a state; and

(e) confine trials strictly to an expeditious hearing of the issues raised by the charges.

VI

EXECUTIVE GROUP

(a) There shall be created at the earliest possible moment an executive group consisting of one representative each of the Soviet Union, the United States, the British Commonwealth and France. Each such representative shall be a member of, or be designated to act for, the military forces of the nation which designates him. The operations of this executive group, so far as within Germany or Austria, shall be subject to the administrative direction of the Control Council for Germany or for Austria, as the case may be. This group shall be assisted by an adequate staff of attorneys and research personnel to compile and analyze data, prepare the charges in the principal case or cases to conform to the proof and arrange the evidence for presentation to the international tribunal in the prosecutions referred to in Articles I and III (a).

(b) The presentation of the arraignment against the chief leaders, as provided in Article I, and of the principal case or cases against the Nazi Organizations before the international tribunal, as provided in subparagraph (a) of

Article III, shall be persons designated by the Soviet Union, the United States, the British Commonwealth and France, each of these countries being entitled to designate one person, who may be its member of the executive group referred to in paragraph (a) of this Article.

(c) The executive group shall also be charged with:

(1) the preparation of plans for, and the furnishing of advice with respect to, the prosecution of individuals to be charged with specific war crimes and atrocities and with complicity (as mentioned in Article III, paragraph (b) above) in the basic criminal plan through membership in one of the organizations hereinbefore mentioned, not only in the national courts of the United Nations but also before occupation or other appropriate tribunals.

(2) planning and assisting in making arrangements for the detection, apprehension, extradition, transfer, trial and punishment of persons charged with war crimes and atrocities or with participation in the basic criminal plan.

(3) planning and recommending suitable, expeditious, non-technical procedures for the swift but fair trial and certain punishment in a manner consistent with the provisions of this Agreement, of those guilty of war crimes and atrocities.

(4) recommending to appropriate governmental authorities of agreements and measures supplemental to or in addition to this Agreement, necessary or appropriate to accomplish the objectives of this Agreement, and

(5) the maintenance of liaison among and with the appropriate military and civil agencies, authorities and commissions of or representing any of the United Nations with respect to the matters dealt with in this Agreement.

VII

(a) The emoluments and expenses of those members of the tribunals provided for in Articles I and IV, designated by the Soviet Union, the United States, the British Commonwealth and France, and of the executive group provided for in Article V (a), shall be borne by the respective Governments just mentioned.

(b) The emoluments and expenses of the staff assisting the executive group, and of the secretarial staffs for the tribunal and the executive group, and incidental expenses, such as rent, heat, light, stationery and printing, shall be borne in equal shares by the Soviet Union, the United States, the British Commonwealth and France.

VIII

All members of the United Nations shall be invited by the Government of the United Kingdom, acting on behalf of the other signatories hereto, to adhere to this instrument. Such adherence shall in each case be notified to the Government of the United Kingdom which shall promptly inform the other parties to this instrument.

Done at ____________ this the ____________ day of ____________ 1945.

DOCUMENT 52

MEMORANDUM RE DOCUMENT ENTITLED, "PUNISHMENT OF WAR CRIMINALS." DATED 28 APRIL, 1945[1]

BY ROBERT H. JACKSON

May 1, 1945

I have two general criticisms of this document which, on the whole, bears evidence of most careful preparation. But I think it should be revised in two general respects.

First, this becomes one of the basic documents in international law. Viewed from the credit it will receive in the future, I think it is too impassioned and gives the impression that it is setting up a court organized to convict. Since this is due to recitals of accusations that are now pretty commonplace and to adjectives that are not necessary to the purpose of the instrument, I think its future credit will be greatly aided if it is a colder toned instrument. What the world is looking for now is not more fiery words which, after all, are pretty much exhausted but evidence of sure footed and discriminating action.

Second, fully appreciating the desirability of committing other of the United Nations to the broadest possible powers in the international tribunal, I think this is too detailed in some respects to serve well as an organic act. We are working in an untried field and dealing with conditions which we can neither control nor anticipate. Every limitation and every mandatory requirement and every qualifying adjective may be seized upon by a defendant as creating possible rights in its observance. The Commission[2] may then be put in the position of having to choose between a disregard of the basic document or of sustaining technical objections. I think procedural matters beyond very basic and general ones should be left in the realm of the Commission's discretion.

Third, while I think it desirable to commit the other United Nations as fully as possible to the method of procedure that we have discussed,[3] unforeseen conditions may make some variation necessary and I am wondering if this instrument does not commit us more inflexibly to a method of procedure than is to be desired. I think that the provisions which indicate the method of presenting the case should be authorizations which we can avail ourselves of as needed but which we can depart from if found expedient without being open to the charge of failing to conform to our authorization or to claim that defendants have obtained some vested rights in a particular method of procedure.

From where I sit one becomes impressed, perhaps over-impressed, with the dangerous quality of adjectives and unnecessary phrases in legal documents for it is surprising how much litigation can be hung on a single word of limitation. Suggestions are too numerous to recite in memoranda and I suggest that we review the document paragraph by paragraph.

DOCUMENT 53

DRAFT EXECUTIVE AGREEMENT[1]

(REDRAFT, APPARENTLY BY COLONEL CUTTER AND JUSTICE JACKSON).

May 2, 1945

I. PARTIES

1. This instrument [of Executive Agreement][2] is entered into by the Governments of the Union of Soviet Socialist Republics, the United States of America, the United Kingdom of Great Britain and North(ern?)[3] Ireland, and the Provisional Government of the French Republic, acting by their respective duly authorized representatives, on their own behalf and on behalf of any other members of the United Nations who [shall] adhere to this instrument as hereinbelow provided.

2. All members of the United Nations shall be invited by the Government of the United Kingdom, acting on behalf of the other signatories hereto, to adhere to this instrument. Such adherence shall in each case be notified to the Government of the United Kingdom which shall promptly inform the other parties to this instrument.

3. For convenience, (a) the four signatories will sometimes be referred to as "the Signatories," (b) the members of the United Nations adhering hereto as provided in the preceding paragraph will sometimes be referred to as "the Adherents," and (c) the Signatories and all Adherents will sometimes be collectively referred to as "the parties to this instrument."

II. POLICY AND PURPOSE

The United Nations have on various occasions pledged themselves that those responsible for the atrocities and crimes committed by the Axis Powers shall not escape punishment. [These atrocities and crimes include those which will be charged as provided in Article III of this instrument.]

The United Kingdom, the United States, and the Soviet Union in the Declaration issued at Moscow November 1, 1943 stated:

> (1) that those German officers and men who have been responsible for or have taken a consenting part in these atrocities "will be sent back to the countries in which their abominable deeds were done in order that they may be judged and punished according to the laws of these liberated countries and of the free governments which will be created therein"; and
>
> (2) that the above declaration was "without prejudice to the case of the major criminals, whose offenses have no particular geographical localizaton and who will be punished by joint decision of the Governments of the Allies."

This instrument is entered into in order to establish the necessary measures for bringing to justice the major criminals referred to above, their principal agents and accessories, and all other offenders who are not sent back for trial to the countries in which their atrocities and crimes were committed.

III. DECLARATION REGARDING THE CRIMINAL~~ITY~~ ~~OF GERMAN~~[4] ACTS [TO BE CHARGED]

1. The parties to this instrument ~~solemnly declare~~ [~~and restate~~][5] [agree to bring to trial,] in the names of their respective peoples ~~that the following acts are criminal, and that the defendants brought to trial as provided in this instrument shall, upon conviction thereof, suffer death or such other punishment as shall be determined under the provisions hereafter.~~ [the persons referred to in Article II for their responsibility for the following criminal acts:]

a. Violation of the customs and rules of warfare.[6]

b. Invasion by force or threat of force of other countries in violation of international law or treaties.

c. Initiation of war in violation of international law or treaties.

d. Launching a war of aggression.

e. Recourse to war as an instrument of national policy or for the solution of international controversies.

2. The foregoing declaration is without prejudice to the right to charge and try defendants under this instrument for violations of law other than ~~that~~

[those] recited above, including but not limited to [atrocities and crimes committed in] violation[s] of the domestic law of any Axis Power or satellite or of any of the United Nations.

IV. DECLARATION REGARDING ACCESSORIAL LIABILITY

In any trial of charges pursuant to this instrument, the prosecution may invoke [where applicable] and the tribunal before which the charges are tried shall recognize and apply the rule of liability, common to all penal systems and included in the general doctrines of the laws of war, that those who participate in the formulation and execution of a criminal plan involving multiple crimes are liable for each of the offenses committed and responsible for the acts of each other.

V. DECLARATION REGARDING DEFENSES

1. No indictment, statement of charges, or other document of arraignment charging violation of law as declared [and restated] in this instrument shall be subject to any allegation of legal insufficiency.

2. The parties to this instrument declare that any defense based upon the fact that the accused is or was the head or purported head or other principal official of a state is legally inadmissible, and will not be entertained by any [~~military~~][7] tribunal before which charges brought pursuant to this instrument are tried.

3. The fact that the criminal acts charged against any defendant hereunder were done pursuant to order of a superior or government sanction may be taken into consideration in determining culpability, either by way of defense or in mitigation of punishment. It shall be discretionary with the tribunal before which the charges are tried whether, and to what extent, the claim of order of a superior or of government sanction shall be taken into consideration.

VI. DUE PROCESS AND DEFENDANTS

In order to insure ~~due process~~ [fair trial] for defendants ~~tried~~ [charged with] crimes pursuant to this instrument, it is ~~agreed~~ [declared that the following is required in order to constitute due process in their behalf:]

1. Reasonable notice shall be given to the defendants of the charges against them and of the opportunity to defend. Such notice may be actual or

constructive.[8] ~~Defendants may be tried in absentia.~~ Any tribunal before which charges are tried pursuant to this instrument shall have the right to determine, in its sole and absolute discretion, what constitutes reasonable notice in any given instance, ~~and in what instances the~~ [to what extent proceedings against] defendants shall be ~~tried in absentia~~ [taken without their presence when they have had reasonable notice and opportunity to appear.(?)] [after notice as hereinbefore provided. (?)][9]

2. The defendants physically present before the tribunal (a) will be furnished with copies, translated into their own language, of any indictment, statement of charges or other document of arraignment upon which they are being tried, and (b) will be given fair opportunity to be heard in their defense personally and by counsel.

3. Groups or organizations may be charged pursuant to this instrument with criminal acts or with complicity therein. In such event:

a. The defendant groups and organizations may be tried by producing before the tribunal and putting on trial such of their number as the tribunal may determine, in its sole and absolute discretion, to be fairly representative of the group or organization in question.

b. Upon conviction of the group or organization thus tried, the tribunal shall make written findings and enter written judgment [finding and adjudicating the guilt of such group or organization and of the members thereof.]

c. Such findings and judgment shall be given full faith and credit in any subsequent trial of a person charged with criminal liability through membership in such group or organization, and in such subsequent trial (1) identification of the defendant as a member of the group or organization in question will constitute conclusive sufficient proof of the guilt of such defendant. ~~unless (2) such defendant satisfies the tribunal that his~~ [the tribunal in its sole and absolute discretion may take into consideration in determining culpability either by way of defense or in mitigation of punishment any relevant circumstances of a defendant's] membership in the group or organization [and relating to the nature and extent of his participation in the activities thereof.] ~~was~~ [~~in consequence~~][10] ~~the result of duress~~ [~~or was nominal only.~~][11]

VII. EVIDENCE AND PROCEDURE

1. Tribunals established pursuant to this instrument shall adopt and apply, to the greatest extent possible, expeditious and non-technical procedures.

2. Such tribunals shall (a) admit any evidence which in their opinion has probative value, (b) confine trials strictly to an expeditious hearing of the

issues raised by the charges, (c) disallow ~~technical or dilatory pleas, motions and objections by defendants~~, [action by defendants the effect of which will be to cause unreasonable delay or the introduction of irrelevant issues or evidence] and (d) employ with all possible liberality ~~the most effective~~ simplifications of proof, such as but not limited to: requiring defendants to make proffers of proof; [~~the reception of summaries of investigations~~] taking judicial notice of facts of common knowledge; and utilizing [reasonable] presumptions.

VIII. TRIBUNALS

1. There shall be set up [one or more] ~~a~~ military tribunal [s] hereinafter referred to for convenience as "~~the~~ ["]International Military Tribunal," for the trial of the leaders of the European Axis powers and their principal agents and accessories. ~~The~~ [Each] International Military Tribunal shall consist of four members and four alternates, to be appointed as follows: One member and one alternate each by the representatives on the Control Council for Germany of the Soviet Union, the United States, the United Kingdom, and France. ~~The members of the [an][12] International Military Tribunal shall be military personnel of the nations of which they respectively are citizens.~~

2. In the event of the death or incapacity of any member of ~~the~~ [an] International Military Tribunal, ~~their~~ [his] alternate shall sit in his stead, and the nation of which he is a citizen shall forthwith appoint another alternate. Three members of the Tribunal shall constitute a quorum, and all actions and decisions shall be taken by majority vote of the members of the Tribunal at any time sitting, except that sentence of death shall not be imposed on the vote of less than three members.

3. ~~The~~ [An] International Military Tribunal may sit in any zone in Germany, Austria or Italy or in the territory of any one of the ~~Adherents~~ [parties to this instrument,] with the consent of such ~~Adherent~~ [party.] It shall have the power to summon witnesses and to compel their attendance, to require the production of documents, to administer oaths, to appoint special masters and other officers, to hold hearings, and generally to exercise in a manner consistent with the provisions of this instrument plenary judicial authority with respect to the trial of charges brought pursuant to this instrument.

4. ~~An~~ [The] International Military Tribunal shall have the power to establish its own rules of procedure, which shall be consistent with the provisions of this instrument.

5. Occupation courts or other tribunals ~~shall~~ [may] be set up by the Signatories, [or any of them,] with the cooperation where feasible of the Adherents, for the trial of ~~lesser~~ offenders [other than those tried before ~~the~~[13]

an International Military Tribunal] who are not sent back for trial to the countries in which their atrocities and crimes were committed, including offenders charged with criminal liability through membership in any group or organization as provided in Article VI of this instrument. To the extent possible, the provisions of this instrument will be applied in the proceedings of such occupation courts and other tribunals.

IX. PUNISHMENT

1. Defendants brought to trial as provided in this instrument shall, upon conviction, suffer death [, reparational labor as may be ordered by the Control Council] or such other punishment [,] as shall be determined by the tribunal before which they are tried and approved by the Control Council. The Control Council may approve, reduce, or otherwise alter the sentences determined by the tribunals, but may not increase the severity thereof.

2. The sentences, when and as approved by the Control Council, shall be carried into execution in accordance with the written orders of the Control Council.

X. EXECUTIVE GROUP

1. There shall be created at the earliest possible moment an executive group consisting of one representative each of the Soviet Union, the United States, the United Kingdom and France. Each such representative shall be a member of, or be designated to act for, the military forces of the nation which designated him. The operations of this executive group, so far as [carried on] within Germany or Austria, shall be subject to the administrative direction of the Control Council for Germany or for Austria, as the case may be. This group shall be assisted by an adequate staff of attorneys and research personnel to compile and analyze data, prepare the charges in the cases of the leaders of the European Axis Powers and their principal agents and accessories to conform to the proof, and arrange the evidence for presentation to the International Military Tribunal in the prosecutions of those cases.

2. The presentation of the cases referred to in the preceding paragraph shall be made by persons designated by the Soviet Union, the United States, the United Kingdom and France, each of these countries being entitled to designate one person, who may be its member of the executive group referred to in the preceding paragraph.

3. The executive group shall also be charged with:

(a) recommending to appropriate governmental authorities of agreements and measures supplemental to or in addition to this Agreement, necessary or appropriate to accomplish the objectives of this Agreement, and

(b) the maintenance of liaison among and with the appropriate military and civil agencies, authorities and commissions of or representing any of the United Nations [in][14] respect to the matters dealt with in this Agreement.

XI. EMOLUMENTS AND EXPENSES

1. The emoluments and expenses of those members of the International Military Tribunal designated by the respective Signatories as provided in Article VIII of this instrument, and of the executive group provided for in Article X of this instrument, shall be borne by the respective Signatories by whom they have been appointed.

2. The emoluments and expenses of the staffs for the International Military Tribunal and the executive group, and incidental expenses, such as rent, heat, light, stationery and printing shall be borne in equal shares by the Signatories.

3. The emoluments and expenses of those occupation courts and tribunals established as provided in paragraph 5 of Article VIII of this instrument in which Adherents participate shall be justly apportioned between the Signatories concerned and the participating Adherents as may be agreed between them.

Done at ____________________ this the ____________________ day of ____________________ 1945

DOCUMENT 54

DRAFT EXECUTIVE AGREEMENT[1]

May 2, 1945

-I[2] PARTIES

1. This ~~instrument of~~ Executive Agreement is entered into by the Governments of the Union of Soviet Socialist Republics, the United States of America, the United Kingdom of Great Britain and Northern[3] Ireland, and the Provisional Government of the French Republic, acting by their respective duly authorized representatives, on their own behalf and on behalf of any other of the United Nations who shall adhere to this instrument as hereinbelow provided.

2. All members of the United Nations shall be invited by the Government of the United Kingdom, acting on behalf of the other signatories hereto, to adhere to this instrument. Such adherence shall in each case be notified to the Government of the United Kingdom which shall promptly inform the other parties to this ~~instrument~~ [Agreement.][4]

3. For convenience, (a) the four signatories will sometimes be referred to as "the Signatories," (b) the members of the United Nations adhering hereto as provided in the preceding paragraph will sometimes be referred to as "the Adherents," and (c) the Signatories and all Adherents will sometimes be collectively referred to as "the parties to this ~~instrument~~ [Agreement]."

~~II.~~ POLICY AND PURPOSE

[4.] The United Nations have on various occasions pledged themselves that those responsible for the atrocities and crimes committed by the Axis Powers [or any officer or agent thereof] shall not escape punishment. These atrocities and crimes include those which will be charged as provided in Article 6 of this ~~instrument~~ [Agreement].

[5.] The United Kingdom, the United States, and the Soviet Union in the Declaration issued at Moscow November 1, 1943 stated:

> (1) that those German officers and men who have been responsible for or have taken a consenting part in these atrocities "will be sent back to the countries in which their abominable deeds were done in order that they may be judged and punished according to the laws of these liberated countries and of the free governments which will be erected therein"; and
>
> (2) that the above declaration was "without prejudice to the case of major criminals, whose offenses have no particular geographical localization and who will be punished by joint decision of the Governments of the Allies".

This ~~instrument~~ [Agreement] is entered into in order to establish the necessary measures for bringing to justice the major criminals referred to above, their principal agents and accessories, and all other offenders who are not sent back for trial to the countries in which their atrocities and crimes were committed.

~~III.~~ DECLARATION REGARDING THE CRIMINAL ACTS TO BE CHARGED

[6.] The parties to this instrument agree to bring to trial, in the names of their respective peoples, the persons referred to in Article 5 for their responsibility for the following criminal acts:

a. Violation of the customs and rules of warfare.

b. Invasion by force or threat of force of other countries in violation of international law or treaties.

c. Initiation of war in violation of international law or treaties.

d. Launching a war of aggression.

e. Recourse to war as an instrument of national policy or for the solution of international controversies.

[7.] This declaration shall also include the right to charge and try defendants under this ~~instrument~~ [Agreement] for violations of law other than those recited above, including but not limited to atrocities and crimes committed in violation of the domestic law of any Axis Power or satellite or of any of the United Nations.

~~IV.~~ DECLARATION REGARDING ACCESSORIAL LIABILITY

[8.] In any trial of charges pursuant to this ~~instrument~~ [Agreement,] the prosecution may invoke where applicable and the tribunal before which the charges are tried shall recognize and apply the [general] rule of liability ~~common to all penal systems and included in the general doctrines of the laws of war,~~ that those who participate in the formulation and execution of a criminal plan involving multiple crimes are liable for each of the offenses committed and responsible for the acts of each other.

~~V.~~ DECLARATION REGARDING DEFENSES

[9.] No indictment, statement of charges, or other document of arraignment shall be deemed legally insufficient which charges violation of law as ~~declared and restated~~ [set forth in] this ~~instrument~~ [Agreement.]

[10.] The parties to this ~~instrument~~ [Agreement] declare that any defense based upon the fact that the accused is or was the head or purported head or other principal official of a state is legally inadmissible, and will not be entertained by any tribunal before which charges brought pursuant to this ~~instrument~~ [Agreement] are tried.

[11.] ~~The fact that the criminal acts charged against any defendant hereunder were done pursuant to order of a superior or government sanction may be taken into consideration in determining culpability, either by way of~~

~~defense or in mitigation of punishment. The tribunal before which the charges are being tried shall determine whether, and to what extent, justice requires that the claim of order of a superior or of government sanctions shall be taken into consideration.~~ [11. The fact that a defendant acted pursuant to order of a superior or government sanction shall not constitute an absolute defense but may be considered either in defense or in mitigation of punishment if the tribunal before which the charges are being tried determines that justice so requires.]

~~VI.~~ DUE PROCESS FOR DEFENDANTS

[12.] In order to insure fair trial for defendants charged with crime pursuant to this instrument, it is declared that the following is required in order to constitute due process in their behalf:

~~1.~~ [a.] Reasonable notice shall be given to the defendants of the charges against them and of the opportunity to defend. Such notice may be actual or constructive. Any tribunal before which charges are tried pursuant to this instrument shall have the right to determine, in its sole and absolute discretion, what constitutes reasonable notice in any given instance.

~~2.~~ [b.] The defendants physically present before the tribunal (a) will be furnished with copies, translated into their own language, of any indictment, statement of charges or other document of arraignment upon which they are being tried, and (b) will be given fair opportunity to be heard in their defense personally and by counsel. The tribunal shall determine to what extent proceedings against defendants may be taken without their presence.

~~3.~~ [c.] Organizations, official or unofficial, may be charged pursuant to this ~~instrument~~ [Agreement] with criminal acts or with complicity therein. ~~In such event,~~

~~a. The defendant organizations may be tried~~ by producing before the tribunal and putting on trial such of their number as the tribunal may determine to be fairly representative of the group or organization in question.

~~b.~~ [d.] Upon conviction of ~~the~~ [an] organization ~~thus tried,~~ [hereunder], the tribunal shall make written findings and enter judgment finding and adjudicating the charges against such organization and the representative members on trial. [~~c.~~] Such findings and judgment shall be given full faith and credit with respect to the criminal ~~character~~ [purposes and activities] of the organization in any subsequent trial hereunder of a person charged with criminal liability through membership in such organization. Upon proof of such membership the burden shall be upon the defendant to establish any circumstances relating to his membership or participation therein which are relevant either in defense or in mitigation.

~~VII.~~ EVIDENCE AND PROCEDURE

~~1.~~ [13.] Tribunals established pursuant to this instrument shall adopt and apply, to the greatest extent possible expeditious and non-technical procedures.

~~2.~~ [14.] Such tribunals shall (a) admit any evidence which in their opinion has probative value, (b) confine trials strictly to an expeditious hearing of the issues raised by the charges, (c) disallow action by defendants the effect of which will be to cause unreasonable delay or the introduction of irrelevant issues or evidence, and (d) employ with all possible liberality simplifications of proof, such as but not limited to: requiring defendants to make proffers of proof; taking judicial notice of facts of common knowledge; utilizing reasonable presumptions.

~~VIII.~~ TRIBUNALS

~~1.~~ [15.] There shall be set up one or more military tribunals, hereinafter referred to for convenience as "International Military Tribunal," which shall have jurisdiction to try the leaders of the European Axis powers and their principal agents and accessories. Each International Military Tribunal shall consist of four members and four alternates, to be appointed as follows: One member and one alternate each by the representatives on the Control Council for Germany of the Soviet Union, the United States, the United Kingdom, and France. [The alternates, so far as practicable, shall be present at the sessions of the tribunal.]

~~2.~~ [16.] In the event of the death or incapacity of any member of an International Military Tribunal, his alternate shall sit in his stead, and the nation of which he is a citizen shall forthwith appoint another alternate. Three members of the Tribunal shall constitute a quorum, and all actions and decisions shall be taken by majority vote of the members of the Tribunal at any time sitting, except that sentence of death shall not be imposed on the vote of less than three members.

~~3.~~ 17. An International Military Tribunal may sit in any zone in Germany, Austria or Italy or in ~~the territory of any one of the parties to this instrument~~ [any other country,] with the consent of such ~~party~~ [country.] It shall have the power to summon witnesses and to compel their attendance, to require the production of documents, to administer oaths, to appoint special masters and other officers, to hold hearings, and generally to exercise in a manner not inconsistent with the provisions of this instrument plenary judicial authority with respect to the trial of charges brought pursuant to this instrument.

~~4.~~ [18.] An International Military Tribunal shall have the power to establish its own rules of procedure, which shall not be inconsistent with the provisions of this instrument.

~~5.~~ [19.] Occupation courts or other tribunals may be set up by the Signatories or any of them, ~~with the cooperation where feasible of the Adherents,~~ for the trial of offenders other than those tried before an International Military Tribunal who are not sent back for trial to the countries in which their atrocities and crimes were committed, including offenders charged with criminal liability through membership in any group or organization as provided in Article b [12 (d)] of this ~~instrument~~ [Agreement.] ~~To the extent possible, the provisions of this instrument will be applied in the proceedings of such occupation courts and other tribunals.~~

~~IX.~~ PUNISHMENT

~~1.~~ [20] Defendants brought to trial before an International Military Tribunal as provided in this ~~instrument~~ [Agreement] shall, upon conviction, suffer death or such other punishment as shall be determined by the Tribunal before which they are tried and approved by the Control Council [acting by majority vote.] The Control Council, [by such vote], may approve, reduce, or otherwise alter the sentences determined by the Tribunal, but may not increase the severity thereof.

~~2.~~ [21] The sentences, when and as approved by the Control Council, shall be carried into execution in accordance with the written orders of the Control Council.

~~X.~~ PREPARATION OF CHARGES AND PROSECUTION

~~1.~~ [22] At the earliest possible time the Soviet Union, the United States, the United Kingdom and France shall each designate a representative, and such representatives acting as a group shall prepare the charges ~~to be prosecuted hereunder~~ [pursuant to Article 6 hereof] and shall institute and conduct the prosecution. [Such representatives shall also prepare and recommend to the Control Council plans for the prosecution and trial of persons charged with liability pursuant to Article 12 (d) through membership in organizations found criminal by an International Military Tribunal.]

~~2.~~ [23] The representatives shall also be charged with:

(a) recommending to appropriate governmental authorities agreements and measures supplemental to or in addition to this Agreement, necessary or appropriate to accomplish the objectives ~~of this instrument~~ [thereof,] and

(b) the maintenance of liaison among and with the appropriate military and civil agencies, authorities and commissions of or representing any of the United Nations with respect to the matters dealt with in this ~~instrument~~ [Agreement.]

~~XI~~. EMOLUMENTS AND EXPENSES

~~1.~~ [24] The emoluments and expenses of those members of the International Military Tribunal designated by the respective Signatories as provided in Article ~~one~~ of ~~the instrument,~~ [Agreement] and of the ~~executive group~~ [representatives] provided for in article 15 [22] of ~~this instrument~~ [Agreement,] shall be borne by the respective Signatories by whom they have been appointed.

~~2.~~ [25] The emoluments and expenses of the staffs for the International Military Tribunal and the ~~executive group~~ [representatives] and incidental expenses, such as rent, heat, light, stationery and printing shall be borne in equal shares by the Signatories.

~~3.~~ [26] The emoluments and expenses of those occupation courts and tribunals established as provided in ~~paragraph 5~~, Article ~~VIII~~ 19 of this [agreement] ~~instrument in which Adherents participate~~ shall be justly apportioned between the Signatories concerned and the [any] participating Adherents as may be agreed between them.

Done at ____________________ this the ______________ day of ______________ 1945.

DOCUMENT 55

EXECUTIVE AGREEMENT
DRAFT NO. 2
(AS DEVELOPED AT SAN FRANCISCO)

May 16, 1945[1]

PARTIES

1. This Executive Agreement is entered into by the Governments of the Union of Soviet Socialist Republics, the United States of America, the United Kingdom of Great Britain and Northern Ireland, and the Provisional Government of the French Republic, acting by their respective duly authorized representatives, on their own behalf[2] and on behalf of any other mem-

bers of the United Nations who shall adhere to this Agreement as hereinbelow provided.

2. All members of the United Nations shall be invited by the Government of the United Kingdom, acting on behalf of the other signatories hereto, to adhere to this Agreement. Such adherence shall in each case be notified to the Government of the United Kingdom which shall promptly inform the other parties to this Agreement.

3. For convenience, (a) the four signatories will sometimes be referred to as "the Signatories," (b) the members of the United Nations adhering hereto as provided in the preceding Article will sometimes be referred to as "the Adherents," and (c) the Signatories and all Adherents will sometimes be collectively referred to as "the parties to this Agreement".

POLICY AND PURPOSE

4. The United Nations have on various occasions pledged themselves that those responsible for the atrocities and crimes committed by the Axis Powers or any officer or agent thereof shall not escape punishment. These atrocities and crimes include those which will be charged as provided in Article 6 of this Agreement.

5. The United Kingdom, the United States, and the Soviet Union in the Declaration issued at Moscow November 1, 1943 stated:

> (1) that those German officers and men who have been responsible for or have taken a consenting part in these atrocities "will be sent back to the countries in which their abominable deeds were done in order that they may be judged and punished according to the laws of these liberated countries and of the free governments which will be erected therein"; and
>
> (2) that the above declaration was "without prejudice to the case of major criminals, whose offenses have no particular geographical localization and who will be punished by joint decision of the Governments of the Allies".

This Agreement is entered into in order to provide for the prompt prosecution and trial of these major criminals including the principal organizations which participated in the commission of crimes and in the execution of criminal plans.[3]

DECLARATION REGARDING THE CRIMINAL ACTS TO BE CHARGED

6. The parties to this Agreement agree to bring to trial before an International Military Tribunal in the names of their respective peoples, the major

criminals, including the principal organizations which participated in the commission of crimes and in the execution of criminal plans.[4]

DECLARATION OF JURISDICTION AND LEGAL PRINCIPLES

7. Any International Military Tribunal created pursuant to Article 15 of this Agreement shall have jurisdiction to hear and decide any charges of criminality based upon the following:[5]

a. Atrocities and offenses against persons or property constituting violations of international law or of the laws, rules and customs of war.

b. Atrocities and offenses committed since 1933 in violation of any applicable provision of the domestic law of ~~any of the parties or of~~[6] any Axis Power or satellite, including atrocities and persecutions on racial or religious grounds.

c. Invasion by force or threat of force of other countries in violation of international law or treaties.

d. Initiation of war in violation of international law or treaties.

e. Launching a war of aggression.

f. ~~Recourse to war as an instrument of national policy or for the solution of international controversies.~~[7]

8. In any trial before an International Military Tribunal, the tribunal shall apply the general rule of liability that those who participate in the formulation and execution of a criminal plan involving multiple crimes are liable for each of the offenses committed and responsible for the acts of each other.[8]

DECLARATION REGARDING DEFENSES

9. No indictment, statement of charges, or other document of arraignment shall be deemed legally insufficient which charges violation of law as set forth in this Agreement.

10. The parties to this Agreement declare that any defense based upon the fact that the accused is or was the head or purported head or other principal official of a state is legally inadmissible, and will not be entertained by any tribunal before which charges brought pursuant to this Agreement are tried.

11. The fact that a defendant acted pursuant to order of a superior or government sanction shall not constitute an absolute defense but may be considered either in defense or in mitigation of punishment if the tribunal before which the charges are being tried determines that justice so requires.

DUE PROCESS FOR DEFENDANTS

12. In order to insure fair trial for defendants charged with crime pursuant to this Agreement, it is declared that the following is required in order to constitute due process in their behalf.

a. Reasonable notice shall be given to the defendants of the charges against them and of the opportunity to defend. Such notice may be actual or constructive. Any tribunal before which charges are tried pursuant to this Agreement shall have the right to determine what constitutes reasonable notice in any given instance.

b. The defendants physically present before the tribunal (a) will be furnished with copies, translated into their own language, of any indictment, statement of charges or other document of arraignment upon which they are being tried, and (b) will be given fair opportunity to be heard in their defense personally and by counsel. The tribunal shall determine to what extent proceedings against defendants may be taken without their presence.

c. Organizations, official or unofficial, may be charged before an International Military Tribunal with criminal acts or with complicity therein by producing before the tribunal and putting on trial such of their number as the tribunal may determine to be fairly representative of the group or organization in question. Upon conviction of an organization hereunder, the tribunal shall make written findings and enter written judgment finding[9] and adjudicating the charges against such organization and representative members on trial.[10]

EVIDENCE AND PROCEDURE

13. Tribunals established pursuant to this Agreement shall adopt and apply, to the greatest extent possible expeditious and non-technical procedures.

14. Such tribunals shall (a) admit any evidence which in their opinion has probative value, (b) confine trials strictly to an expeditious hearing of the issues raised by the charges, (c) disallow action by defendants the effect of which will be to cause unreasonable delay or the introduction of irrelevant issues or evidence, and (d) employ with all possible liberality simplifications of proof, such as but not limited to: requiring defendants to make proffers of proof; taking judicial notice of facts of common knowledge; and utilizing reasonable presumptions.

TRIBUNALS

15. There shall be set up by the Control Council for Germany one or more military tribunals (hereinafter referred to as "International Military Tribunal") which shall have jurisdiction to hear and determine any charges presented pursuant to Article 6. Each such International Military Tribunal shall consist of four members and four alternates, to be appointed as follows: one member and one alternate each by the representatives upon the Control Council for Germany of the Soviet Union, the United States, the United Kingdom and France. The alternate, so far as practicable, shall be present at the sessions of the tribunal. The presiding officer of each International Military Tribunal shall be selected by the members of the tribunal, and, if they are unable to agree, he shall be determined by lot.[11]

16. In the event of the death or incapacity of any member of an International Military Tribunal, his alternate shall sit in his stead. All actions and decisions shall be taken by majority vote of all the members of the tribunal. In the event that the tribunal is in disagreement as to its judgment, the accused may be brought to trial before a second tribunal, no member of which shall have taken part in the first trial.[12]

17. An International Military Tribunal may sit in any zone in Germany, Austria or Italy or in any other country with the consent of such country. It shall have the power to summon witnesses and to compel their attendance, to require the production of documents, to administer oaths, to appoint special masters and other officers, to hold hearings, and generally to exercise in a manner not inconsistent with the provisions of this Agreement plenary judicial authority with respect to the trial of charges brought pursuant to this Agreement.

18. An International Military Tribunal shall have the power to establish its own rules of procedure, which shall be not inconsistent with the provisions of this Agreement.

19. Upon conviction of an organization before an International Military Tribunal, persons charged with criminal liability by reason of membership therein may be prosecuted in occupation courts or other military tribunals established by the Signatories or any of them. In the trial of such prosecutions the legal principles declared in Articles 7, 8, 9, 10 and 11 shall be binding upon the court or tribunal and the findings and judgment of an International Military Tribunal shall be conclusive with respect to the criminal purposes and activities of the organization. Upon proof of membership in such an organization, the burden shall be upon the defendant to establish any circumstances relating to his membership or participation therein which are relevant either in defense or in mitigation. This Agreement shall not in any

way prejudice the creation of other tribunals by the parties to this Agreement, or any of them, for the trial of persons who are not prosecuted before an International Military Tribunal.[13]

PUNISHMENT

20. Defendants brought to trial before an International Military Tribunal as provided in this Agreement shall, upon conviction, suffer death or such other punishment as shall be determined by the Tribunal before which they are tried and approved by the Control Council acting by majority vote. The Control Council, by such vote, may approve, reduce, or otherwise alter the sentences determined by the Tribunal, but may not increase the severity thereof.

21. The sentences, when and as approved by the Control Council, shall be carried into execution in accordance with the written orders of the Control Council.

PREPARATION OF CHARGES AND PROSECUTION

22. At the earliest possible time the Soviet Union, the United States, the United Kingdom and France shall each designate a representative, and such representatives acting as a group shall prepare the charges pursuant to Article 6 hereof and shall institute and conduct the prosecution. Such representatives shall also prepare and recommend to the Control Council plans for the prosecution and trial of persons charged with liability pursuant to Article 12 (d) through membership in organizations found criminal by an International Military Tribunal.[14]

23. The representatives shall also be charged with:

(a) recommending to appropriate governmental authorities agreements and measures supplemental to or in addition to this Agreement, necessary or appropriate to accomplish the objectives thereof, and

(b) the maintenance of liaison among and with the appropriate military and civil agencies, authorities and commissions of or representing any of the United Nations with respect to the matters dealt with in this Agreement.

EMOLUMENTS AND EXPENSES

24. The emoluments and expenses of those members of the International Military Tribunal designated by the respective Signatories as provided in

Article 15 of this Agreement and of the representatives provided for in Article 22 of this Agreement, shall be borne by the respective Signatories by whom they have been appointed.

25. The emoluments and expenses of the staffs for the International Military Tribunal and the representations and incidental expenses, such as rent, heat, light, stationery and printing shall be borne in equal shares by the Signatories.

26. The emoluments and expenses of those occupation courts and tribunals established as provided in Article 19 of this Agreement shall be justly apportioned between the Signatories concerned and any participating Adherents as may be agreed between them.

RETURN OF OFFENDERS TO THE SCENE OF THEIR CRIMES

27. The Signatories agree that the Control Council for Germany shall establish policies and procedures governing (a) the return of persons in Germany charged with criminal offenses to the scene of their crimes in accordance with the Moscow Declaration and (b) the surrender of persons within Germany who are in custody of any of the Signatories who are demanded for prosecution by any party to this Agreement.[15]

Done at ____________________ this the ____________________ day of ____________________ 1945.

DOCUMENT 56

COMMENTS ON DRAFT NO. 2[1]

May 19, 1945

(A) Amend Article 5 (1) and (2) to read:

"(1) that those German officers and men and members of the Nazi Party who have been responsible for or have taken a consenting part in these atrocities 'will be sent back to the countries in which their abominable deeds were done in order that they may be judged and punished according to the laws of these liberated countries and of the free governments which will be created therein'; and

"(2) that the above declaration was 'without prejudice to the case of the major criminals, whose offenses have no particular geographical localization and who will be punished by the joint decision of the Governments of the Allies.' "

Note: Slight changes of language required to conform to official text of Moscow Declaration (U.S. Department of State Bulletin, Volume 9, No. 228, 6 November 1943). Members of the Nazi Party are mentioned in the Declaration and it would seem right to refer to them here.[2]

(B) Amend the paragraph following Article 5 (2) to read:

"This Agreement is entered into in order to provide for the prompt prosecution and trial of the major criminals of the Axis powers, including the persons and organizations who participated or took a consenting part in the formulation and execution of criminal plans, or in the commission of crimes."

Note: Change suggested in order to make clear that Axis criminals, not merely German criminals, are covered by the Agreement. Characterization of organizations as "principal" eliminated. Statement enlarged to correspond with declaration of liability in Article 8. (See (J) below.)

(C) Amend Article 6 to read:

"6. The parties to the Agreement agree to bring to trial before an International Military Tribunal, in the names of their respective peoples, such major criminals, including persons and organizations charged with participating or taking a consenting part in the formulation and execution of criminal plans, or in the commission of crimes."

Note: See (J) below.

(D) Amend Article 7 to read:

"7. In any trial before an International Military Tribunal, the Tribunal shall be bound by this declaration of the parties to this Agreement that the following acts are criminal:"

Note:[3] This restores the language of Draft No. 2-A and parallels the language of Draft No. 3.[4] It is considered essential that the Agreement declare certain acts to be criminal rather than to leave open to future argument the question of the criminality of those acts under existing notions of international or other law.[5]

(E) Amend Article 7, *a* to read:

"a. Atrocities and offenses against persons or property constituting violations of the laws, rules, or customs of war or of the sea, or violations of international law."

Note: Adds the phrase "of the sea." See (I) below.

(F) Amend Article 7, *b* to read:

"b. Atrocities and offenses, including atrocities and persecutions on racial or religious grounds, committed since 1 January 1933—[6]

(i) against nationals of any country, which are in violation of any applicable provision of the domestic law of such country;[7]

(ii) against stateless persons, which are in violation of the principles of criminal law generally observed in civilized states."[8]

OR

"b. Atrocities and offenses, including atrocities and persecutions on racial or religious grounds,[9] committed since 1 January 1933[10] in violation of any applicable provision of the domestic law of any country in which they were committed."

Note: Corresponding text of Draft No. 2 invokes only the domestic law of Axis powers and satellites. This should be broadened. First suggested redraft invokes the national law of the injured person (and general law in the case of stateless persons). Second suggested redraft rests essentially upon territorial theories of criminal jurisdiction. In Draft No. 3 the language used is: "Atrocities and offenses committed since 1933 in violation of any applicable provision of the domestic law of any of the parties or of any Axis Power or satellite, including atrocities and persecutions on racial or religious grounds."

(G) Amend Article 7, *c* to read:

"c. Invasion by force or threat of force of other countries in violation of international law."

Note: See (I) below.

(H) Amend Article 7, *d* to read:

"d. Initiation of war in violation of international law."

Note: See (I) below.

(I) Add after Article 7, *e*:

"International law shall be taken to include the principles of the law of nations as they result from the usages established among civilized people, from the laws of humanity, and the dictates of the public conscience."

Note: Change incorporates the preamble of Hague Convention IV, 18 October 1907, and invokes all sources of international law, whether conventional or non-conventional. This definition will apply to Articles, 7, *a*, 7, *c*, and 7, *d*. The point has been made that the Agreement should contain some general statement of the law which is to be used as a basis of decision in areas not specifically mentioned in the Agreement, for example, the sufficiency in law of various defenses which may be urged, and matters of procedure.

(J) Amend Article 8 to read:

"8. In any trial before an International Military Tribunal the Tribunal shall apply the general rule of liability that those who participate or take a consenting part in the formulation and execution of a criminal plan involving multiple crimes are liable for each of the offenses committed and responsible for the acts of each other."

Note: Adds "or take a consenting part", a phrase which appears in the Moscow Declaration.

(K) Amend Article 9 to read:

"9. No indictment, statement of charges, or other document of arraignment shall be deemed legally insufficient which charges the commission of any criminal act as set forth in this Agreement."

Note: This change depends upon the change noted in (D) above. If change (D) is adopted, there is probably no need for Article 9, and Draft No. 3 in fact eliminates it.

(L) As to Article 12, and the title which appears above Article 12, it has been suggested that the phrase "due process", which has special connotations in Anglo-American law, be eliminated, and blander language submitted.

(M) Amend the first sentence of Article 20 to read:

"20. Defendents brought to trial before an International Military Tribunal as provided in this Agreement shall, upon conviction, suffer death or such other punishment as shall be determined to be just by the Tribunal before which they are tried and approved by the Control Council acting by majority vote."

Note: Addition of the words "to be just" is required in order to exclude the interpretation that punishment for offenses against domestic law (paragraph 7, b) must conform to the penalties provided by such law.

(N) Amend the first sentence of Article 22 to read:

"At the earliest possible time, the Soviet Union, the United States, the United Kingdom, and France shall each designate a representative to act as its Chief of Counsel. Such Chiefs of Counsel, acting by majority vote, shall determine the persons and organizations to be brought to trial before an International Military Tribunal and, acting as a group, they shall prepare the charges and institute and conduct the prosecution."

Note: This adopts the language of Draft No. 3. The corresponding language of Draft No. 2 speaks of "representatives", not of Chiefs of Counsel, and does not specifically provide for selection of defendants by majority vote.

(O) Change references in the balance of Article 22 and in Article 23 to "Chiefs of Counsel".

(P) Article 26 of Draft No. 3 provides that the Control Council for Germany shall establish policies for the return and surrender of persons charged with crime. Article 27 of Draft No. 2 limits this to persons in Germany.

(Q) Probably advisable to amend Articles 4 and 22 by adding "and Article 7" after "Article 6".

The following further points have been suggested for consideration:

I. Should a "plan and combination, etc." be specifically included as an offense under Article 7?

II. Article 19 does not state that findings by an International Military Tribunal shall have any effect in occupational or other military tribunals of adherents, as distinguished from signatories. Was this intended? See Article 26.

III. It seems to be usual in arbitration treaties and the like to specify qualifications of individual members of the Tribunal, and to prescribe an oath of office.

IV. Shall members and staff of the Tribunal be given diplomatic immunity?

V. Shall an official language or languages be prescribed?

VI. Shall a procedure be established for the deposit of accessions to the Agreement, or for signifying nominations by the powers of members of the Tribunal?

VII. Shall provision be made for termination of the Agreement?

VIII. Suppose no Control Council?

DOCUMENT 57

EXECUTIVE AGREEMENT RELATING TO THE PROSECUTION OF EUROPEAN AXIS WAR CRIMINALS[1]
(DRAFTS 3 AND 4)

May 19, 1945

1. *Whereas*: (1) The Declaration issued at Moscow on November 1, 1943 stated that those German officers and men [and members of the Nazi Party][2] who have been responsible for or have taken a consenting part in ~~the~~[3] atrocities and crimes ~~committed by the Axis Powers~~ "will be sent back to the countries in which their abominable deeds were done in order that they may be judged and punished according to the laws of these liberated countries and of the free governments that will be ~~erected~~ [created] therein"; and (2) this

Declaration was stated to be "without prejudice to the case of major criminals, whose offenses have no particular geographical localization and who will be punished by [the] joint decision of the Governments of the Allies";

Now Therefore joint action is necessary to provide for the prompt prosecution and trial of the~~se~~ major criminals [of the European Axis Powers,] including the ~~principal~~ organizations [,] ~~which participated~~ [responsible for or taking a consenting part] in the commission of crimes and in the execution of criminal plans.

2. To provide the necessary practical measures for the achievement of these ends, this Executive Agreement is entered into by the Governments of the Union of Soviet Socialist Republics, the United States of America, the United Kingdom of Great Britain and Northern Ireland, and the Provisional Government of the French Republic, acting by their respective duly authorized representatives. ~~on their own behalf and on behalf of any other members of the United Nations who shall adhere to this agreement as hereinbelow provided.~~

3. All members of the United Nations shall be invited by the Government of the United Kingdom, acting on behalf of the other signatories hereto, to adhere to this Agreement. Such adherence shall in each case be notified to the Government of the United Kingdom which shall promptly inform the other parties to this Agreement.

4. For convenience, (a) the four signatories will sometimes be referred to as "the Signatories," (b) the members of the United Nations adhering hereto as provided in the preceding Article will sometimes be referred to as "the Adherents," and (c) the Signatories and all Adherents will sometimes be collectively referred to as "the parties to this Agreement."

INTERNATIONAL MILITARY TRIBUNALS

5. There shall be set up by the Control Council for Germany one or more international military tribunals (hereinafter referred to as "International Military Tribunal") which shall have jurisdiction to hear and determine any charges presented pursuant to Article 10. Each such International Military Tribunal shall consist of four members ~~and four alternates~~ [each with an alternate] to be appointed as follows: one member ~~and one alternate each~~ by the representatives upon the Control Council for Germany of the Soviet Union, the United States, the United Kingdom and France. The alternate, so far as practicable, shall be present at the sessions of the tribunal. The presiding officers of each International Military Tribunal shall be ~~determined~~ [selected by the members of the Tribunal, and if they are unable to agree, he shall be selected] by lot.

6. In the event of the death or incapacity of any member of an Inter-

national Military Tribunal, his alternate shall sit in his stead [without interruption of the proceedings.] All actions and decisions shall be taken by [majority vote.] ~~majority vote of all the members of the tribunal. In the event that the tribunal is in disagreement as to its judgment, the accused may be brought to trial before a second tribunal, no member of which shall have taken part in the first trial.~~

7. An International Military Tribunal may sit in any zone in Germany, Austria or Italy or in any other country with the consent of such country. It shall have the power to summon witnesses [including defendants] and to ~~compel~~ [require] their attendance [and testimony,] to require the production of documents, to administer oaths, to appoint special masters and other officers, to hold hearings and generally to exercise in a manner not inconsistent with the provisions of this Agreement plenary ~~judicial~~ authority with respect to the trial of charges brought pursuant to this Agreement.

8. An International Military Tribunal shall have the power to establish its own rules of procedure, which shall be not inconsistent with the provisions of this Agreement.

9. This Agreement shall not in any way prejudice the creation of other tribunals by the parties to this Agreement or any of them for the trial of persons who are not prosecuted before an International Military Tribunal [established hereunder].

PRESENTATION OF CHARGES AND PROSECUTION

10. The parties to this Agreement agree to bring to trial before an International Military Tribunal, in the names of their respective peoples, the major criminals of the ~~European Axis Powers~~ including ~~the principal persons and~~ organizations ~~charged~~ [, referred to in Article1.] ~~with participation in the commission of crimes and in the execution of criminal plans.~~ To this end, the Soviet Union, the United States, the United Kingdom and France shall each designate at the earliest possible time a representative to act as its chief of counsel. Such chiefs of counsel, acting by majority vote, shall determine the persons and organizations[4] to be brought to trial before an International Military Tribunal [,] and ~~acting as a group~~ they shall prepare the charges and institute and conduct the prosecution.

11. The chiefs of counsel shall also be charged with:

(a) recommending to appropriate governmental authorities agreements and measures supplemental to or in addition to this Agreement, necessary or appropriate to accomplish the objectives thereof, and

(b) the maintenance of liaison among and with the appropriate military and civil agencies, authorities and commissions of or representing any of the United Nations with respect to the matters dealt with in this Agreement.

DECLARATION OF LEGAL PRINCIPLES

12. In any trial before an International Military Tribunal, the tribunal shall be bound by this declaration of the parties to this Agreement that the following acts are criminal:

a. Atrocities and offenses against persons or property constituting violations of international law, ~~or of~~ [including] the laws, rules and customs of ~~war~~ [land and naval warfare.]

b. Atrocities and offenses[,] including atrocities and persecutions on racial or religious grounds,[5] committed since [1 January 1933][6] in violation of any applicable provision of the domestic law of ~~any of the parties or any Axis Power or satellite~~ [the country in which committed.]

c. Invasion ~~by force or threat of force of other~~ [another] countr~~ies~~[y] ~~in violation of international law or treaties~~ [by force or threat of force, or the] ~~d.~~ initiation of war, in violation of international law[.] ~~or treaties.~~

~~e.~~ [d.] Launching a war of aggression.

~~f. Recourse to war as an instrument of national policy or for the solution of international controversies.~~

["International law" shall be taken to include treaties between nations and the principles of the law of nations as they result from the usages established among civilized peoples from the laws of humanity, and the dictates of the public conscience.]

13. In any trial before an International Military Tribunal, the tribunal shall apply the general rule of liability that those who participate in the formulation ~~[or take a consenting part in]~~[7] ~~and~~ [or] execution of a criminal plan involving multiple crimes are liable for each of the offenses committed and responsible for the acts of each other.

14. In any trial before an International Military Tribunal any defense based upon the fact that the accused is or was the head or purported head or principal official of a state is legally inadmissible and will not be entertained.

15. In any trial before an International Military Tribunal the fact that a defendant acted pursuant to order of a superior or government sanction shall not constitute ~~an absolute~~ [a] defense [per se,] but may be considered either in defense or in mitigation of punishment if the tribunal determines that justice so requires.

~~DUE PROCESS FOR DEFENSE~~
FAIR TRIAL FOR DEFENDANTS

16. In order to insure fair trial for defendants charged with crime pursuant to this Agreement, it is declared that the following [procedure] is required[:]

~~in order to constitute due process in their behalf.~~

a. Reasonable notice shall be given to the defendants of the charges against them and of the opportunity to defend. Such notice may be actual or constructive. An International Military Tribunal shall determine what constitutes reasonable notice in any given instance.

b. The defendants physically present before an International Military Tribunal (a) will be furnished with copies translated into their own language, of any indictment, statement of charges or other document of arraignment upon which they are being tried[;] ~~and~~ (b) will be given fair opportunity to be heard in their defense ~~personally~~ and [to have the assistance of] ~~by~~ counsel. The tribunal shall determine to what extent [and for what reasons] proceedings against defendants may be taken without their presence.

c. Organizations, official or unofficial, may be charged before an International Military Tribunal with criminal acts or with complicity therein by producing before the tribunal and putting on trial such of their number as the tribunal may determine to be fairly representative of the group or organization in question. Upon conviction of an organization hereunder, the tribunal shall make written findings and enter written judgment [on] ~~finding and adjudicating~~ the charges against such organization and the representative members on trial.

EVIDENCE AND PROCEDURE

17. An International Military Tribunal shall adopt and apply to the greatest extent possible expeditious and non-technical procedures.

18. An International Military Tribunal shall (a) admit any evidence which ~~has~~ [it deems to have] probative value; (b) confine trials strictly to an expeditious hearing of the issues raised by the charges, (c) disallow action by defendants which will cause unreasonable delay or the introduction of irrelevant issues or evidence, and (d) employ with all possible liberality simplifications of proof, such as but not limited to: requiring defendants to make proffers of proof; taking judicial notice of facts of common knowledge; and utilizing reasonable presumptions.

PUNISHMENT

19. Defendants brought to trial before an International Military Tribunal as provided in this Agreement shall, upon conviction, suffer death or such other punishment as shall be determined by the tribunal ~~before which they are tried~~ [to be just] and approved by the Control Council acting by majority

vote. The Control Council, by such vote, may approve, reduce or otherwise alter the sentences determined by the tribunal, but may not increase the severity thereof.

20. The sentences, when and as approved by the Control Council, shall be carried into execution in accordance with the written orders of the Control Council.

PROSECUTION OF MEMBERS OF CRIMINAL ORGANIZATIONS

21. Upon conviction of an organization before an International Military Tribunal, persons charged with criminal liability by reason of membership therein may be prosecuted in occupation courts or other military tribunals established by the ~~Signatories~~ [parties] or any of them. In the trial of such prosecutions the legal principles declared in Articles 12, 13, 14 and 15 shall be binding upon the court or tribunal and the findings and judgment of an International Military Tribunal shall be conclusive with respect to the criminal purposes and activities of the organization. Upon proof of membership in such an organization, the burden shall be upon the defendant to establish any circumstances relating to his membership or participation therein which are relevant either in defense or in mitigation.

22. The chiefs of counsel designated pursuant to Article 10 shall prepare and recommend to the Control Council plans for the prosecution and trial of persons charged pursuant to Article 21 with liability by reason of membership in organizations found criminal by an International Military Tribunal.

EMOLUMENTS AND EXPENSES

23. The emoluments and expenses of the members of an International Military Tribunal and their alternates designated as provided in Article 5 of this Agreement and of the chiefs of counsel designated as provided in Article 10 of this Agreement, shall be borne by the respective Signatories by whom they have been designated.

24. The emoluments and expenses of the staffs for the International Military Tribunal and the chiefs of counsel and incidental expenses, such as rent, heat, light, stationery and printing shall be borne in equal share by the Signatories.

25. The emoluments and expenses of those occupation courts or other military tribunals which may be established for the trial of prosecutions instituted in accordance with Article 21 of this Agreement shall be justly apportioned between the Signatories concerned and any participating Adherents as may be agreed between them.

RETURN OF OFFENDERS TO THE SCENE OF THEIR CRIMES

26. The Signatories agree that the Control Council for Germany shall establish policies and procedures governing (a) the return of persons [in Germany] charged with criminal offenses to the scene of their crimes in accordance with the Moscow Declaration and (b) the surrender of persons [within Germany] in the custody of any of the Signatories who are demanded for prosecution by any party to this Agreement.

* * * * * * *

DOCUMENT 58

AN APPROACH TO THE PREPARATION OF THE PROSECUTION OF AXIS CRIMINALITY[1]

BY TELFORD TAYLOR

Early June, 1945

I. GENERAL

1. It is assumed that the two most important things to be accomplished by the Chief of Counsel are:

(a) *Positive*—To give meaning to the war against Germany. To validate the casualties we have suffered and the destruction and casualties we have caused. To show why those things had to be done. The conviction and punishment of Axis criminals are desirable objectives in themselves, but in order to accomplish the larger objectives the conviction and punishment must be obtained by procedures and for reasons which will help to make the war meaningful and valid for the people of the Allied Nations and, it is not beyond hope, for at least some people of the Axis nations.

(b) *Negative*—To establish and maintain harmonious relations with the other United Nations in the preparation and successful prosecution of the case. Incalculable harm can be done to international relations, and to public opinion about the meaning and consequences of the war, if the trial "bogs down" as the result of disagreements among the United Nations, or if the several nations proceed separately and in a spirit critical of each other.

2. The following is based on complete ignorance of, among other things, (a) international plans and time schedules for the holding of the trials,[2] (b) laws of war, rules of international law, and all legal problems relating to the prosecution of war criminals, and (c) the nature and amount of factual material

relating to this case in the hands of O.S.S. in Washington.[3]

3. It is believed that the case breaks generally into two principal parts (each capable of almost infinite subdivision) as follows:

(a) That the defendants *planned* and *launched* illegal wars of aggression, and

(b) That in the course of planning, launching, and carrying on such wars, the defendants committed outrages and offenses, violations of international laws or the public conscience, against their own nationals and the nationals of other countries, both civilian and military. For shorthand convenience, these may be called the "illegal launching" and "commission of atrocities" phases of the case. Under the "Memorandum on Trial Preparation" the preparation of each of these phases is divided between the OSS and the War Crimes Office (JAG).[4]

4. It is also assumed, on the basis of developments to date, that we can plan on sharing the preparation of this case with at least the British and the French.

II. "ILLEGAL LAUNCHING"

5. This phase of the case is based on the assumption that it is, or will be declared, a punishable offense to plan and launch (and lose?) an aggressive war, particularly if treaties are thereby violated. Although the phrase "illegal launching" is a "law idea", and although much legal paraphernalia will be and must be invoked to validate the assumption, the thing we want to accomplish is not a legal thing but a political thing. Its accomplishment depends on persuading the several participating nations to take the political step of committing themselves to this doctrine. Whether the doctrine is presently a judicially valid doctrine is an interesting question, and there will be much interesting and stimulating discussion thereon, but the question will be settled by political acts of the several nations, not by argument before and judicial decision by a tribunal, though such argument and judicial decision might *influence* the political decision.

6. It is important that the trial *not* become an inquiry into the *causes* of the war. It can not be established that Hitlerism was the sole cause of the war, and there should be no effort to do this. Nor, I believe, should there be any effort or time spent on apportioning out responsibility for causing the war among the many nations and individuals concerned. The question of causation is important and will be discussed for many years, but it has no place in this trial, which must rather stick rigorously to the doctrine that planning and launching of aggressive war is illegal, whatever may be the factors that caused the defendants to plan and to launch. Contributing causes may be pleaded by

the defendants before the bar of history, but not before the tribunal.

7. *Ex Post Facto*—Not, I believe, a bothersome question if we keep in mind that this is a *political* decision to declare and apply a principle of international law. It is the governments and people of the participating nations, and not the tribunal, who must be convinced that the principle is valid. Only the most incorrigible legalists can pretend to be shocked by the conclusion that the perpetrator of an aggressive war acts at peril of being punished for his perpetration, even if no tribunal has ever previously decided that perpetration of aggressive war is a crime. And, in any event, the ex post facto question is rendered much easier by the fact of treaty violations, and by the existence of numerous speeches and writings of wise and important men who have been saying for years that it is criminal to launch an aggressive war. Even though no judicial mechanism has heretofore existed to punish the leaders of large nations which violate treaties, a man who violates a treaty must act at peril of being punished by the offended party's employing self-help. The fact that the self-help happens to involve the declaration of a new principle of international law affords the perpetrator no additional ground of complaint.

8. *Elements of Proof*.—We need to establish that one or more of the defendants (a) planned to aggrandize an Axis nation in terms of boundaries and economy, (b) planned to wage aggressive warfare if necessary in order to accomplish the aggrandizement, (c) took action so as to be prepared to wage aggressive warfare, and (d) did launch aggressive warfare. It will also be very helpful to prove that (e) the defendants caused an Axis nation to break treaties in the planning and launching of the aggressive war, and (f) made treaties with the intention of breaking them if necessary to accomplish the aggrandizement.

9. *Evidence*.—*Intentions* of the defendants as made manifest in books, speeches, writings, laws and decrees, correspondence official and otherwise, conversation private and otherwise, etc.; *acts* of the defendants in enabling themselves to wage aggressive warfare and in launching it; *treaties and agreements* and their denunciation or violation.

III. "COMMISSION OF ATROCITIES"

10. The fact that numerous atrocities were committed by Axis personages will be only too easy to prove; in fact we will be in constant danger of being swamped by such evidence. For the Chief Counsel, the nub of the matter will be to prove that the atrocities were directed, encouraged, and assented to by the Axis leaders who are to be the defendants.

11. *Ex Post Facto*.—Many of the atrocities committed by the defendants can be shown to violate international law, the rules of war, or the laws of Axis or Axis-occupied countries. Wherever possible we should show that the

atrocity was committed in violation of previously established law or rule. But if such cannot be established, we need not shy off because of *ex post facto*. No one will be shocked by the doctrine that people who direct or do inhuman and barbarous things in the course of losing a war will be punished. Many would be shocked by the conclusion that such people may go scot-free unless a pre-existent law or rule can be cited. For convenience, however, we may speak of "crimes" where we have a pre-existent rule available and "atrocities" where we are not so sure, but where the inhumanity and barbarity of the act shocks a respectable percentage of the staff members who are told about the act . . .[5]

DOCUMENT 59

AGREEMENT AND CHARTER[1]

August 8, 1945

AGREEMENT by the Government of the United States of America, the Provisional Government of the French Republic, the Government of the United Kingdom of Great Britain and Northern Ireland and the Government of the Union of Soviet Socialist Republics for the Prosecution and Punishment of the Major War Criminals of the European Axis

Whereas the United Nations have from time to time made declarations of their intention that War Criminals shall be brought to justice;

And whereas the Moscow Declaration of the 30th October 1943 on German atrocities in Occupied Europe stated that those German Officers and men and members of the Nazi Party who have been responsible for or have taken a consenting part in atrocities and crimes will be sent back to the countries in which their abominable deeds were done in order that they may be judged and punished according to the laws of these liberated countries and of the free Governments that will be created therein;

And whereas this Declaration was stated to be without prejudice to the case of major criminals whose offenses have no particular geographical location and who will be punished by the joint decision of the Governments of the Allies;

Now therefore the Government of the United States of America, the Provisional Government of the French Republic, the Government of the United Kingdom of Great Britain and Northern Ireland and the Government of the Union of Soviet Socialist Republics (hereinafter called "the Signatories") acting in the interests of all the United Nations and by their representatives duly authorized thereto have concluded this Agreement.

Article 1. There shall be established after consultation with the Control Council for Germany an International Military Tribunal for the trial of war criminals whose offenses have no particular geographical location whether they be accused individually or in their capacity as members of organizations or groups or in both capacities.

Article 2. The constitution, jurisdiction and functions of the International Military Tribunal shall be those set out in the Charter annexed to this Agreement, which Charter shall form an integral part of this Agreement.

Article 3. Each of the Signatories shall take the necessary steps to make available for the investigation of the charges and trial the major war criminals detained by them who are to be tried by the International Military Tribunal. The Signatories shall also use their best endeavors to make available for investigation of the charges against and the trial before the International Military Tribunal such of the major war criminals as are not in the territories of any of the Signatories.

Article 4. Nothing in this Agreement shall prejudice the provisions established by the Moscow Declaration concerning the return of war criminals to the countries where they committed their crimes.

Article 5. Any Government of the United Nations may adhere to this Agreement by notice given through the diplomatic channel to the Government of the United Kingdom, who shall inform the other signatory and adhering Governments of each such adherence.

Article 6. Nothing in this Agreement shall prejudice the jurisdiction or the powers of any national or occupation court established or to be established in any allied territory or in Germany for the trial of war criminals.

Article 7. This Agreement shall come into force on the day of signature and shall remain in force for the period of one year and shall continue thereafter, subject to the right of any Signatory to give, through the diplomatic channel, one month's notice of intention to terminate it. Such termination shall not prejudice any proceedings already taken or any findings already made in pursuance of this Agreement.

In witness whereof the Undersigned have signed the present Agreement.

Done in quadruplicate in London this 8th day of August 1945 each in English, French and Russian, and each text to have equal authenticity.

For the Government of the United States of America
Robert H. Jackson

For the Provisional Government of the French Republic
Robert Falco[2]

For the Government of the United Kingdom of Great Britain and Northern Ireland
Jowitt C.

For the Government of the Union of Soviet Socialist Republics
I. Nikitchenko[3]
A. Trainin

Charter of the International Military Tribunal

I. CONSTITUTION OF THE INTERNATIONAL MILITARY TRIBUNAL

Article 1. In pursuance of the Agreement signed on the 8th day of August 1945 by the Government of the United States of America, the Provisional Government of the French Republic, the Government of the United Kingdom of Great Britain and Northern Ireland and the Government of the Union of Soviet Socialist Republics, there shall be established an International Military Tribunal (hereinafter called "the Tribunal") for the just and prompt trial and punishment of the major war criminals of the European Axis.

Article 2. The Tribunal shall consist of four members, each with an alternate. One member and one alternate shall be appointed by each of the Signatories. The alternates shall, so far as they are able, be present at all sessions of the Tribunal. In case of illness of any member of the Tribunal or his incapacity for some other reason to fulfill his functions, his alternate shall take his place.

Article 3. Neither the Tribunal, its members nor their alternates can be challenged by the prosecution, or by the Defendants or their Counsel. Each Signatory may replace its member of the Tribunal or his alternate for reasons of health or for other good reasons, except that no replacement may take place during a Trial, other than by an alternate.

Article 4.

(a) The presence of all four members of the Tribunal or the alternate for any absent member shall be necessary to constitute a quorum.

(b) The members of the Tribunal shall, before any trial begins, agree among themselves upon the selection from their number of a President, and the President shall hold office during that trial, or as may otherwise be agreed by a vote of not less than three members. The principle of rotation of presidency for successive trials is agreed. If, however, a session of the Tribunal takes place on the territory of one of the four Signatories, the representative of that Signatory on the Tribunal shall preside.

(c) Save as aforesaid the Tribunal shall take decisions by a majority vote and in case the votes are evenly divided, the vote of the President shall be decisive;

provided always that convictions and sentences shall only be imposed by affirmative votes of at least three members of the Tribunal.

Article 5. In case of need and depending on the number of matters to be tried, other Tribunals may be set up; and the establishment, functions, and procedure of each Tribunal shall be identical, and shall be governed by this Charter.

II. JURISDICTION AND GENERAL PRINCIPLES

Article 6. The Tribunal established by the Agreement referred to in Article 1 hereof for the trial and punishment of the major war criminals of the European Axis countries shall have the power to try and punish persons who, acting in the interests of the European Axis countries, whether as individuals or as members of organizations, committed any of the following crimes.

The following acts, or any of them, are crimes coming within the jurisdiction of the Tribunal for which there shall be individual responsibility:

(a) CRIMES AGAINST PEACE: namely, planning, preparation, initiation or waging of a war of aggression, or a war in violation of international treaties, agreements or assurances, or participation in a common plan or conspiracy for the accomplishment of any of the foregoing;

(b) WAR CRIMES: namely, violations of the laws or customs of war. Such violations shall include, but not be limited to, murder, ill-treatment or deportation to slave labor or for any other purpose of civilian population of or in occupied territory, murder or ill-treatment of prisoners of war or persons on the seas, killing of hostages, plunder of public or private property, wanton destruction of cities, towns or villages, or devastation not justified by military necessity;

(c) CRIMES AGAINST HUMANITY: namely, murder, extermination, enslavement, deportation, and other inhumane acts committed against any civilian population, before or during the war;[4] or persecutions on political, racial or religious grounds in execution of or in connection with any crime within the jurisdiction of the Tribunal, whether or not in violation of the domestic law of the country where perpetrated.

Leaders, organizers, instigators, and accomplices participating in the formulation or execution of a common plan or conspiracy to commit any of the foregoing crimes are responsible for all acts performed by any persons in execution of such plan.

Article 7. The official position of defendants, whether as Heads of State or responsible officials in Government Departments, shall not be considered as freeing them from responsibility or mitigating punishment.

Article 8. The fact that the Defendant acted pursuant to order of his Government or of a superior shall not free him from responsibility, but may be considered in mitigation of punishment if the Tribunal determines that justice so requires.

Article 9. At the trial of any individual member of any group or organization the Tribunal may declare (in connection with any act of which the individual may be convicted) that the group or organization of which the individual was a member was a criminal organization.

After receipt of the Indictment the Tribunal shall give such notice as it thinks fit that the prosecution intends to ask the Tribunal to make such declaration and any member of the organization will be entitled to apply to the Tribunal for leave to be heard by the Tribunal upon the question of the criminal character of the organization. The Tribunal shall have power to allow or reject the application. If the application is allowed, the Tribunal may direct in what manner the applicants shall be represented and heard.

Article 10. In cases where a group or organization is declared criminal by the Tribunal, the competent national authority of any Signatory shall have the right to bring individuals to trial for membership therein before national, military or occupation courts. In any such case the criminal nature of the group or organization is considered proved and shall not be questioned.

Article 11. Any person convicted by the Tribunal may be charged before a national, military or occupation court, referred to in Article 10 of this Charter, with a crime other than of membership in a criminal group or organization and such court may, after convicting him, impose upon him punishment independent of and additional to the punishment imposed by the Tribunal for participation in the criminal activities of such group or organization.

Article 12. The Tribunal shall have the right to take proceedings against a person charged with crimes set out in Article 6 of this Charter in his absence, if he has not been found or if the Tribunal, for any reason, finds it necessary, in the interests of justice, to conduct the hearing in his absence.

Article 13. The Tribunal shall draw up rules for its procedure. These rules shall not be inconsistent with the provisions of this Charter.

III. COMMITTEE FOR THE INVESTIGATION AND PROSECUTION OF MAJOR WAR CRIMINALS

Article 14. Each Signatory shall appoint a Chief Prosecutor for the investigation of the charges against and the prosecution of major war criminals.

The Chief Prosecutors shall act as a committee for the following purposes:

(a) to agree upon a plan of the individual work of each of the Chief Prosecutors and his staff,

(b) to settle the final designation of major war criminals to be tried by the Tribunal,
(c) to approve the Indictment and the documents to be submitted therewith,
(d) to lodge the Indictment and the accompanying documents with the Tribunal,
(e) to draw up and recommend to the Tribunal for its approval draft rules of procedure, contemplated by Article 13 of this Charter. The tribunal shall have powers to accept, with or without amendments, or to reject, the rules so recommended.

The Committee shall act in all the above matters by a majority vote and shall appoint a Chairman as may be convenient and in accordance with the principle of rotation: provided that if there is an equal division of vote concerning the designation of a Defendant to be tried by the Tribunal, or the crimes with which he shall be charged, that proposal will be adopted which was made by the party which proposed that the particular Defendant be tried, or the particular charges be preferred against him.

Article 15. The Chief Prosecutors shall individually, and acting in collaboration with one another, also undertake the following duties:

(a) investigation, collection and production before or at the trial of all necessary evidence,
(b) the preparation of the Indictment for approval by the Committee in accordance with paragraph (c) of Article 14 hereof,
(c) the preliminary examination of all necessary witnesses and of the Defendants,
(d) to act as prosecutor at the Trial,
(e) to appoint representatives to carry out such duties as may be assigned to them,
(f) to undertake such other matters as may appear necessary to them for the purposes of the preparation for and conduct of the Trial.

It is understood that no witness or Defendant detained by any Signatory shall be taken out of the possession of that Signatory without its assent.

IV. FAIR TRIAL FOR DEFENDANTS

Article 16. In order to ensure fair trial for the Defendants, the following procedure shall be followed:
(a) The Indictment shall include full particulars specifying in detail the charges against the defendants. A copy of the Indictment and of all the documents lodged with the Indictment, translated into a language which he understands, shall be furnished to the Defendant at a reasonable time before the Trial.

(b) During any preliminary examination or trial of a Defendant he shall have the right to give any explanation relevant to the charges made against him.
(c) A preliminary examination of a Defendant and his Trial shall be conducted in, or translated into, a language which the Defendant understands.
(d) A defendant shall have the right to conduct his own defense before the Tribunal or to have the assistance of Counsel.
(e) A defendant shall have the right through himself or through his Counsel to present evidence at the Trial in support of his defense, and to cross-examine any witness called by the Prosecution.

V. POWERS OF THE TRIBUNAL AND CONDUCT OF THE TRIAL

Article 17. The Tribunal shall have the power
(a) to summon witnesses to the Trial and to require their attendance and testimony and to put questions to them,
(b) to interrogate any Defendant,
(c) to require the production of documents and other evidentiary material,
(d) to administer oaths to witnesses,
(e) to appoint officers for the carrying out of any task designated by the Tribunal including the power to have evidence taken on commission.
Article 18. The Tribunal shall
(a) confine the Trial strictly to an expeditious hearing of the issues raised by the charges,
(b) take strict measures to prevent any action which will cause unreasonable delay, and rule out irrelevant issues and statements of any kind whatsoever,
(c) deal summarily with any contumacy, imposing appropriate punishment, including exclusion of any Defendant or his Counsel from some or all further proceedings, but without prejudice to the determination of the charges.
Article 19. The Tribunal shall not be bound by technical rules of evidence. It shall adopt and apply to the greatest possible extent expeditious and non-technical procedure, and shall admit any evidence which it deems to have probative value.
Article 20. The Tribunal may require to be informed of the nature of any evidence before it is offered so that it may rule upon the relevance thereof.
Article 21. The Tribunal shall not require proof of facts of common knowledge but shall take judicial notice thereof. It shall also take judicial notice of official governmental documents and reports of the United Nations, including the acts and documents of the committees set up in the various allied countries for the investigation of war crimes, and the records and findings of military or other Tribunals of any of the United Nations.
Article 22. The permanent seat of the Tribunal shall be in Berlin. The first

meetings of the members of the Tribunal and of the Chief Prosecutors shall be held at Berlin in a place to be designated by the Control Council for Germany. The first trial shall be held at Nuremberg, and any subsequent trials shall be held at such places as the Tribunal may decide.

Article 23. One or more of the Chief Prosecutors may take part in the prosecution at each Trial. The function of any Chief Prosecutor may be discharged by him personally, or by any person or persons authorized by him.

The function of Counsel for a Defendant may be discharged at the Defendant's request by any Counsel professionally qualified to conduct cases before the Courts of his own country, or by any other person who may be specially authorized thereto by the Tribunal.

Article 24. The proceedings at the Trial shall take the following course:

(a) The Indictment shall be read in court.

(b) The Tribunal shall ask each Defendant whether he pleads "guilty" or "not guilty."

(c) The prosecution shall make an opening statement.

(d) The Tribunal shall ask the prosecution and the defense what evidence (if any) they wish to submit to the Tribunal, and the Tribunal shall rule upon the admissibility of any such evidence.

(e) The witnesses for the Prosecution shall be examined and after that the witnesses for the Defense. Thereafter such rebutting evidence as may be held by the Tribunal to be admissible shall be called by either the Prosecution or the Defense.

(f) The Tribunal may put any question to any witness and to any Defendant, at any time.

(g) The Prosecution and the Defense shall interrogate and may cross-examine any witnesses and any Defendant who gives testimony.

(h) The Defense shall address the court.

(i) The Prosecution shall address the court.

(j) Each Defendant may make a statement to the Tribunal.

(k) The Tribunal shall deliver judgment and pronounce sentence.

Article 25. All official documents shall be produced, and all court proceedings conducted, in English, French and Russian, and in the language of the Defendant. So much of the record and of the proceedings may also be translated into the language of any country in which the Tribunal is sitting, as the Tribunal considers desirable in the interests of justice and public opinion.

VI. THE JUDGMENT AND SENTENCE

Article 26. The judgment of the Tribunal as to the guilt or the innocence of any Defendant shall give the reasons on which it is based, and shall be final and not subject to review.

Article 27. The Tribunal shall have the right to impose upon a Defendant, on conviction, death or such other punishment as shall be determined by it to be just.

Article 28. In addition to any punishment imposed by it, the Tribunal shall have the right to deprive the convicted person of any stolen property and order its delivery to the Control Council for Germany.

Article 29. In case of guilt, sentences shall be carried out in accordance with the orders of the Control Council for Germany, which may at any time reduce or otherwise alter the sentences, but may not increase the severity thereof. If the Control Council for Germany, after any Defendant has been convicted and sentenced, discovers fresh evidence which, in its opinion, would found a fresh charge against him, the Council shall report accordingly to the Committee established under Article 14 hereof, for such action as they may consider proper, having regard to the interests of justice.

VII. EXPENSES

Article 30. The expenses of the Tribunal and of the Trials, shall be charged by the signatories against the funds allotted for maintenance of the Control Council for Germany.

Notes

PREFACE

1. *Report of Robert H. Jackson; Trial of the Major War Criminals before the International Military Tribunal.*

2. Aside from my *Reaching Judgment at Nuremberg*, the past few years have also seen the appearance of Werner Maser, *Nürnberg, Tribunal der Sieger*, Airey Neave, *On Trial at Nuremberg*, and a revised edition of Joe Heydecker and Johannes Leeb, Der *Nürnberger Prozess* (Cologne: 1979).

3. Bradley F. Smith, *The Road to Nuremburg.*

DOCUMENT 1

1. *Declaration of German Atrocities*, in *Foreign Relations of the United States, 1943*, 1:768–69. Winston Churchill proposed the issuance of such a statement, and dispatched a draft to Stalin and Roosevelt on October 13, 1943. The Soviet Union suggested a few additions and rewordings; the most important, for this subject, was the addition of the last clause of the final sentence (*ibid.*, 1:556–57, 768). The declaration, as printed above, is the final form of the document, and includes the Soviet revisions.

After checking the texts for accuracy, I have tried to cite the form of every document most readily available, in this case in the *Foreign Relations of the United States* series.

DOCUMENT 2

1. Walter Bedell Smith Collection of World War II Documents, Box 35, Dwight D. Eisenhower Library, Abilene, Kansas. This directive also ordered the dissolution of the Nazi Party (NSDAP), including the S.A. and the S.S. (pp. 19–20, 56–57), and of the Gestapo and S.D. (p. 74), but not the detention of members of these organizations.

2. No punctuation in the original.

DOCUMENT 3

1. Although this handbook was officially dated September 1, 1944, advance copies circulated in official Washington during the preceding week or two. Like the interim directive printed above, the handbook called for the apprehension of war criminals and the dissolution of the NSDAP. A number of minor errors in German spelling have been corrected. (Walter Bedell Smith Collection of World War II Documents, Box 28, Dwight D. Eisenhower Library, Abilene, Kansas.)

2. Western armies crossed the German border on September 12.

3. *Ordnungspolizei* and *Sicherheitspolizei Befehlshaber* were the commanders of the two main branches of the German police system, the regular police and the security police.

4. *Technische Nothilfe* (Nazi Relief Organization)—this organization and a number of those listed below never enjoyed much power in the Nazi system and had lost most of their moderate influence by the last stages of the war. Much of the information included in this table came from a War Department handbook dating from 1941–1942 and bears little relation to the system of power in late Nazi Germany.

5. Higher S.S. and police chiefs.

6. Inspectors of the *Ordnungspolizei* ("regular police").

7. Inspectors of the *Sicherheitspolizei* ("security police") and the "*Sicherheitsdienst* ("security service") of the S.S.

8. The Nazi party organization was structured geographically into *Gaue* ("regions"), which were in turn subdivided into *Kreise* ("areas"). The *Kreishauptstellungsleiter* was the administrative chief of his area.

9. The *Kreise* were subdivided into *Bereiche* ("zones"). The *Bereichleiter* was the administrative chief of his zone.

10. Nazi town (*Ort*) organizations were subordinate to the *Bereich*. The Nazi leader in a town was the *Ortsgruppenleiter*.

11. The combat (armed) S.S.

12. The *Allgemeine* S.S. was the general S.S.; a *Scharführer* was a platoon leader.

13. The *Sturmabteiling* was the Nazi storm troop (Brown Shirts); a *Sturmbannführer* was a battalion commander.

14. The Hitler Youth; a *Sturmführer* was a company commander.

15. *Nationalsozialistisches Kraftfahrkorps* (Nazi Motor Corps); a *Staffelführer* was a battalion commander.

16. *Nationalsozialistisches Fliegerkorps* (Nazi Flying Corps); a *Sturmbannführer* in this organization was a battalion commander.

17. *Reichsarbeitsdienst* (State Labor Service).

DOCUMENT 4

1. *Foreign Relations of the United States, 1944*, 1:1351–53.

2. See the preceding section of the volume cited in footnote 1.

3. Anthony Eden, later the earl of Avon.

4. The British had reason to believe that the Americans had already assented. On August 7, 1944, Sir William Malkin, the Foreign Office legal specialist who was then visiting Washington, reported to London that in a recent conversation the American State Department legal specialist Green H. Hackworth had declared that the State Department was "definitely opposed to the Commission taking over crimes committed against German Jews etc. in Germany." Hackworth would soon reverse his position. (Sir William Malkin to Frank K. Roberts, August 7, 1944, FO 371/38999/10606, Public Records Office, London.)

DOCUMENT 5

1. This document bears a State Department logged date of August 25, 1944. The *New York Times* of August 29 carried a story on its transmittal. On September 8, the State Department forwarded it to the War Department. See Secretary of War to the Secretary of State, October 27, 1944 (and enclosures) 740.00116 EW/10-2744, Illegal and Inhumane Warfare, National Archives, Diplomatic Branch (the document printed above is taken from that file). See also the War Department preparation papers, McCloy to the Secretary of War, October 27, 1944, Asst. Sect., Box 15, January '43–December '44 File.

2. No point 6 is included in the original document.

3. "Friends of the court."

4. UNWCC.

5. "The legal right to appear and be heard."

DOCUMENT 6

1. Diaries of Henry L. Stimson, August 24, 1944, vol. 48, p. 22, roll 9, Yale University. These briefing notes were prepared by Stimson after a conference with Harry Hopkins, John J. McCloy, and McGeorge Bundy.

DOCUMENT 7

1. *The Morgenthau Diary (Germany)*, 2:443–44.

2. "War Department Handbook of Military Government for Germany."

3. Works Progress Administration, Civilian Conservation Corps, Public Works Administration (New Deal organizations created in 1935 [WPA] and 1933).

DOCUMENT 8

1. From John W. Pehle, executive director of the War Refugee Board, which was established by President Roosevelt in January 1944, largely because of pressure from Secretary of the Treasury Morgenthau, who insisted that something be done for Jews facing the Holocaust. Pehle was a close associate of Morgenthau's. During much of the fall of 1944, Edward R. Stettenius served as acting secretary of state, finally replacing the ailing Hull as secretary in late November. (Asst. Sect., Box 16, Working File. [The document was sent to the War Department on September 4, 1944; see below, document 18].)

2. The Office of War Information, established in June 1942, was directed by Elmer Davis.

3. See below, document 16, for the citations that played a significant role in the development of U.S. war crimes policy.

4. Dubois was another official of the Treasury Department and a close associate of Henry Morgenthau.

5. Herbert Pell, American representative on the UNWCC.

6. See document 4.

7. Not printed. The draft cable contained the argument put forward in the printed letter from Pehle; it was not sent to Mr. Pell by the State Department.

DOCUMENT 9

1. *Foreign Relations of the United States, The Conference at Quebec, 1944*, pp. 76–77.

2. *Geheime Staatspolizei* (Secret State Police). Actually, at this point in the history of the Third Reich, the Gestapo was only one element in the regime's repressive police system.

3. Specifically members of the S.A. (Sturmabteilung d. NSDAP), i.e., the Brown Shirts. But it is not clear whether Stimson sharply distinguished them from the S.S. (Schutzstaffel).

4. International convention designating protections and rights for prisoners of war, signed July 27, 1929.

DOCUMENT 10

1. Expression is vague or awkward at a number of points in this document, but rather than break the flow with an abundance of footnotes, the text appears as it did in the original transcript. RG 153, JAG, Box 1603, File nr. 103-Bk.2-51, Thru. Federal Record Center, Suitland, Maryland.

2. Francis Biddle, attorney general of the United States (and later member of the Nuremberg Tribunal) prosecuted the military trial of the eight Nazi saboteurs in August 1942.

3. He seems to be referring to the investigations made by the Extraordinary State Commission for the Investigation of German Crimes. Professor A. W. Trainin, one of its most prestigious members, was later a Soviet representative at the London Charter conference in the summer of 1945.

4. Presumably he is referring to investigations associated with the UNWCC.

5. Secretary of State Cordell Hull. This was the meeting of the Cabinet Committee on Germany—Morgenthau, Hull, Stimson, and Harry Hopkins.

6. Willard B. Cowles, "Trial of War Criminals by Military Tribunals," *American Bar Association Journal* 30 (June 1944):330–33.

DOCUMENT 11

1. This document was prepared on September 4, 1944, by James W. Riddleberger, Chief Division of Central European Affairs of the State Department, and was

approved without change by Secretary of State Hull. (*Foreign Relations of the United States, The Conference at Quebec, 1944*, p. 96).

2. Italicized in the original.

DOCUMENT 12

1. *The Morgenthau Diary (Germany)*, 2:105–8.

2. All italics, here and below, are in the original.

3. *Nationalsozialistisches Kraftfahrkorps* (Nazi Motor Corps).

4. The Labor Front, or state labor service, was the *Reichsarbeitsdienst*. Strength through Joy (*Kraft durch Freude*) was a Nazi social/recreational program aimed at heightening worker morale.

5. Although the term *Junker* was applied to various Nazi officer cadets, such as those of the S.S., as used here it refers to the great noble landholders of east Prussia. These men were long held to be the basis of conservative Prussian power, but Hitler had already dealt them a severe blow, and Soviet occupation eliminated them.

6. Taken together, primogeniture and entail established that the estates could not be alienated, but had to pass to the eldest (male) heir.

DOCUMENT 13

1. This document, written after the first meeting of the Cabinet Committee on Germany, was a rebuttal to the tough peace plans advocated by the other members of the committee. Although addressed to Henry Morgenthau, copies were sent to the other committee members and to the president. (The papers of Henry L. Stimson (Correspondence Records), September 5, 1944, roll 110 Yale University).

DOCUMENT 14

1. *Foreign Relations of the United States, The Conference at Quebec, 1944*, pp. 124–25.

2. See document 12.

DOCUMENT 15

1. A copy of this paper was discussed with American officials during the Quebec conference and remained in their possession. (*Foreign Relations of the United States, The Conference at Quebec, 1944*, pp. 91–93).

2. War Cabinet W.M. (44) 83rd Conclusions, June 28, 1944, Cab 21, Public Records Office, London. In this meeting an extended discussion occurred about who should be included in a shoot-on-sight list, and the possible dangers of reprisal if such a list became public. Simon was directed at this meeting to produce a clarifying paper. The paper in question (document 15) was not produced for two and a half months, and was not presented to the Cabinet or the Foreign Office before Churchill and Simon had discussed it with the Americans at Quebec. See Bradley F. Smith, *Reaching Judgment at Nuremburg*, p. 30 and related footnotes.

3. Italics, here and below, are as in the original document.

4. W.P. (44) 330, June 16, 1944, Cab 21, Public Records Office, London. The list contained the names of thirty-three Germans and eight Italians.

5. W.P. (44) 345, June 26, 1944, Cab 21, Public Records Office, London. This was a paper by Clement Atlee, who wanted to include industrialists and military leaders in the shoot-on-sight list, and also recommended the inclusion of Franz von Papen and Arthur Seyss Inquart.

6. See Bradley F. Smith, *Reaching Judgment at Nuremburg*, pp. 29–30 and related footnotes.

DOCUMENT 16

1. Preparatory materials for this document may be found in Box no. 4, Trial and Punishment File no. 1, Murray C. Bernays Papers, University of Wyoming, and (under the date of October 27, 1944) in Asst. Sect., Box 15, January '43–Dec. '44 File. The document itself is probably most conveniently located as an appendix to the Stimson to Hull letter of October 27, 1944, printed below as document 18.

2. Italics, here and below, are in the original document.

3. This largely fanciful assertion was carried over into many of the drafts of the evolving Nuremberg plan as a justification for casting the net as wide as possible.

4. Bernays attached the American Jewish Conference Statement of August 25 and the Pehle to Stettinius message of August 28 (documents 5 and 8) as appendixes to his plan (Tabs A and B), and it is the series of statements by Allied leaders mentioned therein to which he is referring.

5. As his appendix Tab C, Bernays included the British aide-mémoire of August 19 (document 4), to which he refers here.

6. He is again referring to the American Jewish Conference and Pehle statements of August 25 and 28. Later the issue did produce a flurry in the press; see, for example, *New York Times*, November 26, 1944, p. 24.

7. Here again he refers to the statements of Pehle and the American Jewish Conference.

8. This refers to a proposal before the UNWCC that a treaty court be established to try Nazi war crimes. The issue was a matter of bitter controversy and ultimately was flatly opposed by the British government; see the aide-mémoire of October 30, 1944, *Foreign Relations of the United States, 1944*, 1:1389–91.

9. This garbled expression is in the original document. Presumably it should have read, "affected participation," etc.

DOCUMENT 17

1. Asst. Sect., Box 15, January '43–December '44 File. Next to Bernays, Colonel Cutter became the most important drafter of the plans for Nuremberg before the London Conference. After the war he was a prominent lawyer in Massachusetts, ultimately serving as a justice of the Massachusetts State Supreme Court.

2. All italics, here and below, are in the original document.

3. This is the Bernays G-1 plan printed above as dcument 16.

4. This file consisted of the British aide-mémoire (August 19, document 4), the American Jewish Conference Statement (August 25, document 5), and Pehle to Stettinius (August 28, document 8). Ultimately the secretary of war took the tack that the UNWCC should not take such action, but dodged the rest of the issue, see below, document 18.

5. Civil Affairs Division.

6. See above, document 16, paragraph 7.

7. A proceeding dealing with right, title, status, etc. by a court not having power over the person of the parties affected.

8. The fear that the Nazi leaders would make propaganda capital out of a state trial plagued American planners until the final days of the IMT.

DOCUMENT 18

1. 740.00116 EW/10-2744, National Archives, Diplomatic Branch.

2. See document 8.

3. See document 5.

4. The European Advisory Commission was established in October 1943 by the Big Three to coordinate Allied policy for Europe. The American representative was

Ambassador John G. Winant. Due in large measure to the caution and confusion in Washington, the commission's promise to unify policy failed to materialize.

5. The Bernays plan, printed above as document 16.

6. Bernays' superior, Major General Stephen G. Henry.

7. War crimes planners became very wary of this theory of subjugation, because German defendants could use it to give a legal gloss to many of their activities in occupied territories. For the problems it caused in the case of the *Protektor* of Bohemia Moravia, Konstantin von Neurath, see Bradley F. Smith, *Reaching Judgment at Nuremberg*, pp. 226–27.

8. James V. Forrestal.

DOCUMENT 19

1. Rosenman Papers War Crimes.

2. These references come from the statement of the American Jewish Conference dated August 25, 1944, printed above as document 5, and they have been published in *Report of Robert H. Jackson*, pp. 9–13.

3. Italics, here and below, in the original document.

4. This odd notion, that Germans forced to stand trial would not yield a record based on duress, remains in a number of the later drafts of the plan.

5. Inclusion of this surprising, and unsupported, assertion is especially difficult to understand.

DOCUMENT 20

1. Asst. Sect., Box 16, Working File.

2. JCS 1067 was the policy directive for postdefeat Germany. Although continually redrafted, the initial arrest categories are in the printed documents 2 and 3.

3. The date Hitler was named chancellor.

DOCUMENT 21

1. Box no. 4, Trial and Punishment File no. 1, Murray C. Bernays Collection, University of Wyoming. (This document is commenting on document 16.)

2. Note General Cramer's very similar observation in his telephone discussion with Secretary of War Stimson, document 10.

3. Brigadier General William E. Hall, commander of the Fifteenth Air Force, was in Bulgaria, almost immediately after the surrender of that country, to head an American war crimes investigatory commission. For his difficulties with Soviet authorities, see *Foreign Relations of the United States, 1944*, 3:470–71, 479–80.

4. Asterisks, here and below, are in the original document.

5. Article 38 treats command relationships to military courts.

6. Or *res adjudicata*, a matter finally decided by a court, which cannot be litigated again between the same parties.

DOCUMENT 22

1. This form of the document was completed on December 4, 1944, and was circulated to the Departments of State, Justice, etc., on December 3–4, 1944. See Judge Rosenman's papers and Asst. Sect. of War's January-April 1945 War Crimes File, as cited in note 4 below.

2. Rosenman Papers War Crimes. All italics, here and below, are in the original.

3. All these citations come from the American Jewish Conference statement (document 5), except the concurrent resolution of March 18, 1943, which condemned atrocities committed in Central and Eastern Europe, especially against Jews, and demanded punishment.

4. The important changes embodied in this draft, compared with the draft of November 11, 1944 (see document 19), are marked in brackets here and below. The changes result primarily from the criticisms of Hackworth, but also include a few rewordings advanced by Colonel Berry of G-1. (Hackworth to the assistant secretary of war, November 16, 1944, Rosenman Papers War Crimes, and Colonel Bernays to Colonel Cutter, November 29, 1944, Asst. Sect., Box 16, January-April 1945 File.)

5. See note 4.

6. See note 4.

7. See note 4.

8. Advocacy of a treaty court is more hesitant in this draft because of the objections of Hackworth. See note 4.

9. See note 4.

10. See note 4.

11. British Aide-Mémoire, October 30, 1944, *Foreign Relations of the United States, 1944*, 1:1389–91. The British paper contended that a UNWCC court was unnecessary, impractical, and outside the mandate of the UNWCC. London did indicate a cautious endorsement of mixed military tribunals, but its main thrust was that war criminals should be tried in the national courts of the individual United Nations. The general tone of the paper showed that Britain (or at least the Foreign Office) viewed any effort to extend the war criminal net with cool, perhaps glacial, suspicion.

12. The whole section of this draft headed "British View" was added to meet Hackworth's views. See note 4.

13. This assertion seems to be based on a clouded letter to McCloy from R. Keith Kane, special assistant to the secretary of the navy (dated c. November 16, 1944, Rosenman Papers War Crimes). But later the secretary of the navy objected to a paragraph similar to the one in this draft, claiming that it overstated Navy disinterest. (Kane to Admiral Davidson, January 25, 1945, RG 165, G-1, Personnel, 000.51, War Crimes, Box 313, Federal Records Center, Suitland, Maryland.)

DOCUMENT 23

1. 740.00116 EW/11-2744, National Archives, Diplomatic Branch.

2. 740.00116 EW/11-1544, National Archives, Diplomatic Branch. In early 1944, the Czech representative on the UNWCC advanced the proposition that the launching of the war should be condemned as a crime, but the proposal was blocked by the British. When the issue was raised again in August, a long debate followed, with a subcommittee declaring tentatively against the proposal in October. (UNWCC, *History of the United Nations War Crimes Commission*, pp. 181–82.) This state of affairs led the American representative, Herbert Pell, to seek instructions from the State Department, which in turn prompted the State Department inquiry to Stimson.

3. When the subcommittee referred to in the previous note made its report, the legal argument against declaring the launching of the war a crime rested on a memorandum by the renowned British authority on international law Sir Arnold McNair. A copy of that memorandum is in Rosenman Papers War Crimes.

4. Herbert Pell, a rather excitable ex-Congressman, who constantly battled what he saw as the overly cautious and hesitant war crimes policy of the State Department.

DOCUMENT 24

1. Asst. Sect., Box 16, Working File. Although Stimson's letter to McCloy is dated November 28, the version of Chanler's memorandum which circulated in the War Department was dated November 30; that version has been printed here.

2. Italics, here and below, are in the original document.

3. Although William Chanler was nominally just a colonel in the Civil Affairs Division of the War department, he was also a member of Mr. Stimson's law firm, his neighbor, and a close personal friend. As such, his views must be given special weight.

4. The Kellogg-Briand Pact.

5. Interdepartmental ad hoc war crimes committee, established on November 9, 1944.

6. The citation in the original document reads: "Statement of Hon. Henry L. Stimson, Secretary of War, Hearings before the House Committee on Foreign Affairs, 77th Congress, 1st Session on H. Res. 1776, pages 103–5."

7. Asterisks are in the original.

8. The citation in the original document reads: "International Law Ass'n., 38 Reports (1935) 66,67."

9. The German occupation of Bohemia and Moravia in March 1939 is legally more complicated than Chanler's presentation indicates because, since there was no resistance by the Czechoslovakian state, there were no casualties and no condition of war.

10. The agreement of September 1938 whereby Germany obtained four-power sanction for the annexation of the Sudetenland of Czechoslovakia.

11. "Living space," a recurrent theme in Hitler's expansionist demands.

12. This view of American history, ignoring such incidents as the Mexican-American War, as well as Chanler's account of the probable attitudes of the other United Nations, may be most charitably characterized as naively indicative of the times.

13. *Stare decisis*, i.e., falling under the rules of precedent.

DOCUMENT 25

1. Brigadier General Kenneth C. Royall, deputy fiscal director and a postwar secretary of the army, was apparently brought into the war crimes picture because McCloy was doubtful about the role of the JAG and was seeking an alternate champion of the conspiracy idea. However, General Royall had as many, if not more, doubts than JAG, and was not a bold champion of the G-1 plan. See Bernays to Berry, December 27, 1944, RG 165, G-1 Personnel, 000.51, War Crimes, Box 313, Federal Records Center, Suitland, Maryland.

The Royall memorandum printed here may be found in Asst. Sect., Box 15, January '43–December '44 File.

2. The exact nature of the materials is not known, but they presumably included the G-1 plan (September 15) and the papers of the British government, the American Jewish Conference, and the War Refugee Board, to which it addressed itself.

3. All italics, here and below, are in the original document.

4. This seems to be a garbled reference to the UNWCC.

5. Note the omission of the Soviet Union.

6. This apparently refers to General Royall's working papers, which do not appear in the files of the assistant secretary of war.

7. See note 6.

DOCUMENT 26

1. Asst. Sect., Box 16, Working File. Although the document was in McCloy's files, it is a photocopy, and the form of the memorandum is very rough, including many penciled rewordings. At the end of the document is what seems to be the signature of General Cramer, the judge advocate general. Typed at the bottom of page one is the name of the apparent author of the memorandum, "Lt. Freeman"; presumably Lt. Alwyn Vernon Freeman of JAG, who in the postwar period become a prominent and highly regarded federal government attorney. The reason why this document was never put in finished form is explained in paragraph 5 of document 30.

2. Major General Stephen G. Henry. The original transmission number was WDGAP 000.5.

3. Document 23 is Stimson's reply to the State Department letter of November 15.

4. See the notes to document 23 for more information on this issue.
The original footnote in this document reads: "Minutes of 36th Meeting, 17 October 1944, Doc. M. 36; cf. also Mr. Pell's letter to the Secretary of State, dated 2 November 1944, No. 18981." These documents and other related materials may be found in *Foreign Relations of the United States, 1944*, 1:1391f.

5. All italics, here and below, are in the original document, but much pencil marking was added to the original document before it was photostated, and some of the underlines may have come from commentators rather than the author.

6. The immediately preceding phrase was a penciled rephrasing.

7. The original footnote reads: "Cf. Par. 4 of his note, UNWCC Document C43, 18 August 1944."

8. "In itself."

9. The original footnote reads: "*Treaties Conventions, etc., between the United States and Other Powers, 1923–1937*, vol. 4, p. 5130."

10. The original footnote reads: "Oppenheim, *International Law*, 6th ed., vol. II, pp. 144–145; Wheaton, *International Law*, 7th ed., vol. II, pp. 89–99; Westlake, *International Law*, vol. II, pp. 3–4, 28; Politis, *The New Aspects of International Law*, pp. 32ff.; Hall, *International Law*, 7th ed., pp. 61 ff; Hyde, *International Law*, 2nd ed., Sec. 596, *et seq.*; Le Fur, *Droit International Public*, p. 541; Fauchille, *Droit International Public*, vol. II, pp. 7–8; Schwarzenberger, in *Czechoslovak Yearbook of International Law*, 1942, p. 77; and compare Halleck, *International Law*, 3rd ed., vol. 1, pp. 493–494, with Nippold, *Die Gestaltung des Völkerrechts nach dem Weltkriege*, Carnegie Ed., pp. 109ff."

11. Seven long paragraphs, covering nine and a half pages of the original document and devoted to showing that aggressive war was not a punishable crime up through the first half of the year 1927, have been omitted.

12. The passage cut here, as well as the next two marked by asterisks, was cut in the original.

13. The original footnote reads: "22 A.J.I.L. [*American Journal of International Law*], 1928, pp. 356–357. Cf. also, Alvarez, *Le Panaméricanisme et la Si Conference Panaméricane*, pp. 74 ff.; Urrutia, *La Continent American et le Droit international*, pp. 96 ff."

14. The faulty paragraph numbering here and in the sections immediately following is an error made in the original document.

15. The original footnote reads: "*Treaties, Conventions, etc.* vol. 4, p. 4793."

16. The original footnote reads: "*Ibid*, p. 5132."

17. The original footnote reads: "For detailed treatment of these questions, see Wright, "The Meaning of the Pact of Paris," in 27 *A.J.I.L.*, 1933, pp. 39 ff.; and Wehberg, *The Outlawry of War*, pp. 82 ff."

18. The original footnote reads: "Thus Borchard, in 23 *A.J.I.L.*, 1929, p. 118: 'No conceivable wars have been excluded from the list of permitted wars.' "

19. The original footnote reads: "Cf. the *Case of the Factory at Chorzon*, Judgments of the Permanent Court of International Justice, Series A, no. 9, pp. 27–28; I. Hudson, *World Court Reports*, p. 663." Number error that follows, in original.

20. The original footnote reads: "Wehberg, *op. cit.*, p. 87."

21. The original footnote reads: "Oppenheim, *International Law*, vol. II, p. 157."

22. The original footnote reads: "Oppenheim, *op. cit.*, pp. 157–158."

23. The original footnote reads: "*International Law*, 2nd ed., paragraph 59a."

24. An offense rather than a crime.

25. Paragraph 6 of the original manuscript, which has been omitted here, contained a long discussion of the "Commission on the Responsibility of the Authors of the War and on Enforcement of Penalties" in 1919 and its conclusion that launching World War I and the invasions of Belgium and Luxembourg could not properly be designated as crimes.

26. See the first page of this document and related notes.

27. See the first page of this document and document 23.

28. In light of the current historical argument over how central Hitler's anti-Semitism was to his whole policy, as well as a much more sophisticated discussion of what one means by "planning" or "intending" extermination, the assertions in this section seem very old-fashioned.

29. The original footnote reads: "Cf. *The Treatment of Polish Nationals in Danzig*, Hudson, *World Court Reports*, pp. 804–805; and, for a general discussion, Freeman, *The International Responsibility of States for Denial of Justice*, pp. 522 ff."

30. The following sentence was a last-minute revision of the original document, added on a supplementary page.

31. A short phrase, partially illegible in the original document, referring to a possible application of one of the conclusions of the UNWCC, has been omitted.

32. The original footnote reads: "*The American Journal of International Law*, 1944, p. 689."

33. *Condominium* is legal joint dominion or joint ownership.

DOCUMENT 27

1. Asst. Sect., Box 16, Working File. A copy of this memorandum went to McCloy on January 1, 1945. The importance of this memorandum has a special dimension, because its recipient, Francis Biddle, later became America's senior tribunal member at the main Nuremberg Trial and its author, Herbert Wechsler, served as one of Mr. Biddle's chief advisors during the first half of the trial.

2. This is document 22. Precisely which documents were supplied by Hackworth is unknown, but they probably included the British aide-mémoires of August 19 and October 30, 1944.

3. All italics, here and below, are in the original document.

4. "There cannot be a crime without law."

5. See document 22, for discussions of the British aide-mémoire of October 30, 1944.

DOCUMENT 28

1. This document was found in the files of the Justice Department, and appears to be an opinion dictated by Attorney General Francis Biddle. In an interview on May 8, 1975, Herbert Wechsler, the former assistant attorney general, expressed the view that it was most likely the product of a dictation by Biddle. The memorandum clearly seems to have been produced in response to document 22. All italics are in the original document.

2. The irony, that Biddle himself would be the American chief judge at the trial, should be noted.

DOCUMENT 29

1. Secretary of State Edward R. Stettinius. *Foreign Relations of the United States, Conferences at Malta and Yalta, 1945*, p. 401.

2. Herbert Pell.

DOCUMENT 30

1. Asst. Sect., Box 16, January–April 1945 File. Both Colonel Bernays and Major Brown were officers in G-1 Personnel.

2. All italics, and indications of omitted sections, both here and below, appear as they do in the original document.

3. This explanation and justification was revised and expanded, but it remained one of the foundations of American war crimes policy up through the London Conference and the trials of the major war criminals.

4. Omitted from the original.

5. The original citation reads: "P. J. Noel-Baker, *The Geneva Protocol*, London, 1925."

6. The original citation reads: "Memorandum by Professor Lauterpacht to the International Commission for Penal Reconstruction and Development in July 1942." Both this material and the document referred to in the following notes were sent to Bernays on December 30, 1944, by Katherine Fite of the State Department Legal Office. (File 740.00116 EW/13-1944, Illegal and Inhumane Warfare, National Archives, Diplomatic Branch.

7. Trainin's book was translated into English (London, 1945), but American war crimes planners depended on fragments until December 1944, when, as indicated in the previous note, Fite sent them a full translation.

8. With due allowance for tunnel vision, the dangers inherent in phrases like these would, one might assume, be evident to nearly anyone, but not a word of caution regarding them appears in the American documents.

9. The confusion inherent in the numbering of the Hague Convention results from the fact that a series of conventions, many of them dealing with aspects of naval warfare, were made in 1907. Convention IV, mentioned here, concerned land warfare, while Convention III, cited in the following paragraph, concerned the necessary procedures for indicating the start of hostilities.

DOCUMENT 31

1. Rosenman Papers War Crimes. A second copy is in the Joseph E. Davies Papers, War Criminals, Container 93, Folder K, Library of Congress. This major redraft of document 22 resulted from the meetings following January 8 with representatives of Justice, State, and War, as well as Judge Rosenman and Ambassador Davies. A note of January 19 from Cutter to McCloy states that this paper includes "Mr. Biddle's (Wechsler's?) and Mr. Hackworth's changes." (Asst. Sect., Box 16, Working File).

This draft includes a great deal of rewording and expansion of the earlier arguments, and it is especially important that it lays heavy emphasis on the aggressive war charge and places great stress on the need for a treaty court.

2. All italics, here and below, are in the original document.

3. Note that in neither of the first two cases cited was there an armed clash.

4. The introduction of this argument, at a time of great concern in the American

government about postwar occupation problems, is noteworthy.

5. At this point, and repeatedly below, the charge of aggressive war has been introduced into this draft.

6. Here again, there is obviously great uneasiness in a number of quarters about the possible implications of such a precedent.

7. This is the only draft of the document in which this problem is stated so baldly.

DOCUMENT 32

1. Joseph E. Davies Papers, War Criminals 1944, Container 93, Folder J., Library of Congress.

DOCUMENT 33

1. Asst. Sect., Box 16, Working File. This file also contains a note by General Royall dated January 18, 1945, praising this draft, so it had at least limited circulation. Prepared in the JAG, it was a counterproposal to the Bernays-Wechsler-Hackworth draft (document 31). All italics are in the original document.

2. The emphasis on treatment of prisoners of war (POWs) is sharply different from the Bernays-Wechsler-Hackworth draft.

3. Note the inclusion of Italy in this document, here and below.

4. The document ignores the problem of immunity for heads of state.

5. Note that this conclusion clashes sharply with that of the Bernays-Wechsler-Hackworth draft.

6. The Czech village of Lidice was obliterated by the Nazis in retaliation for the killing of Reinhard Heydrich by a Czech/(British-trained) partisan team.

7. Why only these three countries are specified here—note that even Denmark is omitted—and why the three particular examples, especially Bulgaria, are chosen in paragraph 10 is a total mystery.

8. This is the only reference to abuse of women in any of the extant American records regarding war crimes planning.

9. The Rules of Ground Warfare.

10. The Molotov statement cited here is published in *Report of Robert H. Jackson*, pp. 15–17.

11. This statement shifts the tone of the British document, which flatly rejected a treaty court and only hesitantly voiced some sympathy for the idea of mixed military tribunals. (Aide-Mémoire, October 30, 1944, *Foreign Relations of the United States, 1944*, 1: 1389–91.)

12. Paragraph 2 was omitted in the original document.

13. This is the only point in the document where the tone regarding conspiracy rings close to that of the Bernays-Wechsler-Hackworth draft, but note document 29, in which the president had already indicated sympathy for a conspiracy approach.

DOCUMENT 34

1. Joseph E. Davies Papers, January-May 1945, Container 16, War Crimes, Library of Congress. This document consisted of a two-page preface and a five-page memorandum (the introductory two pages of the memorandum have not been printed here, see note 5 to this document). According to a note in Ambassador Davies' hand, the memorandum was given to the president and Secretary of State Stettinius before they left for Yalta, but as any one who has used Ambassador Davies papers will understand, such notes must be accepted with extreme caution. The Ambassador assembled these papers in preparation for writing his memoirs, and he was not troubled by any reticence in magnifying his own role. There are instances in the papers where the ambassador rewrote documents for inclusion in his proposed memoirs, and the rewrites often contain significant variations from the originals. The document printed here is by all indications an original document of January 1945, but as to what was done with it and to whom it was circulated, cautious conclusions are advisable.

2. This fragmentary expression is in the original document.

3. This is the first appearance of the phrase "crimes against humanity" in the extant war crimes planning documents. It could indicate that Ambassador Davies caught the drift of the ideas of Hersch Lauterpacht and others before most of his contemporaries; it might also be another case of postwar revision—see notes 1 and 4 to this document.

4. Again this vagueness of expression is in the original document, and suggests that little or no serious revision was made subsequently.

5. Two pages of introduction, covering four paragraphs of the situational summary, have been omitted.

6. "Not inherently unlawful (i.e., not contrary to natural law), but made unlawful by statute."

7. "Collateral opinions of a judge or judges."

8. This is another of the careless expressions which indicates that this document was a hurried dictation of January 1945 rather than a careful postwar revision.

DOCUMENT 35

1. *Foreign Relations of the United States, Conferences at Malta and Yalta, 1945*, pp. 403–8.

2. Tab letters have been omitted. For the specific statements, see document 31.

3. Document 1.

4. The Soviet Union did not join because it contended that, given Britain's insistence on Dominion representation, it was underrepresented.

5. Cecil Hurst, chairman of the UNWCC in 1943 and 1944, was replaced by Lord Wright of Australia.

6. Italics in the original.

7. The text of the statement was published in *Report of Robert H. Jackson*, pp. 12–13.

8. Underlined in the original.

9. All words and phrases simply placed in brackets were additions to the January 19 draft.

10. All words and phrases placed in brackets and lined out—[~~lined out~~]—were cut from the January 19 draft.

11. Phrase was bracketed in the January 22 original.

12. The first three bracketed words were added, and the last bracketed word was cut from the January 19 draft.

13. See note 10 to document 33.

DOCUMENT 36

1. This document was drafted by Bernays and Hackworth on January 19–20, 1945, and was sent to the president's secretary together with the Three Secretaries Memorandum for use at the Yalta conference. (Bernays Memorandum for Record, January 20, 1945, Asst. Sect., Box 16, Working File; Hackworth to Rosenman, January 20, 1945, in *Foreign Relations of the United States, Conferences at Malta and Yalta, 1945*, p. 408.)

DOCUMENT 37

1. Rosenman Papers War Crimes. After the Treasury Department learned that its representatives would not be able to attend the general war crimes meeting on January 18, Morgenthau's aides planned to forward a stiff paper reiterating the shoot-on-sight proposal. Upon being informed that all others concerned with the issue were unanimously in favor of trial but that they would not push the treaty idea or permit obstacles to extradition, Treasury moderated its stand, and the memorandum printed here was dispatched to Rosenman. Although Secretary Morgenthau signed the cover letter, he apparently never even saw the document, depending solely on a summary of its contents provided by his assistants. (*The Morgenthau Diary (Germany)*, 2: 890f.)

2. Insufficient attention has been paid to the role the fight over war criminal policy played in developing the American stand at Yalta, which conceded to the Soviets the right of return of all Soviet nationals after the war—note that in this sentence the crucial noun is not *German*, but *person*.

3. There was a general feeling in the West, both among government officials and among the public, that the war criminal policy of the First World War, culminating in the failure to extradite the kaiser from the Netherlands and the modest rulings of the German Leipzig trails, was totally ineffective and a sham.

4. The trial of two dozen plus American pro-Fascists and right-wing cranks was marked by long delays and tragicomic antics by the defendants. The trial ended abruptly, and symbolically, near the close of 1944 with the collapse and death of the judge.

5. Line markings in the original.

6. Asterisks in the original.

DOCUMENT 38

1. Diaries of Henry L. Stimson, January 19, 1945, vol. 49, pp. 57–58, roll 9, Yale University.

2. Note that Stimson omits the State Department.

3. On January 18 occurred the final meeting of the committee, out of which the draft of January 19 was produced, and this, with minor rewordings, was the finished document for the president of January 22 (document 35). Stimson did not attend the meeting of January 18, but had a luncheon engagement with Judge Rosenman immediately after it, and took the opportunity to chat with those who had attended the meeting.

DOCUMENT 39

1. Asst. Sect., Box 16, Working File.

2. Deputy fiscal director in the War Department, and a postwar secretary of the army.

3. Note that the memorandum for the president of January 22, 1945, based the court proposal on an executive agreement, not a treaty.

4. European Theater of Operations, commanded by General Eisenhower.

5. See document 25.

6. The problem of superior orders plagued the early efforts of the war crimes planners, and in October 1944 G-1 and JAG prepared a revision of the *Field Manual on*

Rules of Land Warfare (FM 27-10) so as to weaken the superior orders defense. A major factor in this revision was the desire to facilitate enemy war crimes prosecution. See General (Myron C.) Cramer to G-1, October 4, 1944, RG 153, JAG, Box 1606, Folder 103-24, Federal Records Center, Suitland, Maryland.

DOCUMENT 40

1. *Foreign Relations of the United States, 1945*, 3: 471–73.

DOCUMENT 41

1. Memorandum from General Weir to McCloy, March 27, 1945 (the note indicating that these were the General's rough ideas was written on the document in pencil). (Asst. Sect., Box 16, Working File.)

2. Paragraph 3 merely noted the kind of details, "size and composition of the court," etc., that would need agreement.

3. This statement may exaggerate the contrast, but the adversary system generally does grant more protection to the accused.

4. This idea was utilized in the American plan and led to long circular debates at the London conference. See *Report of Robert H. Jackson*, pp. 338f.

5. The clouded expression used here is in the original document.

DOCUMENT 42

1. Rosenman Papers War Crimes. Internal evidence shows that this was a State Department document prepared as background for Rosenman's talks with the British.

2. This passage marks an early appearance of two ideas that were to cause much trouble for war crimes planners: placing the burden of proof on the members of organizations and the use of criminal-organization labor for reconstruction.

DOCUMENT 43

1. Joseph E. Davies Papers, January-May 1945 File, Container 16, Library of Congress.

DOCUMENT 44

1. Rosenman Papers War Crimes. On March 26, a slightly revised version of the implementing instrument of January 20, 1945, had been prepared (a copy is in the same file). Then, in Cutter's words, "when we first arrived" in London (i.e., on April 3), he prepared the more extensive revisions printed here. See note of April 10, 1945, Cutter to Rosenman, Asst. Sect., Box 15, Alphabetical File.

2. Note that this provision was added immediately after the briefing of Judge Rosenman sketched out in document 42.

3. The proposal to make the executive group, i.e., the later prosecution staff, subject to the Control Council was hotly debated in following months until it was flatly vetoed by Justice Jackson and President Truman. When General Lucius Clay tried to champion the idea in mid-May, he was slapped down hard, a rebuff he took with good grace. The exchanges between McCloy, Eisenhower, and Clay, DTG 091945Z, May 9, 1945, are in the War Crimes File, Box 7, of the Rosenman papers.

4. This little acorn grew into the great spreading oak of courtroom trial lawyers that appeared at Nuremberg.

DOCUMENT 45

1. Simon to Rosenman, April 6, 1945, *Foreign Relations of the United States, 1945, 3: 1158–61.*

2. Here again is the peculiar inference that most of the Jewish victims were German nationals.

3. "An enemy of humanity."

4. The use of the term *intermediate class* by the British to refer to the prosecution of organizations, some of which had hundreds of thousands of members, is at the least inappropriate.

DOCUMENT 46

1. This revision, as worked out by Cutter, may best be studied in the form in which it was handwritten and stapled into the April 3 revision of the implementing instrument. See Asst. Sect., Box 16, January-April 1945 File.

2. Number omitted from the original.

3. What a Soviet joint-prosecutor would have done with this paragraph, if it had been retained in the final document, is difficult to imagine.

DOCUMENT 47

1. Colonel R. A. Cutter to Assistant Secretary of War John J. McCloy, April 7, 1945, Asst. Sect., Box 15, Alphabetical File.

2. The portion omitted lists the enclosures and what else Cutter was doing to notify Washington officials of developments in London.

3. European Advisory Commission members, i.e., the United States, the Soviet Union, Great Britain, and France.

DOCUMENT 48

1. Enclosure in W.P. (45) 281, May 3, 1945, CAB 65, Public Records Office, London.

2. Misprinted in the original as "it."

3. Note that there is no mention of French or German legal concepts. It might also be noted that Lord Simon was not far from the mark regarding some of the later reactions to the Nuremberg Trial.

4. A copy of Lord Simon's paper was given to Judge Rosenman on April 21 and was forwarded to John J. McCloy on April 23, but the last three sentences of the British document as printed here were omitted from the paper given to the Americans. (Rosenman to McCloy, April 23, 1945, Asst. Sect., Box 16, January-April 1945 File.

DOCUMENT 49

1. Draft of argument in favor of trial, April 20, 1945, under an April 23, 1945 cover letter from McCloy to Secretary of War Stimson. (Asst. Sect., Box 16, January-April 1945 File.) Although the official transmissions indicate that this paper was drafted after Lord Simon's April 16 paper was officially received in Washington, the argument moves so close to the positions of the British paper that one suspects unofficial communication put it in American hands before April 21, 1945.

2. Much of this argument is taken directly from the notes that McCloy prepared for his talks with the British on April 16. (Ibid., Box 15, Alphabetical File.)

3. An error in the original made this word "by."

4. A reverse error in the original made this "be."

5. The murky expression here is in the original document.

6. The planning session of August-October 1944 for the creation of the United Nations Organization.

7. The immediately preceding three words were typed in as an addition.

8. An interesting veiled reference to American fears about Soviet secret police methods.

DOCUMENT 50

1. Memorandum of April 25, 1945, Asst. Sect., Box 15, Alphabetical File; Memorandum of April 27, 1945, Rosenman Papers War Crimes. With the exception of one revision made in the April 27 draft (as noted in the text below) all words lined out ~~(lined-out)~~ were words in the April 25 draft that were cut in the April 30 version. Similarly, all words in brackets were added in the April 30 version.

2. The original note concluded: "page 10" (of the original document).

3. The original note concluded: "page 6."

4. The original note concluded: "page 7."

5. The words *or at least* were first added, then cut, in the April 30 version.

6. For no apparent reason, the adjectival form, *Hitlerite*, which had been taken over from the Soviets, was not used on this occasion.

7. Note that, perhaps unconsciously, the specific term *conspiracy*, rather than *criminal enterprise* or *common plan*, slips back in here.

8. This passage was added in the April 27 version after the first seven lines of the original April 25 version were cut.

9. All of section IV draws heavily on document 49, but note that heavy cuts were also made.

10. It would be difficult to find a passage in any other 1945 document that so clearly expresses the traditional progressive values and ideas of punishment as does this section.

11. An error in the letter sequence crept in here, but it was corrected in the printed version.

12. Note the early impact of the stories, arising in the first areas of occupation, that German civilians had not known of the horrors perpetrated by the Nazi regime.

13. The distinction between "Slavic" and "Continental" legal systems is interesting. Obviously Slavic areas are on the continent, and nearly as obviously, Western officials were more concerned about the peculiarly communistic elements of Soviet law than they were about any special "Slavic" features.

14. This phrase indicates the real Western worry, the Soviet use of forced confessions and show trials.

15. In fact this prediction was incorrect; the Americans continued to try to make aggressive war the central issue until the final days of the trial.

DOCUMENT 51

1. "Punishment of War Criminals," April 28, 1945, Rosenman Papers War Crimes. This document contains the revisions of April 3 and 10 that Colonel Cutter made in Hackworth's January 20, 1945 implementing instrument. In addition, Cutter made substantial revisions between April 10 and 28.

2. Obviously this retains the hope that the arraignment idea could be sold back to the British.

3. This is the first draft that omits any representation for the smaller United Nations.

4. This is the first appearance of the notion, later controversial, that the bench should control defense witnesses.

5. Here again a provision for small-power representation was cut.

DOCUMENT 52

1. The document carries a note "Rec'd from Mr. Justice Jackson 1 May 45," Asst. Sect., Box 15, SF File.

2. I.e., a tribunal.

3. It is symptomatic that in his first memorandum as Chief of Counsel, Justice Jackson stressed at two points that he wished to put considerations of legal drafting ahead of factors that would ease dealings with the Allies.

DOCUMENT 53

1. Murray C. Bernays Collection, Box no. 4, Trial and Punishment File no. 2, University of Wyoming.

2. All words and phrases in brackets are additions made by Colonel Cutter and Colonel Bernays on May 2, 1945. (Ibid.)

3. Parenthesis and question mark are in the original document.

4. All words and phrases lined out ~~(lined out)~~ were deletions made during the revision by Colonel Cutter and Colonel Bernays on May 2, 1945.

5. The phrase "and restate" was added, then cut, by Colonel Cutter and Colonel Bernays.

6. The order of items a through e was greatly altered by Colonel Cutter and Colonel Bernays. The original order placed item d first, then e, b, c, and a.

7. Colonel Cutter and Colonel Bernays added, then cut, the word *military*.

8. "Constructive notice" means sufficiently broad publicity so that the individual in question should reasonably be assumed to have learned of it.

9. These two bracketed phrases, each ending in a question mark, were added in the revision by Cutter and Bernays.

10. The phrase "in consequence" was added, then cut, by Cutter and Bernays.

11. The phrase "or was nominal only," was added, then cut, by Cutter and Bernays.

12. The word *an* was added, then cut, by Cutter and Bernays.

13. The word *the* was added, then cut, by Cutter and Bernays.

14. The word *in* has been added by the editor to clarify meaning.

DOCUMENT 54

1. Rosenman Papers War Crimes.

2. Words and phrases lined out here and below were deletions made on the plane trip to San Francisco, May 2, 1945, by Cutter, Wechsler, and Rosenman. See Cutter to the War Department, May 4, 1945, Murray C. Bernays Collection, Box No. 4, Trial and Punishment File no. 2, University of Wyoming.

3. Brackets around the letters *ern* and a following question mark were deleted in the final revision made by Cutter, Wechsler, and Rosenman.

4. All words and phrases in brackets, here and below, were added in the final revision made by Cutter, Wechsler, and Rosenman.

DOCUMENT 55

1. Asst. Sect. Box 15, SF File. The document, prepared by Colonel Cutter to pull together the various changes suggested by the Allies and the redrafting work of McCloy, Wechsler, and Cutter himself, bears a stamped date of May 16 but may have been produced a few days earlier.

2. Sir William Malkin of the British Foreign Office wanted to end the sentence here, but this was one of the few points in which Cutter's redraft did not meet his wishes. See Malkin note, May 5(?), 1945, ibid.

3. This paragraph, emphasizing prosecution of criminal organizations and "criminal plans," was taken from an undated draft partial revision prepared by the American group (McCloy, Wechsler, and Cutter) in San Francisco. (Rosenman Papers War Crimes.)

4. This paragraph, emphasizing the same points as the previous one was taken from the undated partial draft prepared in San Francisco. (Rosenman Papers War Crimes.)

5. This redraft, containing numerous changes in paragraph 7, was also taken from the partial draft prepared in San Francisco by the Americans (Rosenman Papers War Crimes). Sir William Malkin and Jules Basdevant of France had both asked for changes in paragraph 7 during the meeting of May 5. Basdevant wanted the charges made more specific, and both he and Malkin raised the issue of conflicting legal opinion on the criminality of aggressive war. Other doubts about this paragraph may have been raised at the May 8 meeting of legal specialists for the four powers, but the extant notes are too short and cryptic to allow a solid opinion. See Asst. Sect., Box 15, SF File (notes of meetings on May 5 and 8).

6. Lined out in the original document.

7. Lined out in the original document.

8. The simplified wording utilized here was suggested by Sir William Malkin. (Note by Malkin May 5(?), 1945, Asst. Sect., Box 15, SF File.)

9. The original wording is "findings," apparently a typing error, although the wording of the whole paragraph is murky.

10. This redrafted paragraph was taken from an undated partial redraft prepared by the American group—McCloy, Wechsler, and Cutter—in San Francisco (Rosenman Papers War Crimes). Note, too, that a portion of the earlier formulation of this paragraph was moved to paragraph 19.

11. This redrafted paragraph was taken from an undated American partial redraft prepared in San Francisco, but the suggested revision came from Sir William Malkin. (Rosenman Papers War Crimes, and notes of May 5 meeting, Asst. Sect., Box 15, SF File.)

12. See note 11.

13. After questions about the organizational provisions in the original executive agreement were raised during the May 5 meeting by a number of those present, this paragraph was prepared by the American group in San Francisco.

14. This paragraph came from an American partial draft prepared in San Francisco. (Rosenman Papers War Crimes.)

15. This paragraph, initially labeled 19½, was inspired by Soviet questions about jurisdiction raised at the May 5, 1945 meeting. For the drafts see Rosenman Papers War Crimes; for notes of the May 5, 1945 meeting see Asst. Sect., Box 15, SF File.

DOCUMENT 56

1. Asst. Sect., Box 15, SF File. No author of the document is indicated but internal evidence suggests that Hackworth and Wechsler may have had a hand in its preparation. The detailed knowledge of diplomatic-legal documents points to Hack-

worth. The reliance on legal theory, the reference to what was done in the San Francisco (where Wechsler was present), and the fact that many of these suggestions were taken into the final document by a committee of which Wechsler was a member, all point to the assistant attorney general (see document 57).

2. This reference indicates the work of a State Department legal specialist, i.e., Hackworth.

3. "No" is written in the margin in what may be Colonel Cutter's hand.

4. Draft 2-A was one of the partial revisions prepared in San Francisco. Draft 3 is document 57.

5. This passage, with its detailed knowledge of what went on in San Francisco, points to Wechsler.

6. This date is obviously an error; January 30, 1933, the date Hitler was named chancellor, was surely intended.

7. "No" is written in the margin in what may be Colonel Cutter's hand.

8. "No" is written in the margin in what may be Colonel Cutter's hand. There are also a few large, inked check marks in the margin, but their import is not clear.

9. "Perhaps" is written in the margin in what may be Colonel Cutter's hand.

10. Again, this was surely intended to be January 30, 1933.

DOCUMENT 57

1. S.F. Conference File, Box 3, Papers of Samuel J. Rosenman, Harry S. Truman Library, Independence, Missouri. Draft 4, showing the changes from draft 3 in Bernays' hand, is from the Murray C. Bernays Collection, Box no. 4, Trial and Punishment File no. 2, University of Wyoming. Another copy with the same changes, presumably in Cutter's hand, is in Asst. Sect., Box 15, SF File. A Cutter note to Rosenman, May 24, 1945, attached to a third copy of draft 4 explains that the revision from draft 3 to draft 4 was made by Cutter, Bernays, Wechsler, Jackson, and three officials of the chief of counsel's new staff—Colonel Kaplan, Shea, and Alderman. (Rosenman Papers War Crimes.)

2. All words and phrases in brackets, here and below, were added in draft 4.

3. All words and phrases lined out, here and below, were deleted in draft 4.

4. "Organization" was singular in the original, presumably a typing error.

5. The phrase beginning with the word *including* and ending with the word *grounds* was moved from the end of the paragraph to this position in draft 4.

6. A mistaken reference to the date of Hitler's *Machtergreifung*, i.e., January 30, 1933.

7. This phrase was first added and then lined out in draft 4.

DOCUMENT 58

1. (Before June 5, 1945) RG 165, G-1 Personnel, 000.5, War Crimes, Box 314, Federal Record Center, Suitland, Maryland. Although this thirteen-page analysis of the case by Telford Taylor was criticized by Colonel Bernays (Bernays to Alderman, June 5, 1945, RG 165, G-1 Personnel, 000.5, War Crimes Box 314, Federal Records Center, Suitland, Maryland) Alderman himself praised it without qualification in a memorandum for Justice Jackson (June 5, 1945, Murray C. Bernays Collection, Box no. 4, Trial and Punishment File no. 3, University of Wyoming). It has been included here, in abbreviated form, to indicate that Justice Jackson's staff did not lack individuals prepared to take a hard and realistic view of the nature of the case.

2. At this point, there were in fact no such plans or schedules.

3. Office of Strategic Services, the improvised World War II Central Intelligence Agency. The OSS was charged with the duty of collecting the evidence for half the case in the early planning, but by July Jackson's staff concluded that OSS resources and abilities had been grossly overrated and the case ultimately rested mainly on captured enemy records. See Bradley F. Smith, *Reaching Judgment at Nuremberg* (New York, 1977), pp. 53f.

4. The six-page Memorandum on Trial Preparation is a staff estimate of what would have to be established to prove the basic charges set in the draft executive agreement. The Memorandum on Trial Preparation was approved by Justice Jackson on May 16, 1945. A copy of the Memorandum on Trial Preparation is in RG 238, Office of the Chief of Counsel for the Prosecution of Axis Criminality, Box 33, National Archives, Modern Military Branch.

5. The remaining nine pages of Colonel Taylor's memorandum, omitted here, surveyed possible sources of evidence for the various aspects of the case. Taylor's main points were that there was better evidence in Europe than Ameica, that British intelligence sources were better than those in Washington, and that the main operation of case preparation should be moved to Europe. Although these points were contested by others, including Colonel Bernays, Taylor was proven right, but with poetic justic he was the one chosen to stay behind and head the Washington office until the early fall of 1945.

DOCUMENT 59

1. *Report of Robert H. Jackson*, document 60, pp. 420–28. It may appear inconsistent to include this document after leaping over all the documentation of the London conference of June-August 1945. However, since this is the culminating document in the whole developmental process it is indispensable for comparative study. It is not possible at this time to select the salient materials produced at London

before the completion of the Agreement and Charter. As I indicated a few years ago (*Reaching Judgment at Nuremberg*, p. 314, n. 17), the common assumption that the documents contained in the *Report of Robert H. Jackson* are the best or most representative materials is not necessarily correct. At that time (1975–1977) I had found additional stenographic records of various sessions in the Bernays papers and the British Foreign Office Records. Since then the papers of the Earl of Kilmuir (Sir David Maxwell-Fyfe) have been deposited in the Churchill Archives Centre, Cambridge University, and the records of the British War Crimes Executive (LCO 2, 2985) have been opened to study at the Public Records Office, London. In addition, more files from the records of the Office of Chief of Counsel for the Prosecution of Axis Criminality (RG 238) are now open in the Modern Military Branch of the National Archives. A long and exhaustive study of the London conference needs to be done. Until it is, inclusion of the Agreement and Charter standing on their own, without any other materials produced in the summer of 1945, most accurately reflects the state of our existing knowledge.

2. French alternate tribunal member during the major Nuremberg trial.

3. Soviet tribunal member during the major Nuremberg trial.

4. Due to inconsistencies in punctuation between the Russian and the French-English versions of Article 6, paragraph (c), a formal revision was made on October 6, 1945, changing this semicolon to a comma. (*Report of Robert H. Jackson*, document 61, p. 429.)

Bibliography

Rather than repeat the same listings of unpublished sources and books with only minor rewordings from one volume to another, I have restricted this bibliography to works cited in the notes. For a comprehensive recent bibliography of published material, see Werner Maser, *Nürnberg, Tribunal der Sieger* (Düsseldorf and Vienna, 1977). For a more extensive listing of unpublished sources, see Bradley F. Smith, *The Road to Nuremberg* (New York, 1981).

ARCHIVE AND MANUSCRIPT COLLECTIONS

United States

Diplomatic Branch, National Archives, Washington, D.C.
- 740.00116 EW, General European War File
- 740.00116, Illegal and Inhumane Warfare

Dwight D. Eisenhower Library, Abilene, Kansas
- Walter Bedell Smith Collection of World War II Documents

Federal Records Center, Suitland, Maryland
- RG 165, Personnel Records, G-1
- RG 153, Judge Advocate General's Office

Harry S. Truman Library, Independence, Missouri
- Papers of Samuel I. Rosenman

Library of Congress
- Joseph E. Davies Papers

Modern Military Branch, National Archives, Washington, D.C.
- RG 107, Assistant Secretary of War, 000.5, War Crimes
- RG 107, Secretary of War, 000.5, War Crimes

RG 238, Office of Chief of Counsel for the Prosecution of Axis Criminality

United States Justice Department
War Crimes Files

University of Wyoming
Murray C. Bernays Papers

Yale University
Diaries and Papers of Henry L. Stimson

Great Britain

Public Records Office, London
CAB 65, War Cabinet Minutes
CAB 21, War Cabinet Committee on War Crimes
FO 371, Foreign Office General Diplomatic Series

PUBLIC DOCUMENTS (UNITED STATES GOVERNMENT)

Foreign Relations of the United States, 1943. Vol. 1. Washington, 1963.

Foreign Relations of the United States, 1944. Vols. 1 and 3. Washington, 1965 and 1966.

Foreign Relations of the United States, 1945. Vol. 3. Washington, 1968.

Foreign Relations of the United States, The Conference at Quebec, 1944. Washington, 1972.

Foreign Relations of the United States, Conferences at Malta and Yalta, 1945, Washington, 1955.

Morgenthau Diary (Germany), The. 2 Vols. Washington, 1967.

Nazi Conspiracy and Aggression. 11 Vols. Washington, 1946–1947.

Report of Robert H. Jackson, United States Representative to the International Conference on Military Trials, London, 1945. Washington, 1949.

Trial of the Major War Criminals before the International Military Tribunal. 42 Vols. Washington, 1949.

BOOKS

Maser, Werner. *Nürnberg, Tribunal der Sieger*. Düsseldorf and Vienna: Econ Verlag, 1977.

Neave, Airey. *On Trial at Nuremberg*. New York: Little, Brown, 1979.

Smith, Bradley F. *Reaching Judgment at Nuremberg*. New York: Basic Books, 1977.
———. *The Road to Nuremberg*. New York: Basic Books, 1981.
UNWCC. *History of the United Nations War Crimes Commission*. London, 1948.

PERIODICALS

The American Bar Association Journal
The New York Times

Index